LAUNCHED INTO ETERNITY

LAUNCHED INTO ETERNITY

CRIME AND PUNISHMENT, HITMEN AND HANGMEN

DAVID LESLIE

BLACK & WHITE PUBLISHING

First published 2017
by Black & White Publishing Ltd
Nautical House, 104 Commercial Street
Edinburgh EH6 6NF

1 3 5 7 9 10 8 6 4 2   17 18 19 20

ISBN: 978 1 78530 137 7

A CIP catalogue record for this book is available from the British Library.

Typeset by Iolaire, Newtonmore
Printed and bound by MBM Print, East Kilbride

MIX
Paper from
responsible sources
FSC® C117931

CONTENTS

'Death is Nature's remedy for all things, and why not Legislation's? Accordingly, the forger was put to Death; the utterer of a bad note was put to Death; the unlawful opener of a letter was put to Death; the purloiner of forty shillings and sixpence was put to Death; the holder of a horse at Tellson's door, who made off with it, was put to Death; the coiner of a bad shilling was put to Death; the sounders of three fourths of the notes in the whole gamut of crime, were put to Death. Not that it did the least good in the way of prevention . . .'

Charles Dickens, *A Tale of Two Cities* (1859)

PROLOGUE

The crowd was sparse, the numbers kept down by cold and heavy rain that had fallen since dawn. But the 2,000 or so, most of them young women, who were there that Tuesday morning on 12 May 1868 would remember every detail of what they were about to see. Their eyes were on a swarthy, apparently bored young man standing a few feet above them. His name was Robert Smith. He was moments from death and in dying he would create history, because chance had decreed that this pathetic farm labourer, aged just nineteen, condemned for sickening attacks on a girl of nine and an adult woman, would forever be remembered as the last person to be publicly executed in Scotland.

Before the month was out politicians had endorsed a bill ordaining that future judicial executions must take place in prisons, out of public view with just a handful of official witnesses present. Nobody was prepared to openly admit it, but the fact was that for decades watching an execution had been a popular free entertainment available to the highest and lowest in society. Hangings were frequently rowdy, boisterous, with troops needed to help police control crowds. Reformers felt that no matter what their crimes those about to die were entitled to do so in dignity and solemnity. Even distinguished authors such as Sir Walter Scott, Thomas Hardy and Charles Dickens had vied for prime spots from which to watch these spectacles. And however briefly they might be in the limelight, the fact was that condemned men and women became minor celebrities. Just three years before executioner Thomas Askern from York put the noose around the neck of Robert Smith, a near riotous crowd said to number up to 80,000 and including drunks, prostitutes and pickpockets had watched as Doctor Edward Pritchard was hanged at Glasgow. And so politicians had acted with the result that Smith's hanging was a much more humble affair. Mindful of the forthcoming legislation the authorities decided to make it difficult for the public to watch his demise by erecting the gibbet in the yard of Dumfries prison thus limiting the room available for spectators.

The young man's crimes had caused alarm and distaste throughout Britain. 'Horrible Murder in Dumfries-shire' trumpeted the *Blackburn Standard* while the *Illustrated Police News* carried a report of a 'Barbarous Murder and Attempted Murder near Annan'. The victim was little Thomasina Scott, one of the eleven children of a shoemaker and his wife. Her mother had given Thomasina ten shillings with which to buy the family shopping and she set off happily, skipping and singing. When it began to rain she sheltered in the neighbouring home of Jane Crichton, where she discovered another visitor, Smith, who offered to accompany the youngster on the road to Annan once the rain eased off. Thomasina was never seen alive again; she was lured by Smith into a plantation, where he raped and strangled her then stole her ten shillings.

Then he set about eliminating the only witness to his link with the dead girl; creeping back to first shoot unsuspecting Jane Crichton in the head before stabbing her in the neck and choking her. She survived because Smith was interrupted by two callers to her home who sounded the alarm and her attacker was arrested after a massive manhunt. He made a full confession.

At eight minutes past eight Askern shook him by the hand then withdrew the bolt, women shrieking as the teenager dangled and struggled in agony as he choked for two minutes before dying. The official time of death was registered as 8.15 a.m.

Askern was paid twenty guineas, a fee originally destined for official hangman William Calcraft, who had to turn down the job when his employers at Newgate prison in London appointed him to execute Irishman Michael Barrett, aged twenty-seven, on the same day that Smith was due to hang. Barrett was a determined member of the Fenians group bent on achieving the creation of an independent Irish Republic. He had been arrested in Glasgow for having a gun and was accused of being part of a gang that set off a bomb in Clerkenwell, London, killing a dozen people and severely injuring scores of others. Barrett protested his innocence, claiming he was in Glasgow when the bomb went off and at his trial produced half a dozen witnesses to back him up.

Such was the strength of belief that he was the victim of a miscarriage of justice that his execution was respited while the authorities went through the motions of investigating Barrett's alibi. But his hopes of a reprieve were dashed and two weeks after Smith dropped to his doom, Barrett became the last person to be publicly hanged in England. The free show might have been over, but it would be 130 years before capital punishment was finally outlawed in the United Kingdom.

1

CRIME AND PUNISHMENT

Relaxing in heated cells surrounded by personal comforts and watching satellite television, prisoners today still find plenty to complain about. In some cases the legal system even financially assists perpetrators of the vilest crimes to sue for what the average man or woman in the street would regard as the most spurious reasons. There are cases on record where the government has been faced with claims for compensation over allegations that include an inmate being injured during a football match; hurt in a game of cricket; being issued with dirty underwear; losing false teeth while exercising; losing expensive designer clothes; being handed a faulty computer games console; having mail opened; a non-smoker being told to share a cell with a smoker; an inmate even demanding money because he was injured in a failed escape attempt.

A male rapist demanded compensation on grounds that he was refused treatment to stop him reoffending; another said his sex life was ruined after he slipped in a prison shower; yet another wanted recompense for having suffered depression while in jail. Complaints about food are frequent, while compensation claims by former and current inmates forced into the age-old daily ritual of slopping out cost the taxpayer tens of millions of pounds. Judges sentencing those guilty of shocking offences find their own options manacled by human rights regulation. One classic case is that of Thomas McCulloch and Robert Mone, who murdered three men while escaping from the State Hospital at Carstairs in 1976. A judge sentenced them to 'natural life' in prison but both used human rights legislation to obtain specific lengths of imprisonment, with the result that McCulloch was released and Mone continues to legally fight for freedom.

How does crime and punishment in the present compare to that of the past?

In days long gone laws and penalties were basic. The Celts who settled Scotland before the birth of Christ were likely to drown thieves who stole food; bury alive couples who committed adultery; burn any man or woman suspected of worshipping an unrecognised god and crudely strangle a murderer. Vikings who made Scotland their home introduced courts that could order thieves to have their hands chopped off or made slaves to their victims; protagonists in disputes to fight to the death; murderers or rapists to be hanged from a tree, while the offence of sabotaging or stealing a longboat usually found the culprit taken out to sea, weighed down by heavy stones and dropped overboard. Even those we might think of as minor offenders – someone who stole a cow or a sheep or a man's wife, or an unmarried woman finding herself pregnant – could expect to be banished, ordered to stay away from Viking communities and warned that should they attempt to return they would be executed. For most it was the equivalent of being condemned to die of starvation or simply freeze to death. As *Launched Into Eternity* will demonstrate, it was a type of punishment that would come to affect thousands of Scots.

By the Middle Ages Scotland had seen the arrival, although mainly relatively short-lived, of Normans and Saxons with their own regimes of crime and punishment. As the newcomers were forced out, the clan system developed; its power and religious beliefs would be the frequent cause of suspicion by the various monarchies and lead to increasingly savage forms of punishment, along with the growth of a legal system in which the upper classes introduced and enforced laws intended to ensure fear kept commoners submissive and ambitious only for simple survival.

Torture became an element in punishment; men might have their hands or ears cut off for even the tiniest thefts; beheading and disembowelling following hanging were introduced; in towns and villages throughout the country carpenters were ordered to build stocks in which offenders could be held, their heads and hands or legs clamped through tiny holes and at the mercy of anyone wanting to pelt them with stones or stinking rubbish. Perceived challenges to the power of those who ruled were ruthlessly dealt with and a man or woman might be accused of witchcraft for the simple kindness of healing a neighbour or even a pet. The ordering of executions became ever more commonplace. In Scotland 'The Maiden', an early and crude form of guillotine, began slicing off heads in 1564 and remained in use until 1708. Its use, guaranteeing a relatively painless death, was principally for ending the lives of aristocracy. Ordinary miscreants were forced to suffer at the often incompetent hands of hangmen.

Imprisoning a man or woman was not a popular option because it meant he or she having to be maintained by a lord or the local burgh. At first there were no buildings specifically set aside as prisons; culprits might find themselves thrown into a castle dungeon or even merely a pit, often shackled to the walls or floor without sanitation or water and with rats and vermin for company. At Dunstanburgh Castle in Northumberland a weak underground spring running through the dungeon was the sole means of water and thirsty prisoners were forced to lick it. Usually unless a prisoner had means to pay a jailor for food or clothing he or she would simply have to go without for days. At least the cost factor encouraged trials to come hard on the heels of an arrest, and at trials sentences of imprisonment were rare.

With the development of local government, burghs erected tolbooths, from which authorities conducted all their business, with prisons incorporated into them. And yet just as civilisation appeared to be taking root, legal savagery bloomed. So did the number of crimes for which death was the penalty. The consequence of all this was that now the ability of man to invent ever more terrible forms of cruelty was seen at its worst.

Those accused of witchcraft had very little chance of proving their innocence and avoiding appalling suffering. The Survey of Scottish Witchcraft, a database compiled by Julian Goodare, Lauren Martin, Joyce Miller and Louise Yeoman, identified 3,837 people alleged to have been involved in the activity between 1563 and 1736, three-quarters of them women. According to the survey the purge against witches began in earnest during the reign of King James VI of Scotland after the boat on which he and bride-to-be Anne of Denmark were sailing was caught in a severe storm in 1590. James became convinced witches at North Berwick had called up the storm and a series of trials followed, resulting in the execution of more than seventy people in which most were tied to a stake where they were strangled and then their bodies burned. Among them was Agnes Samson, who was accused of 'Assembling at North Berwick with six men and ninety women, all witches and of having raised storms and kissed the devil's a**e.'

Broadsides were news sheets usually detailing notable events, matters of interest, trials and executions and generally sold on the streets of Scotland for a penny each. One published in Edinburgh in 1826, which referred to the accusation against Agnes, announced it included accounts of 'the most remarkable Trials and Executions which took place in Scotland for above 300 years against the persons who suffered for Witchcraft, Adultery, Fornication'. It read like a horror comic, beginning with the tragic case of Thomas Aikenhead, a twenty-year-old student who became the last person in Britain to be put to death for blasphemy. The broadside told its readers that Aikenhead, 'For denying the Trinity, and the authority of the Scriptures and for maintaining the Eternity of the world,' was found guilty and sentenced, 'To be taken to the Gallow-fee on the 8th of January 1697, between the hours of two and four in the afternoon, and to be hanged, his body to be buried at the foot of the gallows and his moveable estate to be forfeited. Mercy was asleep as well as Justice and Science; so the dreadful sentence was executed!'

In comparison with the fate of others Aikenhead's was a relatively painless death, which was more than could be said for that originally planned for Jesuit John Ogilvie after his trial at Glasgow in 1615. Son of a wealthy Banffshire estate owner, he was ordained a Catholic priest on the Continent in 1610. He defied a ban on Catholicism in Scotland by sneaking back to his homeland under a false name, was caught and convicted of refusing to swear allegiance to King James I and sentenced to be immediately hanged and quartered. The broadside revealed that at least while he was hanged that same afternoon, the quartering was dispensed with. For the same offence years later Thomas Richards from Wigtownshire was sentenced to spend a month in a Glasgow jail where 'his ears were cropt' and he was shipped off to Jamaica and sold as a slave. 'He had six good horses taken from him; many of his goats were shot, and his house plundered, without any compassion showed to his wife and four small children.'

The paper said Alice Pearson from Byre Hills, Fifeshire, was convicted of witchcraft in 1688, strangled and burned. The catalogue of horror went on to the case of Euphan McCalzeane, tried for witchcraft in 1591: 'A lady possessed of a considerable estate in her own right. She was the daughter of Thomas McCalzeane, Lord Cliftenhall of the Senators of the College of Justice; she was burned alive and her estate confiscated.' Four years later a similar fate befell Patrick Lawrie and then in 1619 Isobel Young of East Barns was tried for 'having by enchantment stopped a mill twenty-nine years before; she was strangled and burned.' Sometimes the charges leading to execution could sound bizarre. In 1630 Alex Hamilton 'was convicted on his own confession of having had many meetings with the devil from whom he once received a severe drubbing for not keeping an appointment'. In 1649 Janet Brown was executed 'for having a meeting with the devil and of renouncing her bilotism [sic]'. According to the broadside, Elspeth Rule was burned on the cheek and banished from Scotland for life for witchcraft. The paper went on to claim that after a witch was condemned in 1722, 'The devil has never been seen in Scotland since.'

The difference in attitudes to sex-matters between the seventeenth and twenty-first centuries is shown by the case in 1617 of John Guthrie, who was convicted of 'notorious adultery', taken straight from court to the Cross of Edinburgh and hanged. Ten years later Patrick Robertson and Marion Kempt were accused of 'adulterous commerce with each other' and hanged on a gibbet at the Castle hill. Sex cost Sawney Cunningham his life in 1635. When his pretty wife admitted a Glasgow lawyer was determined to sleep with her, Cunningham encouraged the liaison and the couple tricked the love-struck lawyer into turning up at their home with money, where he was bludgeoned to death and his body dumped into a cellar. Later Sawney murdered his uncle, an act predicted to him by a female astrologer who also correctly forecast that he would be hanged at Leith.

A year later the citizens of Edinburgh had the chance to watch the execution of another notable Patrick McGregor, infamous leader of an outlaw gang that caused terror and mayhem across Aberdeenshire. He was known as Gilder Roy and in a terrible night he murdered his own mother for her money in the family home in Perthshire, raped his sister and then a maidservant. He fled to France and then Spain, where he committed a number of robberies before returning to Scotland and forming a gang of highwaymen. After three of his men were arrested and executed, McGregor captured the judge who condemned them and hanged him. He was eventually betrayed by a mistress and hanged in chains between Edinburgh and Leith.

Poison would become the means of committing a number of Scotland's most horrendous murders, but one of the earliest recorded cases in which it was the preferred method was that of George Clerk and John Ramsay, hanged at Edinburgh on 1 March 1765. They worked for and lived with their victim, wealthy merchant John Anderson, and regularly stole his money. They also ridiculed the businessman by slipping drugs into his drinks so they could poke fun of him when he became drunk. Later they would admit it gave them the murderous idea of putting poison into his spirits. Eighteen months after they dangled, the chemist's apprentice who supplied the poison was banished for life, a fate most believed to be remarkably painless.

But when it came to punishment, the real butchery was yet to begin.

2

HANDS OFF

Throughout history religious differences have divided nations and been the source of violent conflict, terror and barbarism. Scotland is no different. During the seventeenth century Covenanters, members of a Presbyterian movement opposed to any interference by Stuart kings in their church, were at the centre of major upheaval and bitter armed disputes that spread to England and Ireland. The movement was ruthlessly crushed and an eight-year period of bloodshed up to 1688 when many Covenanters were killed, was named the Killing Time by historian Robert Wodrow in *The History of the Sufferings of the Church of Scotland from the Restoration to the Revolution*, published in 1721–22.

Particularly gruesome was the execution at Edinburgh on 30 July 1680 of David Hackston, a highly active and militant Covenanter who had been present the previous year when a gang ambushed and assassinated James Sharp, Archbishop of St Andrews. After his capture by soldiers in Ayrshire, Hackston knew to expect no mercy. The Privy Council ordered magistrates at Edinburgh to meet him and three other prisoners and, 'Mount him on a bare-backed horse, with his face to the horse's tail, and his feet tied beneath his belly, and his hands flightered with ropes; and the executioner, with head covered, and his coat, lead his horse up the street to the tolbooth, the said Hackston being bareheaded; that the three other prisoners be conveyed on foot, bareheaded, after him, with their hands tied to a goad of iron.' The authorities went into similar detail for his execution six days later, commanding that he should be 'drawn backwards on a hurdle to the Mercat Cross and there at the cross of Edinburgh, and there upon a high scaffold erected a little above the cross have his right hand struck off and after some time to have his left hand struck off, and then to be hanged up and cut down alive, and the bowels taken out, and his heart to be shown to the people by the hand of the hangman, and his heart and bowels to be burnt in the presence of the people, in a fire prepared for that purpose upon the scaffold, and afterwards to have his head cut off, and his body divided into four quarters, and his head to be affixed on the Netherbow, and one of his quarters with both of his hands to be affixed at St Andrews, another quarter at Glasgow, the third at Leith, the fourth at Burntisland, and that none presume to be in mourning for him, nor he to have a coffin, and that none be on the scaffold with him but two baillies, four officers, the executioner and his servants, and this sentence to be put in execution against him this thirtieth day of July instant, betwixt three and five o'clock in the afternoon.' It added that the name of Hackston should never again be mentioned, while all his property was to be confiscated.

Three years later the only actual assassin of the Archbishop to be captured was put to death when Andrew Guilline was sentenced to have his hands cut off before he was hanged, beheaded and his body left hung in chains on Magus Moor, the spot in Fife where Sharp was murdered. However, things did not go according to plan when the executioner arrived drunk and took a sickening series of axe blows to chop off the hands and had to hack at the stomach to remove the bowels. Weeks afterwards Guilline's body was stolen by friends who were later transported.

In 1685 seventeen Covenanters were executed together at Inveraray, one having his arms sliced off before his hanging. But it was another incident that most reflects the cruelty to which the Covenanters were subjected. Margaret Wilson, aged eighteen, and her widow friend, Margaret McLachlan, sixty-three, were sentenced to death by drowning at Wigtown after refusing to swear an oath admitting James VII of Scotland was the rightful head of the Church. Scotland's Privy Council granted both women a reprieve, but this was ignored and on 11 May 1685 the women were chained to stakes in the Solway Firth. They sang and prayed as the tide came in, closed over their heads and drowned them.

It wasn't only the condemned who suffered. More than 100 Presbyterians were captured and sentenced to be hanged, drawn and quartered after a battle between soldiers and Covenanters in the Pentland Hills on 28 November 1666. Most of the executions took place at Edinburgh but the authorities were keen for the general population to be made aware of what happened to those refusing to bow to the authority of the King. As a result it was decided to put eight men to death at Ayr and two each at Dumfries and Irvine. The task of performing the executions was one for the hangmen of each town. At Edinburgh the post was held by Harry Ormiston, while William Sutherland was his Irvine counterpart – and he was about to find himself at the centre of an astonishing and terrifying row, as he revealed in an interview with historian Wodrow.

The problem began when the Ayr hangman, 'being unwilling to imbrue his hands in the blood of these good men', refused to hang the eight and, 'No other could be found to undertake this hateful work.' Following the Ayr hangman's decision William Sutherland was ordered to do the job. He too refused and was dragged from Irvine to Ayr, and when he again refused he was put in the stocks and not allowed food or drink. When he persisted he was tied to a stake and troopers ordered to point their guns and shoot him. It was a bluff but when that didn't work Wodrow reported that they covered his face and after a little the soldiers were ordered to run in upon him with a shout, and all the noise they could make. 'Thus they resolved to make him feel the fear of death, though he escaped the pain of it. And this was his martyrdom, which he underwent with a great deal of composure and resolution.'

Sutherland wasn't a Covenanter but he respected their beliefs. Finally the powers that be relented and simply jailed him. The desperate authorities persuaded one of the eight condemned, Cornelius Anderson, to hang his colleagues by promising his life would be spared and he performed the executions at Ayr and Irvine and then promptly dropped dead. Two years later, on 17 February, church minister James Renwick became the last of the Covenanters to be executed when he was hanged in the Edinburgh Grassmarket two days after his twenty-sixth birthday. He was dead when his head and hands were cut off and fixed to gates around the city.

In the meantime the business of judicial killing had gone on as usual. The Covenanter executions had been an especially busy time for Ormiston, whose death in 1684 was marked by an elegy in a special broadside that also revealed his successor to be another Sutherland, James.

> All Strumpets for Sculdudrie Sin,
> To Leith Wynd Foot Condem'd to spin,
> Let Tears like Tweed from Tinto rin,
> Weep for auld Hary,
> For Sutherland will Taun your Skin,
> And never spare you.

Covenanters died because of their passion for their beliefs. While schoolmaster Robert Carmichael's zeal didn't cost his life, it had devastating consequences for him. In 1700 Carmichael, the schoolmaster at Moffat, now a busy spa town in the Annandale Valley close to the M74 motorway, flogged one of his pupils, John Douglas, so brutally that the youngster died. Realising he was facing a murder charge, Carmichael took to his heels, hiding out with friends hoping the fuss would subside, but he was eventually arrested and accused of, 'Beating and dragging the boy and giving him three lashings without intermission.' His punishment seemed appropriate. He was initially jailed in the Edinburgh Tolbooth but then hangman Sutherland arrived with a guard, stripped the schoolmaster to the waist, pinioned his arms and dragged him first to the Lawnmarket where he was, in accordance with his sentence, 'lashed by seven severe stripes'. Whip in hand Sutherland hauled his victim to the Cross where he gave him 'six sharp stripes' and then pulled the now bleeding teacher to the Fountain Well to receive 'five more stripes'. The ordeal was not over. Although Carmichael was taken back to the tolbooth for a doctor to examine his injuries, he remained in prison until he was declared fit for the final part of the sentence, which was for him to be, 'Banished from Scotland for life, never to return thereto under all the highest pains.'

Sea captain William Kidd must have wished he had never returned to his native Britain. But he did so in chains. Born in Greenock in the 1640s, Kidd spent most of his time switching between honest sailor and pirate, mainly in the Caribbean. He was arrested in Boston along with a number of crewmen, including one Darby Mullins, and sent to London where at the Old Bailey they faced a series of charges that included murder and piracy. All were condemned but then reprieved, with the exception of Kidd and Mullins, who were hanged at Execution Dock, Wapping, on 23 May 1701. Like so many doomed others, Kidd's suffering was worsened by bungling at his hanging. As he dropped with the noose around his neck the rope snapped and Kidd, despite being drunk, fell shaken and shocked only to be carried back on to the scaffold where a new rope was fixed and he dropped for a second time, this time fatally. More than a century and a half later a report of the trial was read by Robert Louis Stevenson, who included the name 'Darby' as a character in his adventure story *Treasure Island*.

Seven years after Captain Kidd was hanged, his body left in chains to be covered by the tides, another Scot would inspire a remarkable and ageless story. Alexander Selkirk, son of a shoe-maker from Lower Largo in Fife, had become a seaman with a reputation as a troublemaker and whose meddling led to his being cast away in 1704 on a remote island 420 miles from the coast of Chile. He remained there for four years before being rescued and almost immediately returned to seafaring. Four years before Selkirk's death in 1723 at the age of forty-seven, writer Daniel Defoe published *The Life and Surprising Adventures of Robinson Crusoe* based on the Scot's experiences.

Absence was the cause of a particularly brutal murder in 1708. Soldier David Blyth Horner from Saline in Fife had been posted abroad and while he was away his brother William began an affair with the soldier's wife Elison. William ignored warnings to stop the relationship and set up home with her. But when Elison's husband returned she announced she was ending the affair. During a night out heartbroken William fatally stabbed her in the neck. He was sentenced to be hanged in chains but refused to confess to the killing; however, a remarkable incident produced a dramatic change of heart by the condemned man. A few days before he was to hang, a set of chains was brought to the tolbooth for him to try on to make sure they fitted. It was a form of made-to-measure chaining. As soon as they were on Horner pleaded for a minister to whom he made a full confession, begging forgiveness.

In 1715 Jacobite supporters of James Francis Edward, Prince of Wales and son of the deposed James VII of Scotland and II of England, rose with the aim of putting him on the throne of England as James III and in Scotland as James VIII. By the time he landed at Peterhead from France in December 1715, his Jacobites had already been routed the previous month at the Battles of Sheriffmuir and Preston. James briefly held court at Scone Palace near Perth, but dogged by illness and depression and about to be encircled by government forces fled back to France. His had been a brief and unsuccessful flirtation with power, but it would ultimately have devastating consequences for Scotland.

While the government and King debated how to penalise those Scots who supported James and tried to ensure there was no repeat of the little invasion, cruelty continued unabated. Regrettably for him Patrick Hamilton literally lost his head when he fell in love with a teenage beauty in Edinburgh and after discovering she had another suitor killed his rival. Because Hamilton came from aristocracy he was condemned to be beheaded, a punishment normally reserved for that class. It was to take place at the Grassmarket on 5 September 1716. A broadside expressed sadness for his folly and demise, telling its readers:

> My weeping Muse proceed with mournful Tone,
> And with great Floods of brekish Tears bemoan,
> The fatel End of this brave Hamilton,
> Who might for Beauty equal Absolom;
> A stately Youth, of honoured Birth and Blood,
> Who likewise had an Education Good,
> But was by youthful Passions led astray,
> And in a Fit, rashly a Man did Slay,
> Which tho' not out of Malice, or Envy,
> The Law requires that for it he should Die;
> Accordingly, the Sprightly Youth was led
> Unto the Scaffold and his Blood their shed,
> That thereby he might in some part Attone,
> For th' undesigned mischief he had done.

While there was sympathy for the young man, there was none for Robert Irvine. He was chaplain to wealthy Edinburgh merchant and Baillie James Gordon and responsible for educating the businessman's sons, John and Alexander. Almost certainly Irvine suffered some form of mental blackout because on Sunday 28 April 1717 he took the youngsters for a walk and slit both their throats with a penknife. He then cut his own throat and threw himself into a quarry pond but was caught and survived. Asked why he committed the terrible deeds Irvine told prosecutors it was a 'Temptation of the Devil' and he had planned the murders for several days. There would never be mercy for such wickedness and on the afternoon of 1st May hangman Sutherland shackled Irvine's hands over a wooden block sited between Edinburgh and Leith, chopped them off and then hanged him. The severed hands were stuck on poles outside the city prison and his body dumped in the same quarry where he had tried to kill himself. In a broadside about the murders it was said that Irvine confessed, 'That his Sins, particularly this of deliberate and wilful Murder, were of so heinous a Nature and of so deep a Dye, that he was afraid that God would not have Mercy on him and had particularly this Expression, The Snares, Fire and Brimstone would be his Portion.'

His punishment was deliberately meant to make him suffer pain; that inflicted in November 1718 on murderer John Grant of Carron in Aberdeenshire was intended to humiliate. He was ordered to be hanged with the axe he used to commit the killing tied around his neck.

By 1723 the British parliament was in desperate need of a scapegoat on whom it could shoulder blame for a massive economic downturn. Even royalty and the rich had suffered horrendous financial losses with the collapse of the South Sea Company, partly owned by the government. For the poor the consequences were catastrophic; jobs were lost, families turned out of their homes and forced to beg. In the country many turned to illegal poaching. Two poaching groups were especially active in Hampshire and Windsor Forest. They were conspicuous through blacking their faces to disguise their features. Wealthy landowners who largely controlled parliament demanded action and claimed the poaching gangs were linked to Jacobites who had fought for the Old Pretender. The result was the passing in 1723 of the Black Act, which laid down the death penalty for more than fifty offences including being found armed and with a blackened face in a forest or royal park, stealing or killing cattle, setting fire to corn, hay, straw, wood, houses or barns, damaging a fish pond, sending anonymous letters demanding money or venison, trying to rescue a prisoner or shooting at anyone. Poaching deer would be punished by a fine and then transportation. It was the start of years of terror as year by year the number of capital offences was increased and hangmen were kept on their toes.

One who would not be involved was William Sutherland. A year earlier in 1722 the magistrates at Edinburgh decided enough was enough as far as their executioner was concerned. He was frequently drunk, consorted with prostitutes, beat his wife and bungled hangings. Finally he was sacked, suffered the humiliation of being whipped just as he had done to so many others and then banished from the capital.

3

BEYOND THE SEAS

As the population of Britain increased, so did the number of those the state regarded as unwelcome and unwanted because they were at odds with the law. Lawbreakers weren't only those committing murder, stealing, poaching, having illegitimate babies, indulging in adultery or pinching horses or cows; they included men and women who challenged authority. In any revolt one huge problem facing the victors was what to do with those they defeated. Battles during the Civil War between 1642 and 1651 over who had the right to rule Britain threw up tens of thousands of prisoners, many of them Scots.

Following the Battle of Dunbar in September 1650 when English Parliamentarian forces under Oliver Cromwell routed a Scottish army led by David Leslie, who was loyal to Charles II, around 5,000 Scots prisoners were marched off south. Half naked, starving, desperately ill from an outbreak of cholera and suffering from untreated wounds, men in the miserable column began dying in their droves, their bodies sometimes left to rot or dumped into unmarked pits. Their destination was the Thames but by the time they reached the south of England just over 1,000 remained alive. Why London? Because Cromwell and his cohorts had decided how to get rid of these agitators before they could stir up further rebellion.

Early in the seventeenth century England had come up with a plan that would resolve the question of how to deal with its unwanted masses. Simply putting them in prison and maintaining them was rapidly creating a mounting and unsustainable financial burden on civil administrators. At the same time Britain was anxious to build up its colonies 3,000 miles away across the Atlantic. Labour was needed there and in 1615 it was decided to begin shipping felons to America, initially to the mainland, principally to Maryland, Virginia and then later to settlements in the Caribbean, mainly Barbados and then Jamaica and eventually the Leeward Islands.

This was just another form of slavery; a largely disorganised system in which groups of convicts were put in the hands of agents, who made deals with individual ship owners to take human cargoes on voyages lasting around two months in often unseaworthy vessels and in filthy conditions. Deaths at sea were frequent. When they landed some were even sold, but most were distributed among plantation owners or businessmen who were made responsible for them. This was the fate of the remaining Scots survivors from the debacle of the Battle of Dunbar. They were not alone for long. Exactly a year later, on 3 September 1651, at the Battle of Worcester, Cromwell smashed another Royalist army, capturing 10,000 prisoners. The English among them were recruited into his ranks but for an estimated 8,000 Scots a nightmare voyage to America beckoned. They found themselves chained alongside the likes of religious protesters, prostitutes, murderers and thieves, some of whom were no older than nine or ten.

The monetary benefits from the emptying of English jails eventually spread to Scotland and gradually courts began pronouncing the dread sentence that a culprit would be 'Banished Beyond the Seas', usually for seven or fourteen years but increasingly for life. Being caught returning before the expiration of a sentence almost certainly guaranteed a public flogging, a spell in jail and then transportation for life. However, the dumping of tens of thousands of felons on their doorsteps was not going down well with some colonists. In 1651 even before huge cargoes of Scots soldiers had arrived, colonists in Virginia demanded that contracts to ship Scots were put on hold, 'Till assurance be given of their not being carried where they may be dangerous.' Many of the colonists were deeply religious and the situation was not helped by the transporting from Leith to Virginia by order of Edinburgh magistrates of around fifty 'lewd' women and thirty others caught 'walking the streets after ten at night'. Some colonies tried passing legislation to stop the imposition on them of convicts or prisoners, but were overruled by the British monarchy. However, the irritation of the colonists over the transportation issue was further aggravated when the uprisings by supporters of the Old and Young Pretenders saw more Scots taken in battle, in particular following the defeat at Culloden, and shipped off.

While Scottish courts were much more reluctant than those in England to use the transportation option, the miserable trail up the steps of the scaffolds continued to be well worn, although not always with the result judges had intended. September 1724 saw one of the most remarkable episodes in Scottish legal history when mother-of-two Maggie Dickson was sentenced to death. Separated from her fisherman husband after he was press ganged into the Navy, she found work at an inn in Kelso, where she had an affair and discovered she was pregnant. Desperate to keep her condition a secret she continually denied she was expecting, but after the discovery of the body of a newborn baby on the banks of the Tweed a surgeon reported the infant had been alive when it was born and gossips pointed the finger of guilt at Maggie, who was arrested, charged with infanticide, found guilty and ordered to be executed at Edinburgh Grassmarket. A broadside printed at the time revealed, 'While she lay in confinement she was extremely penitent, and acknowledged that she had in many instances, neglected her duty, and likewise that she had been guilty of fornication; but to the last denied murdering the child, or that she had the least intention of so doing. Her reason for concealing the birth of the child was for fear of being made a public example in the church, and a laughing-stock to all her neighbours. She said she was suddenly taken in labour, sooner

17

than she expected, and her agonies not only prevented her from getting assistance, but also left her in a state of insensibility, so that what became of her child she could not say. When she was brought to the gallows she behaved in the most penitent manner, but still denied her guilt, after which she was turned off, and hung the usual time.'

Then came an astonishing development. 'When cut down her body was given to her friends, who put her into a coffin, in order to carry it to Musselburgh, for interment; but the men who had charge of the corpse stopped at a village called Pepper Mill about two miles from Edinburgh in order to get some refreshment, leaving the cart with the body near the door. While they were drinking one of the men thought he saw the lid of the coffin move, and going towards the cart, uncovered it, when he could perceive the woman to move, and she arose upright in her coffin; upon which he and others took to their heels, almost killed with fear. A gardener who was drinking in the house went up to the coffin, and had the presence of mind to open a vein, and within an hour afterwards she was so well recovered as to be able to go to bed. Next morning she walked home to Musselburgh.'

There was even more good news for Maggie. Scots law decreed that, 'Every person upon whom the judgment of the court has been executed, has no more to suffer, but must be forever discharged.' So, officially dead, she was able to remarry her husband and resume life in which she became known as 'Half-Hangit Maggie' without the fear of rearrest. A pub named after her is a popular attraction in the Grassmarket.

Three years later in March 1727 another woman followed Maggie on to the same scaffold, when a Mrs McLeoid was sentenced to die for forgery, despite maintaining she was innocent. A broadside told, in verse, what it claimed were her final words, some of which were:

> My loving Husband he is gone,
> and left me here forlorn,
> Because for Forgery I am seiz'd,
> which makes my Heart to mourn.

I never Forg'd in my Life,
nor khew [sic] what it did mean,
I never could incline my Heart,
to act such horrid Sin.
But yet I apprehended was,
and cast in Prison strong,
For Forgery, which grieves my Heart;
but those that did me Wrong,
I leave them to the Judgment Day
when they must all appear,
To answer for that Blood, was shed,
was purchased so dear.

The gibbet was equally busy elsewhere. Regularly judges were expected to travel around the various circuits, holding court in towns and cities that included Perth, Dumfries, Aberdeen and Glasgow. Sometimes that meant a long, cold, bumpy and occasionally dangerous coach journey to Inverness where some must have wondered whether the effects of the travel had left judges irritated and in a frame of mind to take out their discomfort on the unfortunates appearing before them. It probably seemed that way to Archibald Gillespick Donn in May 1721 when he was given the death sentence for just a couple of minor thefts. In 1725 Archibald Campbell, a tinker from Urquhart, and Donald McKinnon from Loch Arkaig in Lochaber were told they would hang together 'till they are dead and their moveable goods and gear inbrought to his majesties'.

At Inverness, Ewan McGoilvain, a former smith in Achnacarry, Lochaber, heard a judge at Inverness tell him he was to be 'hanged by the neck upon a gibbet till he be dead and thereafter to be hung in chains of iron upon the same gibbet for ye barbarous murder of John Cameron in Clunes and Dougald McDonald in Invergarry'.

At times sentences seemed to vary between being silly or barbaric. In Edinburgh in 1729 two women were jailed just for wearing men's clothes while that same year at Execution Dock in London John Gow, a native of the Orkneys, was sentenced to be pressed to death. It was a horrific punishment ordered simply because Gow refused to offer a plea to a charge of piracy; it involved increasing amounts of huge stones being piled on his chest until his ribs caved in and he was crushed. As the sentence was about to be carried out Gow changed his mind, pleaded guilty and was sentenced to hang. But the drama did not end there. On the gibbet his friends, determined to end his misery quickly, pulled his legs but did so with so much force that the rope broke and he had to be strung up again, this time successfully.

Documents held at the Highland Archive Centre in Inverness reveal there was no let-up in the issuing of death sentences. In 1736 Donnichie was condemned for theft and murder and told he would be joined on the scaffold by Duncan Buy alias Cameron, convicted of murdering Katherine Fraser.

If others elsewhere in the Highlands felt they were being deprived of seeing the hangman at work, they were given the satisfaction in 1741 of hearing the fate of Duncan McQueen and Angus Buchanan for the murder and robbery of James Orr. While McQueen was to die on the Gallows Muir at Inverness, Buchanan was ordered to be taken back to the town tolbooth and kept there until soldiers could take him to Portree in the Isle of Skye so he could be hanged there on the same day as his accomplice. It meant the authorities at Inverness had to fork out the cost of his imprisonment and that incurred by the troops. The issue of cost was one of which the burgh was becoming increasingly aware.

4

BONNIE PRINCE CHARLIE

If the treatment meted out to Cromwell's Scottish prisoners seemed harsh, it was as nothing compared with what was to come. The Old Pretender had twice tried to seize the throne of Britain that he claimed as the son of King James II of England and Ireland (VII of Scotland) was rightfully his. An attempted landing in the Firth of Forth in 1708 had to be aborted when the French ship carrying him was scared off by English naval vessels, while the rising of 1715 had been a short-lived disaster. Now he was living in Rome under Papal protection, largely a figure of curiosity to travellers, leaving his son Charles to try to succeed where he had failed.

As young Charles – Bonnie Prince Charlie – was laying plans from bases first in Rome then in France for a landing in Scotland from which to mount an invasion of his own, word from spies of this next possible rising reached the ears of George II, his ministers and younger son William, Duke of Cumberland, known to his followers as 'Sweet William'. Scots would come to give him a very different tag. The Duke was just twenty-two when, in 1743, concern arose over the invasion prospect. Some Scotsmen, as an alternative to starvation and homelessness, had joined a number of clan-based British infantry companies to patrol or watch for troublemakers mainly in the Highlands and were known to

Gaelic speakers as Am Freiceadan Dubh – the Black Watch. By 1743 these companies were officially the 42nd Regiment of Foot. The majority, when they joined up, did so believing they would remain in Scotland. Now the presence there of armed, trained troops whose loyalties were primarily to their homeland was causing alarm in London. Their very existence meant the Young Pretender might arrive to discover a ready-made army at his disposal and so it was decided to move them south and station them around the capital.

The excuse given when they were ordered to march off was that the King wanted to see for the first time his Highland regiment, but by the time the Scots reached London they had discovered His Majesty was in Europe and a rumour began that an inspection by him was merely an excuse to draw them from Scotland and their real destination was the West Indies. Angry and disillusioned, 109 men deserted and set off back to Scotland in May. They were pursued by three troops of dragoons who caught up and surrounded them in a wood in Northamptonshire. After surrendering, the Scots, their arms tied behind their backs, were force marched back to London, thrown into the Tower and then sentenced to death by a court martial as the rest of the regiment was being shipped over to Flanders where it would fight with distinction under the Duke of Cumberland. All but three of the condemned men were reprieved. Corporals Malcolm and Samuel Macpherson, alleged to have been the ringleaders, and Private Farquar Shaw, who was accused of struggling with a sergeant, were executed by firing squad at the Tower of London in July. The others involved in the mutiny were separated and dispatched to join other regiments in Minorca, Gibraltar, America and the West Indies.

Meanwhile on the European mainland Bonnie Prince Charlie was finalising his arrangements to arrive in Scotland. As he did so Highlanders were preparing to heed the call to arms that would inevitably arrive. Such issues seemed to be evolving too far off to interest young men in Edinburgh who had other matters to concern them. In 1744 a group of enthusiasts formed the Honourable Company of Edinburgh Golfers and played on a five-hole course over Leith Links. They and others took the game seriously. Two locals were hauled before magistrates and fined for riding their horses over the course.

The following year the Young Pretender landed. Initially his campaign went well but then it ran out of steam and his supporters were massacred at Culloden in April 1746 by forces under the Duke of Cumberland, including units of the Black Watch. Now the twenty-four-year-old Duke was about to demonstrate his reputation as a butcher to the cost of those taken prisoner and countless others throughout the Highlands accused of supporting the Jacobites. The *Glasgow Journal* reported in its issue of 19 May 1746 that the Duke had written to the King to say that, 'The number of prisoners increases at Inverness. The prisons at Aberdeen, Montrose and Stirling are filled and prisoners are continually brought into Perth, Dunfermline, Dundee, Irvine and Dumfries.'

The newspaper also offered a remarkable insight into the behaviour of some of the Prince's officers. 'John Hay, a Scotchman, who calls himself a Captain and Paymaster of Lord John Drummond's Regiment, surrendered himself to the Lord Justice Clerk and was, by his Lordship, committed to our Castle. This man says that the French viz Drummond's Regiment, the Irish Picquet at Fitz James's Horse at the time of the late battle amounted to between 6 and 700 men, that of the first, 50 were killed in the battle and of the second about 100. He further says that he parted from the person called Lord John Drummond at Ruthven, who took the money belonging to the Regiment from him and divided it amongst his officers desiring every one to shift for himself as he intended to do, that the rebels had not received any pay for some weeks before the Battle; that the night before they were extremely harassed by marching and counter marching and before they could get any refreshment they were surprised by the Duke's quick march.'

The *Glasgow Journal* also gave a hint that the King acting on advice from Cumberland had made up his mind to treat his prisoners with the same disregard for mercy as had Cromwell. In a report dated 13 May it stated, 'We are assured that his Majesty has been pleased to order such of the Rebel private men as his Royal Highness shall think proper objects of his Majesty's clemency to be transported to some of His Majesty's American colonies.' So the lucky ones would live but never see Scotland again.

Cumberland's venom against the defeated men was not helped by an incident reported in the same newspaper. 'Two soldiers belonging to the Garrison of Fort William having been fishing, were attacked by some vagabond Camerons who cut off their arms and left them in that shocking condition.' Little wonder then that its readers saw on 24 July that, 'Seventeen rebels were condemned in London to be hanged, drawn and quartered.' The paper also had news from 'Sky', using a different spelling for the island we know as Skye. Dated 17 July its report revealed, 'We hear that Mr Sullivan, two Irish officers and two other gentlemen who either cannot or will not speak English are taken in the Isle of Sky. The Pretender is said to be there in women's clothes. The Hussars commanded by an Aid de Camp are gone in quest of him.'

Four days later it was the turn of the captured Earl of Kilmarnock, Earl of Cromartie and Arthur Elphinston, Lord Balmerino, to be tried for high treason. The *Newgate Calendar*, a newsletter published from time to time and dealing principally with executions, described in detail their appearance on Monday 28 July 1746 before 136 of their fellow peers and the grisly outcome for two of them.

'About eight o' clock in the morning, the three rebel lords, prisoners in the Tower, were carried from thence in three coaches, the Earl of Kilmarnock, with Governor Williamson, and another gentleman, captain of the guard, in the first, the Earl of Cromartie; attended by Captain Marshall, in the second: and Lord Balmerino, attended by Mr Fowler, gentleman gaoler, who had the axe covered by him, in the third, under a strong guard of foot-soldiers to Westminster Hall. William Earl of Kilmarnock was brought to the bar and his bill of indictment for high treason read, to which his lordship pleaded Guilty, and desired to be recommended to his Majesty for mercy. Then George Earl of Cromartie was brought to the bar, &c, who also pleaded Guilty

24

and prayed for mercy, After which Arthur Lord Balmerino was brought to the bar, &c. who pleaded Not Guilty, alleging that he was not at Carlisle at the time specified in the indictment, whereupon six witnesses for the crown were called in and examined, whose evidence was distinctly repeated by the reading-clerk, proving that his Lordship entered Carlisle (though not the same day) sword in hand, at the head of a regiment called by his name, Elphinston's Horse.'

Like his friends Cromartie was also convicted but was later pardoned after successfully arguing the charge against him was inaccurate. But Balmerino and Kilmarnock were told they would be beheaded on 18 August.

The *Calendar* described that terrible day. 'At six o'clock a troop of life-guards, one of horse-grenadiers, and 1000 of the foot guards, (being fifteen men out of each company,) marched from the parade in St James's park through the city to Tower-hill, to attend the execution of the Earl of Kilmarnock and the Lord Balmerino, and being arrived there, were posted in lines from the Tower to the scaffold, and all round it. About eight o'clock the sheriffs of London, with their under-sheriffs, and their officers, viz. six serjeants at mace, six yeomen, and the executioner, met at the Mitre tavern in Fenchurch-street, where they breakfasted, and went from thence to the house lately the Transport-office on Tower-hill, near Catherine-court, hired by them for the reception of the said lords, before they should be conducted to the scaffold, which was erected about thirty yards from the said house. At ten o'clock the block was fixed on the stage, and covered with black cloth, and several sacks of sawdust were brought up to strew on it; soon after their coffins were brought, covered with black cloth, ornamented with gilt nails, &c. On the Earl of Kilmarnock's was a plate with this inscription, "Gulielmus. Comes. de Kilmarnock decollatus, 18 Augusti, 1746, Ætat. suæ 42, " with an earl's coronet over it, and six coronets over the six handles; and on Lord Balmerino's was a plate with this inscription, "Arthurus Dominus de Balmerino decollatus, 18 Augusti, 1746, Ætat. Suæ 58, " with a baronet's coronet over it, and six others over the six handles.

'At a quarter after ten the sheriffs went in procession to the outward gate of the Tower, and, after knocking at it some time, a warder within asked, "Who's there?" The officer without answered, "The Sheriffs of London and Middlesex." The warder then asked, "What do they want?" The officer answered, "The bodies of Earl of Kilmarnock, and Arthur, Lord Balmerino," Upon which the warder said, "I will go and inform the Lieutenant of the Tower," and in about ten minutes the Lieutenant of the Tower, with the Earl of Kilmarnock, and Major White with Lord Balmerino, guarded by several of the warders, came to the gate; the prisoners were there delivered to the Sheriffs, who gave proper receipts for their bodies to the Lieutenant, who, as is usual, said, "God bless King George"; to which the Earl of Kilmarnock assented by a bow, and Lord Balmerino said, "God bless King James."

'The Earl then, with the company kneeling down joined in a prayer delivered by Mr Foster: after which, having sat a few moments, and taken a second refreshment of a bit of bread and a glass of wine, he expressed a desire that Lord Balmerino might go first to the scaffold; but being informed that this could not be, as his lordship was named first in the warrant, he appeared satisfied, saluted his friends, saying he should make no speech on the scaffold, but desired the ministers to assist him in his last moments, and they accordingly, with other friends, proceeded there with him. The multitude, who had been long expecting to see him on such an awful occasion, on his first appearing on the scaffold, dressed in black, with a countenance and demeanour, testifying great contrition, shewed the deepest signs of commiseration and pity; and his lordship, at the same time, being struck with such a variety of dreadful objects at once, the multitudes, the block, his coffin, the executioner, the instrument of death, turned about to Mr Hume (a minister), and said, "Hume! This is terrible"; though without changing his voice or countenance.

'After putting up a short prayer, concluding with a petition for his Majesty King George and the royal family, in verification of his declaration his speech, his lordship embraced, and took his last leave of his friend. The executioner, who before had something administered to keep him from fainting, was so affected with his lordship's distress, and the awfulness of the scene, that on asking him forgiveness, he burst into tears. My lord bid him take courage, giving him at the same time a purse with five guineas, and telling him that he would drop his handkerchief as a signal for the stroke.

'He proceeded, with the help of his gentleman, to make ready for the block, by taking off his coat, and the bag from his hair, which was then tucked up under a napkin cap, but this being made up so wide as not to keep up his long hair, the making it less occasioned a little delay; his neck being laid bare, tucking down the collar of his shirt, and waistcoat, he kneeled down on a black cushion at the block, and drew his cap over his eyes, in doing which, as well as in putting up his hair, his hands were observed to shake; but, either to support or for a more convenient posture of devotion, he happened to lay both his hands upon the block, which the executioner observing, prayed his lordship to let them fall, lest they should be mangled or break the blow.

'He was then told, that the neck of his waistcoat was in the way, upon which he rose, and with the help of a friend took it off, and the neck being made bare to the shoulders, he kneeled down as before: in the meantime, when all things were ready for the execution, and the black baize which hung over the rails of the scaffold, having, by direction of the colonel of the guards or the sheriffs, been turned up that the people might see all the circumstances of the execution; in about two minutes (the time he before fixed) after he kneeled down, his lordship dropping his handkerchief, the executioner at once severed his head from his body, except only a small part of the skin, which was immediately divided by a gentle stroke; the head was received in a piece of red baize, and with the body immediately put into the coffin. The scaffold, was then cleared from the blood, fresh sawdust strewed, and, that no appearance of a former execution might remain, the executioner changed such of his clothes as appeared bloody.'

The gruesome account which was said to have been published by the authority of the sheriffs said it had been claimed in some versions of the events that, 'The Lord Kilmarnock requested his head might not be held up as usual, and declared to be the head of a traitor; and that, for this reason that part of the ceremony was omitted, as the sentence and law did not require it; but we are assured that his lordship made no such request; and further, that when he was informed that his head would be held up, and such, proclamation made, it did not affect him and he spoke of it as a matter of no moment. All that he wished or desired was, 1. That the executioner might not be, as represented to his lordship, "a good, sort of man," thinking "a rough temper would be fitter for the purpose." 2. That his coffin, instead of remaining in the hearse, might be set upon the stage: and, 3. That four persons might be appointed to receive the head, that it might not roll about the stage, but be speedily, with his body, put into the coffin.

'While this was doing, the Lord Balmerino, after having solemnly recommended himself to the mercy of the Almighty, conversed cheerfully with his friends, refreshed himself twice with a bit of bread and a glass of wine, and desired the company to drink to ain degrae to haiven, acquainting them that he had prepared a speech which he should read on the scaffold, and therefore should there say nothing of its contents. The under-sheriff coming into his lordship's apartment to let him know the stage was ready, he prevented him by immediately asking if the affair was over with the Lord Kilmarnock, and being answered "It is," he inquired how the executioner performed his office, and upon receiving the account, said it was well done; then addressing himself to the company, said, "Gentlemen, I shall detain you no longer," and with an easy unaffected cheerfulness he saluted his friends, and hastened to the scaffold, which he mounted with so easy an air as astonished the spectators; his lordship was dressed in his regimentals, a blue coat turned up with red, trimmed with brass buttons, (and a tie-wig,) the same which he wore at the battle of Culloden; no circumstance in his whole deportment shewed the least sign of fear or regret, and he frequently reproved his friends for discovering either upon his account.

'He walked several times round the scaffold, bowed to the

people; went to his coffin, read the inscription, and with a nod, said, it is right; he then examined the block, which he called his pillow of rest. His lordship putting on his spectacles, and taking a paper out of his pocket, read it with an audible voice, which, so far from being filled with passionate invective, mentioned his majesty as a prince of the greatest magnanimity and mercy, at the same time that, through erroneous political principles, it denied him a right to the allegiance of his people: having delivered this paper to the sheriff, he called for the executioner, who appearing, and being about to ask his lordship's pardon, he said, "Friend, you need not ask me forgiveness, the execution of your duty is commendable;" upon which, his lordship gave him three guineas, saying, "Friend, I never was rich, this is all the money I have now, I wish it was more, and I am sorry I can add nothing to it but my coat and waistcoat, which he then took off, together with his neck-cloth, and threw them on his coffin; putting on a flannel waistcoat, which had been provided for the purpose, and then taking a plaid cap out of his pocket, he put it on his head, saying he died a Scotchman; after kneeling down at the block to adjust his posture, and shew the executioner the signal for the stroke, which was dropping his arms, he once more turned to his friends, and took his last farewell, and, looking round, on the crowd, said, "Perhaps some may think my behaviour too bold, but remember, Sir (said he to a gentleman who stood near him) that I now declare it is the effect of confidence in God, and a good conscience, and I should dissemble if I should shew any signs of fear."

'Observing, the axe in the executioner's hand as he passed him, he took it from him, felt the edge, and returning it, clapped the executioner on the shoulder to encourage him; he tucked down the collar of his shirt and waistcoat, and shewed him where to strike, desiring him to do it resolutely, for in that, says his lordship, will consist your kindness. He went to the side of the stage, and called up the warder, to whom he gave some money, asked which was his hearse, and ordered the man to drive near. Immediately, without trembling or changing countenance, he again knelt down at the block, and having with his arms stretched out, said, "O Lord, reward my friends, forgive my enemies, and receive my soul," he gave the signal by letting them fall. But his uncommon firmness and intrepidity, and the unexpected suddenness of the signal so surprised the executioner, that though he struck the part directed, the blow was not given with strength enough to wound him very deep; on which it seemed as if he made an effort to turn his head towards the executioner, and the under jaw fell, and returned very quick, like anger and gnashing the teeth; but it could not be otherwise, the part being convulsed. A second blow immediately succeeding the first, rendered him, however, quite insensible, and a third finished the work.'

The *Glasgow Journal* described the executions the following day of some of those rebels who had been ordered to be hanged, drawn and quartered. Among them were John Sanderson and Thomas Syddall, Captains in the Manchester regiment; David Morgan, described as a Counsellor at Law, Andrew Blood and two others named Townley and Dawson.

Its report began by relating that on the same day as Balmerino and Kilmarnock had perished, the men were informed it was their turn tomorrow. 'They seemed not at all shocked but rather cheerful. The next morning they were called up about six o'clock and unloosed from the floor to which they had been chained down ever since the sentence of Death was passed upon them. They then ordered coffee to be got ready for their breakfast as soon as they were brought down into the yard. And after breakfast they had their irons knocked off. When the halter was put about Syddall he was observed to tremble very much although he endeavoured to conceal his disorder from the spectators by taking a pinch of snuff and as the executioner was fastening his hands and lifting up his eyes said, "Oh Lord Help Me". When they had finished their devotions, every one of them took some written papers out of the book which Morgan held in his hand and threw them among the mob. The contents of the papers were that they died in a just cause, that they did not repent of what they had done and doubted not that their deaths would be revenged with several other treasonable expressions.

'They were then tied up to the Gallows and in about five minutes the executioner cut down the body of Mr Townley and laid it on a stage for the purpose. The body being stript and laid at length having some signs of life in it, the executioner struck it several blows on the breast, then cut off his head, took out his bowels and flung them into the fire near the gallows. Dawson was the last and when the executioner had thrown his heart and bowels into the fire the spectators gave three loud huzzas at the same time crying out 'God Bless King George and all the Royal Family'. When he had done the executioner put the heads with the embowelled bodies into coffins, laid them in sledges and they were carried to the New Gaol.'

Eight months later on 9 April 1747, eighty-year-old Lord Lovat met his bloody end. The *Newgate Calendar* described him as 'very large and unwieldy in his person' and related that, 'At five o'clock he arose, and asked for a glass of wine-and-water, and at eight o'clock he desired that his wig might be sent, that the barber might have time to comb it out genteelly, and he then provided himself with a purse to hold the money which he intended for the executioner. At about half-past nine o'clock he ate heartily of minced veal, and ordered that his friends might be provided with coffee and chocolate, and at eleven o'clock the sheriffs came to demand his body. He then requested his friends to retire while he said a short prayer; but he soon called them back, and said that he was ready.

'When his lordship was going up the steps to the scaffold, assisted by two warders, he looked round, and, seeing so great a concourse of people, "God save us," says he, "why should there be such a bustle about taking off an old grey head, that cannot get up three steps without three bodies to support it?"

'Turning about, and observing one of his friends much dejected, he clapped him on the shoulder, saying: "Cheer up thy heart, man! I am not afraid; why should you be so?" As soon as he came upon the scaffold he asked for the executioner, and presented him with ten guineas in a purse, and then, desiring to see the axe, he felt the edge and said he "believed it would do".

'He ordered his cap to be put on, and, unloosing his neckcloth and the collar of his shirt, knelt down at the block, and pulled the cloth which was to receive his head close to him. But, being placed too near the block, the executioner desired him to remove a little farther back, which with the warders' assistance was immediately done; and, his neck being properly placed, he told the executioner he would say a short prayer and then give the signal by dropping his handkerchief. In this posture he remained about half-a-minute, and then, on throwing his handkerchief on the floor, the executioner at one blow cut off his head, which was received in the cloth, and, with his body was put into the coffin and carried in a hearse back to the Tower, where it was interred near the bodies of the other lords.'

The old man had led a remarkable life, even raping his reluctant heiress bride in order to inherit his title and her fortune. For that he had been outlawed but he ingratiated himself by fighting on the side of the King against the Old Pretender, only to switch sides with deadly results.

5

THE OLD BILL

It was with good reason that the Scots, transported to the Americas, many of whom had married and settled down and no longer looked on themselves as British but American, had no love for the English monarchy. Now they were joined by Jacobite rebels bitter at their callous treatment after the 1745 uprising. While dissent among the exiles in America continued to ferment, back in Scotland the death sentences, especially in the Highland birthplaces of so many of the rebels, continued to teem down. No wonder then that at every court accused men and women dreading the inevitable harshness of their punishments failed to appear and were outlawed while others took advantage of crumbling tolbooths or poor security to escape.

Judges rarely accepted defence challenges and a defendant was not allowed to give evidence at his or her own trial. Juries were largely comprised of men from the wealthy upper classes – well-to-do businessmen and property owners with little or no understanding of what it was like to be poor or hungry. Even when a jury, giving a guilty verdict in one of the now fast-increasing number of capital cases pleaded for an accused to be shown mercy, the odds on that leading to a reprieve were long. Mostly, once a judge put on the black cap and pronounced the death sentence, the scaffold loomed.

Such a grim prospect faced one-time army sergeant major John Young. He had fought bravely in Flanders for the Duke of Cumberland, acted gallantly despite being on the losing side against the Jacobite rebels at the Battle of Falkirk Muir in January 1746 and was commended for his courage at Culloden. He was highly thought of by his superiors and eventually became regimental paymaster. Then it all went wrong. He helped a recruit named Parker engrave a plate to counterfeit Bank of Scotland notes. For a while the scheme worked well and the pair seemed well on the way to getting rich. But a pile of banknotes supplied to a businessman were discovered to be fakes; Young's quarters were searched, wads of notes discovered and when Parker saved his own skin by giving evidence against him, Irish-born Young was condemned for forgery after a day-long trial.

As was the normal practice the judge who sentenced him laid down a two-hour period – between two and four in the afternoon – in which he was to be executed on 19 December 1748. Young was popular with his fellow Edinburgh Tolbooth inmates and as he languished in the condemned cell was assured by them that if he had not been hanged by four o'clock then the sentence would become invalid and he would have to be freed. Now he was convinced he had discovered a loophole in the law allowing him to escape death and so on 19 December he barricaded himself in his cell with the result that when the jailer arrived to hand him over to the hangman, he could not get in. Pleadings for Young to open up were ignored and with the official execution party including armed troops waiting anxiously in the corridor outside the cell, it was decided to send for workmen; but a gang of carpenters and blacksmiths could not budge the door. Masons reckoned they could knock through the wall without the whole building falling down but the plan was rejected as too risky.

Finally even though the four o'clock deadline had passed, carpenters began hacking a hole in the ceiling from the cell above. They broke through and the cell door was opened but even then Young refused to go quietly and snatching a musket from one of the soldiers threatened to shoot anyone trying to disarm him. However, after a brief stand-off half a dozen soldiers suddenly dropped through the opening and even though one was battered on the head by Young the convict was overpowered and hauled off to the scaffold where his protests that it was now six o'clock and no one had authority to hang him were ignored and he was hanged.

Others condemned to the same fate went more quietly. A year after Young met his doom Kenneth McDonald was condemned to death at Inverness for murder, giving the tolbooth jailer a problem. The prison was small but there was already someone else in the condemned cell; Marjory McEanduy was facing death for murdering her own child, a common offence of the time and the jailer was officially ordered to make sure McDonald and McEanduy were kept apart even though both were due to die on the same Gallows Muir scaffold. That same year Donald Fraser Younger had been convicted of theft and murder and in addition of being 'habite and repute a vagrant and of bad fame in the County'. He too was to die at Gallows Muir, as was Thomas Findlater, found guilty of rape.

The anti-establishment feeling in the Highlands persisted with these sentences, which often appeared unduly harsh, and it was hardly surprising to many when on 14 May 1752 Government Factor Colin Roy Campbell of Glenure, known as the Red Fox because of his brightly coloured mop of hair and his vigorous persecution of suspected Jacobites, was shot dead in Appin. The chief suspect, Allan Stewart, also known as Alan Breck Stewart, disappeared and the authorities prosecuted James Stewart, who was hanged on 8 November 1752 at Ballachulish, even though the evidence against him was virtually non-existent. The incident was dramatised by Robert Louis Stevenson in *Kidnapped*.

As if there was not already a feeling among Scots of injustice, unfairness and cruelty, the government seemed determined to use fear as a means of subjugating the poor and any of its opponents. The Murder Act of 1751 gave judges authority to order that murderers should be hanged in chains and/or face the humiliation of having their bodies publicly dissected in order that their remains would never have a burial. The act further said that death sentences should, whenever possible, be carried out within two days of being pronounced. One of the first to suffer this ghastly indignity was farm worker Christian Phren, put to death at Aberdeen for killing her newly-born illegitimate baby and then trying to conceal both her pregnancy and the murder by burning the infant's body. However, the charred remains were discovered and according to the *Glasgow Journal* she was made to wrap the little grisly mess in her apron and carry it until she reached the tolbooth. As was the discretionary rule with regard to anyone convicted of murder, the judges sentenced her to be fed only bread and water until she was hanged after which her remains were given to local surgeons to carve up in order to increase their knowledge of the workings of the human body. There seemed no limit to the cruelty of the judiciary. Despite the abhorrence of such a punishment, in April 1753 Anne Williams was burned at the stake near Gloucester, having been convicted of murdering her husband William by poisoning him, a crime under English law regarded as a form of treason.

The lucky ones were still being packed off to the Americas, but there the ill feeling at being the equivalent of a refuse tip for unwanted British and a golden egg eaten by the English Crown was mounting. The writing might not have been on the wall, but a hint of the importance of Britons being made aware of the atmosphere in America was demonstrated by the *Glasgow Journal* when it published the contents of a letter written by a man in Philadelphia to his friend in Bristol. The cause of his gripe was the passing of the 1765 Stamp Act, which forced the colonies to pay tax to London on most documents.

'I make no doubt you have been informed by letters from your friends, as well as by our public newspapers of the great commotion throughout our colonies in general, which daily increase on account of the late Stamp Act for raising money among us. What adds to our uneasiness is, that we hear our brethren in England censure us severely, from a mistaken opinion that we are unwilling to pay our proportion towards relieving the nation from the heavy burden of debt it now groans under.'

Unrest on the other side of the Atlantic was not the only matter alarming the government. Trouble was looming on the home front. In May 1765 the *Glasgow Journal* reported that up to 50,000 weavers had gathered in Spitalfields, London, and marched to Westminster, their womenfolk carrying French-made silk hand-kerchiefs as flags and the men wearing red cockades in their hats. It was said that they stopped the carriages of members of parliament, 'praying to them to take pity on the poor weavers'. Soldiers called out to protect property were pelted with stones when the protest turned violent. In decades to come weavers and the lack of opportunities would feature prominently in the story of crime and punishment in Scotland.

The Crown's response to the march for pity was to come down even harder on those it wanted to prune from society. In 1765 Humphrey Ewing and Matthew Jack, convicted of defrauding the revenue by manipulating tobacco weights, were ordered to stand at Glasgow Cross between the official drummer and the hangman for half an hour at midday with their hands tied behind their backs and a label on their chests bearing the words, 'Convict of withdrawing his Majesties' weighs and substituting false weighs in place thereof', and then to be given fifteen lashes on their naked backs. That was just half of their ordeal. On the next market day they would undergo a repeat of the punishment at Greenock.

Humiliating though the sentence was the pair were lucky when compared to others. While they were being taunted, John Davidson, convicted of stabbing and wounding his wife, was ordered to be whipped through the streets of Aberdeen and then banished to the American plantations for seven years. He was followed by Alexander Smith from Corbrach, who was jailed then whipped through Aberdeen for being 'a person of bad character'.

The value of transportation to the authorities was shown by an item in the *Glasgow Journal* in May 1765 reporting that the Aberdeen gaol was almost, following the arrests of a number of 'thieves, vagrants and hurdy beggars, full of such bandits', and the local magistrates were in the process of setting up a House of Correction to which culprits would be sent and made to perform hard labour. Full jails meant rising bills to the local community;

execution and transportation kept the numbers incarcerated down.

Documents held at the Highland Archive Centre give a fascinating insight into the cost of crime and punishment. The Doomster, sometimes called Dempster, was the man appointed to relay a death sentence to a condemned person. It was a post peculiar to Scotland and formally abolished in 1773 – to save money – and to many it was thought unnecessary as the death sentence was in any case announced by a judge. But the Doomster, who often doubled as public executioner, cost money. At the double execution in 1736 of John McDonnichie and Duncan Buy for theft and murder, the Doomster was paid £1 7s (£270 in 2017 values), but there were many other charges including one resulting from the escape of the pair and recapture. Five soldiers from Lord Lovat's company were paid £5 (£1,000) for chasing and holding on to the two after they briefly got away from the Inverness Tolbooth.

The bills continued to mount up. 'Postage of a letter, candles and watching the malefactors and the Dempster for whiping and cords' set the burgh back £1 16s (£360). Then there were 'cords for laying two men, cash paid to the gravedigger and carrying the coffin' which came to £1 4s (£240). Someone needed to be paid ten shillings (£100) for 'carrying the ladders to and from the gallows'; cash to the Borrow (Burgh) Officers and 'lights for watching' amounted to a total of £2 8s (£495). There was even two shillings needed for a 'dram', presumably to the two men on their way to the scaffold.

Everything had its price, as the documents reveal. On 22 April 1737 'Ropes to bind the woman that was to be whipped and banished' cost eight shillings and the hangman received six shillings for carrying out the punishment. A week later the hangman was given fifteen shillings and four pence for 'whooping two women and for cords'. The Inverness hangman complained his room at the tolbooth was cold and so he was provided with a nightcap costing the burgh eight shillings. He was given the task by the magistrates of 'shaving the head of Macdonald the Beggar' for which he pocketed twelve shillings. Poor Macdonald's woes were not over. On 6 May 1737 the hangman received another twelve shillings for 'Putting a maid in the pillory and whooping Macdonald the Beggar.'

Following the execution on the Gallows Muir of a man named Evans at Inverness in March 1738, local blacksmith Fraser Smith received £1 4s for 'loosing iron chain from the gallows and carrying to town,' while the hangman collected twelve shillings for 'burying Evans' bones'. In April 1739 the burgh treasurer forked out fifteen shillings for 'a razor to the hangman for cutting a thief's ear, a gamlet [gimlet], a cord and his wages'.

The average hanging set the burgh back just over £5 as was demonstrated by the costs incurred for the holding of McQueen and Buchanan in 1741 (see Chapter 3) prior to the execution locally of McQueen and that of Buchanan at Portree. 'Candles for the courthouse and carrying the carpet along which the judges walked to and from the church; maintenance of two criminals under sentence of death; maintenance to the hangman during his confinement and until the execution; ropes "groat and small [sic]" for the execution of two men and paid to the executioner; fees to the executioner for that execution; candles to the town guard in time of the execution; bedding for the criminal under sentence of death.' It all totted up to £11 15s (£2,400) but in this case there was an extra cost for the burgh to meet, one that would not go down too well. As two men were sentenced to death the Inverness hangman vanished and the town had to cough up £1 4s to a pair of locals to hunt through the various taverns for him. Once found he was ordered to stay at the tolbooth, resulting in another extra bill for his 'confinement'.

In contrast was the annual bill for celebrating the King's Birthday. The burgh lashed out £46 (£9,400) in 1739 for claret to drink his health. By 30 October 1745, three months after the Young Pretender had arrived in Scotland and on the same day as he was discussing with his chief officers whether or not to invade England, the Inverness treasurer was recording that the burgesses were raising their glasses to George II and in doing so knocking back £58 (£11,800) worth of claret.

The treasurer's minute book records that following the death of the Doomster in 1733 he paid a total of £3 12s for 'burying the

Doomster; broad linen for a shroud and candles'. All sorts of bills had to be met. In 1744 six shillings was paid for 'a lock for hand-cuffs for a woman in gaol for murdering her child', while the hunt for yet another alleged child killer, the unfortunate Marjory McEanduy, set the burgh back £4 4s to 'Him that went in search' of her and £11 9s 6p for her maintenance before her execution. When the executioner announced his uniform was threadbare the treasurer had to dip into burgh funds and pay out £11 8s for a new outfit with mohair buttons. Keeping men and women in a tolbooth that was in continual need of repair wasn't the only burden on burgh finances. In 1767 when a group of prisoners escaped the treasurer had to pay £18 to three men who went in search of them.

Costs were constantly rising. The bill for hanging James Taylor in 1766 came to £19 14s (£3,200), although the accused man did his best to avoid conviction and so save the burgh money only to discover mercy was an expensive commodity and death the cheapest option. Taylor from Pluscardine, Elginshire, charged with housebreaking and robbery, knew the noose awaited him if he was convicted and attempted a bizarre way out by feigning madness. His wild antics startled guards taking him to Inverness for his trial and a jury had first to decide whether he really was mad. It concluded he was simply pretending, but he was not giving up.

The *Scots Magazine* said that, 'During the whole trial, at reading the verdict and even at receiving sentence, he continued his frantic behaviour, singing, whistling, dancing and talking incoherently to those around him; but all that was thought to be affectation.' The verdict was guilty, the sentence death and a cold entry in the minute book.

When it hanged Kenneth Leal on 7 July 1773, the burgh, forked out £20 2s (£2,830), which included five shillings for the 'consta-bles for drink after the execution'.

Leal, a messenger at arms from Elgin, had been finding the costs of supporting his wife and eight children increasingly diffi-cult to meet. He held up the local mail coach and thought he had got away with £270 (£37,800). But he had been recognised, was arrested and at Inverness convicted of robbery and sentenced to death. Leal begged to be transported, pointing out that would save money because his death would mean the authorities having to support his family. But it was a plea never likely to win sympathy and he was hanged at the same spot where he committed the hold-up.

Crime was expensive to its victims as well as to those having to deal with the culprits but there was little, if any, evidence to support the theory that injecting extreme pain into punishments would deter criminals. In November 1765 Alexander Provan was dragged from the Paisley Tolbooth to the scaffold, where the right hand with which he had murdered his wife was hacked off by the hangman, who then strung him up. His treatment seems savage to those living in the twenty-first century, but it was relatively humdrum when compared to the hanging and disembowelling that followed the 1745 uprising. But the example of Provan did nothing to halt a regular flow of domestic murders, some bordering on the barbaric.

Attempts at cracking down hard on crime were not limited to those from the establishment. Farmers throughout Scotland were becoming increasingly fed up with their livestock and horses being stolen. They were frequently in a position to vent their anger on defendants because farmers and estate owners regularly sat on juries. John MacLeod from Cromarty was sentenced to be executed at Inverness on 4 July 1767 for stealing horses and cattle and resetting them knowing they were stolen. After his capture he had been held with an accomplice in the tolbooth at Dingwall to await trial and they escaped, but MacLeod was recaptured. It was undoubtedly this that went against him when appeals for mercy were submitted to the King, whose agent wrote to the authorities saying the doomed man was, 'Not found, after the most mature deliberation, any way entitled to the Royal mercy and that the law was to take place against that unhappy man.'

Farmers in Midlothian banded together and formed a society to investigate and prosecute cattle thieves, with the result that in June 1766 Thomas Orr was convicted at Stirling of stealing a black horse and a bay mare from two parks and sentenced to death. Five years later the same fate beckoned to butcher James Hogg from Stirling, who stole cows from a local farm. But Hogg saved his neck by deciding to make a full confession. Owning up saved him from the gallows, but not from being whipped through the town before he was shipped to the plantations.

6

DOWN UNDER

The days when shiploads of Scots criminals crossed the Atlantic were numbered. Men and women from the stinking, cholera-riddled closes and streets of Glasgow, Edinburgh and Aberdeen, from villages and farms, had met with mixed fortunes – some literally sold into slavery. Others had risked hanging by absconding, lured by talk of gold strikes in the north and west; a few had used their old contacts in Scotland to cash in on the thriving tobacco trade that made millionaires of merchants in Glasgow. The transportees had come from a vast range of backgrounds; there were men and women of evil, men of business, artisans, and women of the night, there were the cunning, the idle and even the odd man of God.

Adultery was regarded as a direct insult to God because adulterous couples were seen to have violated sacred marriage oaths and it had for centuries been a capital offence in Scotland. Men had been executed for sex outside marriage and while adultery still had serious consequences for offenders and was an offence, it was no longer treated as a hanging crime. Usually allegations concerning the sexual behaviour of ministers would initially be dealt with internally by the Church authorities themselves, who could hand miscreants on to the Crown for prosecution. In the mid-1760s such a situation arose on Orkney when Thomas Lyell, ordained minister of Lady Parish in 1754, found himself at the centre of a scandal that in modern times would have sent tabloid journalists scurrying to the island.

According to gossip no sooner had he taken up his post than Lyell began sleeping with one of his maidservants, teenager Elspeth Smith, who had become pregnant as a result. When word of her plight leaked out, she was secretly taken to the home of friends of the minister and after a few days put on board a boat to Leith and from there sent to Edinburgh, where she gave birth in 1756. She and the child were being maintained by Lyell. Six years later another of his employees, housekeeper Margaret Scott, found herself pregnant and immediately fingers pointed at the minister, who protested to Church officials seeking to have him dismissed that his brother David, who lived with him, was the father; a fact David and Margaret later admitted to a Church commission investigating complaints of 'indecencies and immoralities' against the minister. The commission decided to dismiss the complaints against Lyell on the grounds of irregularities in the way the local presbytery had handled them, but other ministers persisted with attempts to get rid of Lyell, who was finally sacked in 1768. At least he avoided the criminal courts.

Not so fortunate was William Nisbet, minister in the neighbouring united parishes of Firth and Stenness in the Stewartry of Orkney. At the same time as scandalmongers were condemning Lyell, married Nisbet was under fire for having a married parishioner as his mistress. In 1763, while still a bachelor, he and the woman had been openly living together in the manse. He eventually agreed to demands from the presbytery to move her out, but then cheekily set her up in a building just twenty yards away. In 1764 Nisbet took another woman as his wife, but Church officers who believed this would put an end to the illicit relationship were shocked to discover that soon after the marriage the mistress was back living with the Nisbets. Not surprisingly Mrs Nisbet walked out. Once again the minister was ordered to get rid of his mistress and this time he set her up in a house half a mile away where, in 1765, it became obvious she was pregnant. While the Church dithered over what to do next, the civil authorities at Inverness, well aware of the goings-on, stepped in and Nisbet found himself convicted of committing adultery both before and after his marriage by a jury at a Circuit Court hearing. A few decades earlier he could have expected to be strung up; but the sentence he was given was tantamount to ending the life he had known. He was ordered to be chained in the Inverness Tolbooth for two months and fed only on bread and water, and then sent to the Thames hulk prison ships, where he would be kept until a boat took him to the plantations in the Americas, where he was to remain for the rest of his life.

In puritanical Scotland there was no mercy for a minister seen to put sex before godliness. The *Scots Magazine* of June 1766 quoted from various Scots legal annals. 'Open, manifest, and incorrigible adulterers, after the Kirk censures executed upon them, shall be denounced rebels and their goods escheat. Open and manifest adulterers, after due monition made to them to abstain, shall be punished to the death,' it proclaimed, making no secret of what it felt the punishment ought to have been.

Despite the growing ill feeling in the colonies towards Britain, Scotland continued sending its wayward citizens to the Americas. In many cases offenders facing execution discovered that begging to be transported could often be a means of avoiding the noose. Penny-pinching towns and cities realised that such an option saved on the costs of maintaining culprits in prisons and avoided bills for hanging. Further, the quicker transportees could be moved south to the Thames prison ships to await a boat over the Atlantic, the better, because once over the border it was up to the English authorities to look after them. In May 1765 the *Glasgow Journal* reported that Catharine Finlay, daughter of a Falkirk weaver, facing execution for killing her infant child, had pleaded to be banished and was told she would be transported 'Beyond the Seas' for the remainder of her life but if she ever returned to Scotland she would be hanged. A month later Christian Robertson, convicted at Perth of picking a man's pocket, successfully begged to be transported instead of strung up. That same year John Davidson was whipped through Aberdeen for stabbing his wife and then transported, while Mary Lawson from nearby Monymusk successfully petitioned for banishment to the Americas after murdering her baby.

Sentences were generally harsh but in the case of Agnes Weir in 1766 many felt the judges to be unduly lenient, possibly because she came from what was regarded as a middle-class background. Agnes was married to a Glasgow merchant but the two frequently argued, sometimes the disputes ending in violence by one or the other. One night she slashed him across a leg with a chopping knife, which broke, splintering the bone. It was a freak accident that ended in tragedy because infection set in and he died four days later. She was charged with 'beating and wounding her husband in a most inhumane manner which was suspected to have been the cause of his death'. Unlucky or not, she was facing the death penalty, but then in a surprise move the prosecution decided there wasn't enough evidence to convict her of a capital offence and she was told she would be transported for life. Friends of her late husband at least had the satisfaction of hearing that before she left Scotland she was to be twice whipped on her bare back through the streets of Glasgow.

The transportation ships continued to make their way across the Atlantic, but on their return masters were reporting their arrivals were being increasingly treated with hostility. It was obvious Britain and especially its convicts were not welcome and resentment of Crown authority finally exploded on 16 December 1773 when a shipment of tea from the East India Company was thrown into the harbour at Boston, Massachusetts. The British government's response to the Boston Tea Party was to close Boston harbour and from that there was no way back. Bitterness developed into full-scale hostilities in 1775, with battles at Lexington and Concord. The following year, shortly after George Washington, whose English great-grandfather had emigrated to Virginia in 1656, was appointed commander-in-chief of the American forces, the country's Congress issued its Declaration of Independence. The war that followed dragged on until 1783, when Britain accepted defeat and the transportation route to the colonies, crossed by an estimated 50,000 to 100,000 criminals, was closed.

In England the authorities had seen the writing on the wall some time earlier and had looked about the world for another cesspit into which to dump those seen as the dregs of society. As the years drifted by and prisons began filling up, the search became ever more frantic and the situation was not helped by judges who continued to send prisoners to banishment over the seas. Hugh Ross had been sentenced to hang at Inverness in 1785 for stealing sheep but following a plea for mercy was reprieved and told he was to be transported instead. Normally he would have found himself in the Thames hulks within a matter of weeks, but these too were filled to overflowing and so he had to lie in the Inverness Tolbooth, which was rapidly becoming busy. Tolbooth records report that Ross was joined there by Donald McAskill, Joseph Hay, Daniel Gordon and Angus Bayne Kennedy, all ordered to be transported, and in May 1786 by Christopher and Duncan McRae who, like him, had originally been sentenced to death. The same records show that in 1786, 'These seven remain in jail for transportation.'

While they languished, as did hundreds of others in prisons all over Britain, a decision was taken on their destination. In 1688 the explorer William Dampier – the man who piloted one of the vessels that rescued Scot Alexander Selkirk (see Chapter 2) – had landed in Australia and when he eventually returned to Britain he wrote a book about his findings. In 1770 Captain James Cook claimed what is now New South Wales for the British Crown and soon the first settlers were heading down under. Britain wanted Australia developed and realised that in convicts it had a ready supply of labour to help build settlements. It had found a replacement for America and in May 1787 the first convoy of transports set sail, arriving at Port Jackson, Sydney, on 26 January 1788. Gradually the Thames hulks and English prisons were emptied, making room for Scots to be moved south, although it was not until April 1789 that the Inverness jailer recorded that 'Angus Bayne Kennedy was delivered to the Sheriff Depute for transportation.'

Among the 582 male, 192 female and fourteen child felons in the eleven ships making up that initial convoy – the First Fleet

– was Caysy Hancock, aged forty-two, sentenced at Aberdeen Court of Justiciary to fourteen years transportation for assault and attempted robbery. A brick maker, he was the only Scot on board the 335-ton wooden-hulled *Charlotte*, and after his sentencing had been shipped south and held in the hulk ship *Dunkirk* at Plymouth until the First Fleet was ready to sail. Hancock and the others endured a journey that for a landlubber must have been a nightmare. They were at sea for thirty-six weeks, the voyage taking them from Plymouth, south-west to Rio de Janeiro, where they took on fresh water and food, then east to Table Bay, Cape Town before finally arriving in Botany Bay late in January 1788, a distance of around 17,000 miles. Once he had been disembarked Hancock's building skills were soon put to work helping erect the homes and schools around which Sydney would develop. He remained in Australia until his death at the age of seventy-six in 1821.

With a nearly empty vast land to fill, the flow of convicts ran faster than ever. One of the very first women from Scotland to be sent down under was Helen Robinson, convicted at Stirling and shipped off on the *Earl Cornwallis*, which left London in August 1800, arriving in New South Wales ten months later. An average 2,000 felons were set off on the arduous voyage every year until the last convict vessel docked in 1868. In February 1794 the *Surprize* left London carrying thirty-three male convicts, fifty-eight female prisoners, a consignment of troops to guard the felons, and a number of families and individuals classed as 'free settlers' who had decided to leave Britain and make a new life for themselves in New South Wales. Her departure excited more than the usual interest because among the prisoners were four men who had become known as the Scottish Martyrs. Maurice Margarot, aged forty-eight, Thomas Muir, twenty-eight, Unitarian minister the Reverend Thomas Fyshe Palmer, forty-six, and William Skirving, forty-eight, had been sentenced to transportation for life simply because they advocated political reform. A fifth Martyr, Joseph Gerrald, aged thirty-two, would follow them to Australia the following year.

Challenging the authority of the establishment at this time

was to invite trouble. The government, still smarting over the loss of America and now nervous by events over the Channel in France, would inevitably wreak vicious revenge on any attempts to reform the system under which a handful of powerful families controlled the affairs of the country. Since the surrender of the Bastille in 1789 and the decimation of the French aristocracy Britain was becoming divided between an establishment determined to cling on to control and those who wanted the working classes to have a say in government. Any hint of revolution invited cruel revenge. A government spy had infiltrated the reform movement in Scotland and reported links with alleged revolutionaries in Ireland and those in France. In 1793, following a series of trials in Scotland, the Martyrs were sentenced to transportation. They knew they were in for a hard time, especially Muir, who was regarded as the leading light.

The *Annual Register* reported in December 1793 that Muir and Palmer had arrived in London from Leith and were immediately sent on board hulk prison ships moored in the Thames at Woolwich. 'They were in irons among the convicts and were ordered to assist them in the common labour on the banks of the river.' When the Master of the *Surprize*, Patrick Campbell, announced he was ready to sail, the prisoners, who had been moved to Newgate prison, were marched on board to jeers and insults from passing Londoners and chained below decks. Among the others were six soldiers convicted of desertion and who would be suspected of plotting a mutiny during the voyage and immediately clapped in irons. At least the Martyrs had Scots for company, including James Beerhope, convicted at Edinburgh of stealing watches; William Carswell and Donal Turner from Edinburgh; John Grant convicted at Edinburgh of forgery; John Campbell, Thomas Dick, John Henderson, John Mackenzie and Thomas Morrison all from Glasgow; Neil MacIntosh and Malcolm McLellan from Inveraray; James McKay, found guilty at Edinburgh of robbery and sentenced to hang but then reprieved and instead ordered to be transported for life, and convicted robber John Stirling from Edinburgh. Among the free settlers was James Ellis, a close friend of Palmer, who had decided to accompany the radical to Australia.

The convict ship arrived at Rio de Janeiro on 2 July but Campbell reported in his log that the pipe from which the *Surprize* would get fresh water had broken and so the crew had to fill casks from a supply miles away and roll them to the ship. This delayed the departure and when the surgeon announced that a number of those on board including Muir were ill, it was decided to wait a few more days to allow them time to recover. It was August before the voyage resumed but the newly built *Surprize* sailed well and arrived at Sydney in late October. There was some sympathy for the Martyrs among colony officials, who treated them not as convicts but political prisoners, but they still longed to be back in Britain, and yet none lived to see old age. Not long after arriving Muir escaped and after a series of adventures reached revolutionaries in Paris, where he died in 1799, while Palmer served out his fourteen-year sentence and along with Ellis set sail for home but the pair were shipwrecked, and captured by the Spanish, which were then at war with Britain. The minister died in 1802. Once his sentence expired Margarot returned to England, where he died, penniless, in 1810. Skirving died in New South Wales in 1796 while Gerrald, already seriously ill with tuberculosis when he reached Australia in November 1795, died of the disease a few months later.

If the savagery of the sentences meted out to the Martyrs was meant to discourage others from demanding change then it failed. Long before the *Surprize* left London others were already active with campaigners in Scotland determined to win independence. One of these was George Mealmaker, a Dundee weaver and member of a group that formed itself into the Society of the United Scotsmen. At his trial for sedition in 1798 the indictment alleged that he and his supporters intended to, 'Create in the minds of the people a spirit of dissatisfaction and disloyalty to the King and the established government and ultimately to stir them up into acts of violence and opposition to the laws and constitution of this country.' It went on to claim Mealmaker and fellow independence seekers plotted to organise secret clubs and had written and distributed a pamphlet entitled 'The Moral and Political Catechism of Man or a Dialogue Between a Citizen of the World and an Inhabitant of Britain'.

From the start of his trial in Edinburgh in January 1797 it was obvious the judges were set on ensuring he was convicted, likening him and another accused to French revolutionaries. Mealmaker was sentenced to transportation for fourteen years but had to lie in prisons in Scotland and England before being taken on board the *Royal Admiral* in May 1800 and arriving at Port Jackson in November. But it had been a dreadful voyage during which fever killed forty-three prisoners. Among the 299 men who embarked with Mealmaker were weaver Andrew Kellock, aged twenty-seven, convicted at Perth of stealing cloth; James Grant, forty, sentenced at Aberdeen for housebreaking, and Hurley brothers Timothy, thirty, and Patrick, twenty-six, ordered at Ayr to be whipped through the streets of the town and then transported for forgery. At Parramatta, now a suburb of bustling Sydney but at the time a township in its own right, the government had set up a weaving factory employing mainly women convicts and Mealmaker's weaving skills were soon put to use with his appointment as supervisor. He had left behind in Edinburgh a wife and children but in New South Wales became lonely and disillusioned, finding solace in drink. Not long after, fire destroyed the factory and he died destitute from alcoholism.

Other transportees settled more comfortably. Anne Young and her sister Euphemia from Aberdeen together with others had been convicted of 'stealing and theftuously carrying away a piece of dark coloured cloth'. They left on the *William Pitt* in July 1895, arriving nine months later. In New South Wales Anne married farm worker James Parker and as far as records were concerned disappeared; Euphemia lived with Irish convict Patrick Hanrahan, marrying him in 1816. The couple had five children but in 1823 she left and set up home with Frederick Morgan. They were still together when she died in 1850.

While there were exceptions, for the vast majority transportation was as good as a life sentence whether it was to New South Wales or the colony on Van Diemen's Land – Tasmania – which opened in 1822. Few could afford a ticket back to Scotland once their sentence had expired; a handful like Thomas Muir tried escaping but returning home early meant at best a second, longer sentence of transportation and at worst execution. And it wasn't only the lowly who found themselves on an unwanted trip at sea. In 1812 a judge at Glasgow spared Robert Rennie but told him he was to spend the remainder of his life in Australia for the heinous crime of stealing a cow. Rennie was shipped off on board the *Earl Spencer* and found himself in the midst of a remarkable motley crowd of convicts that included a Captain Davidson, several bankers' clerks, men known as Luddites and a gang of smugglers convicted of helping in the escape of French prisoners. Also on board was ex-soldier William McLeod, convicted at Perth of shop-breaking. McLeod had served his country with courage and distinction, fighting in the July 1806 Battle of Maida in Calabria, Italy, during the war against Napoleon and then taking part in actions in Egypt, but his valour earned no mercy and he was told to serve the next fourteen years in Australia. However, the old soldier would never see action down under, dying during the voyage.

Another who discovered that gallantry counted for nothing when it came to pinching animals was Robert Fenton who appeared at the same court as McLeod and was found guilty of stealing sheep. His counsel pleaded for mercy on the grounds that he had a family and a few years previously had ignored the risk to his own life when he twice rushed into a blazing building through fierce flames to haul barrels of gunpowder to safety, saving the property and the lives of locals trapped in their homes. He was still sentenced to seven years transportation.

Once they found their feet in Australia a few convicts failed to resist the temptation to stray back into their old, devious ways even though the penalties for lawbreaking were even more severe than those back in Britain. In 1823 the *Caledonian Mercury* reported that, 'Letters have been received in Edinburgh from Van Diemen's Land giving the most favourable reports of that interesting colony. It has been found that tobacco grows in that genial climate, with the greatest luxuriance, and is of very superior quality. Several valuable well-bred horses had arrived safely from England; and no less than forty-nine large ships had been in Hobart Town Harbour from England alone, during the last ten months, most of them richly laden with all kinds of merchandise, and passengers of the highest respectability from mother country.'

But the same letters suggested that not all the new Tasmanians were respectable: 'The convict, John McDougal, of ship-sinking notoriety, is walking about here like a gentleman, and advising in the newspapers for business as a general agent and accountant. When the ship arrived with him, he was brought ashore by the Governor's boat, separate from the other prisoners, in plain clothes, instead of the convict dress [of yellow cloth] so as to save his feelings. He pretends that he has not a stiver [small amount of money] in the world, and that he was preparing to send home documents to prove who were the guilty parties – a post too late for himself however.' McDougal had been convicted by the High Court of Admiralty in 1821 of having in June 1816, 'feloniously sank and destroyed, after having abstracted the cargo, the vessel called the *Friends of Glasgow*, by means of boring holes in the bottom of that vessel for the purpose of defrauding and prejudicing the underwriters or owners of the vessel or goods'. McDougal was a nineteenth-century version of a confidence trickster, pretending to be mad and claiming that if he was given a light sentence he would give details of other ships he had helped sink. Now it appeared he had fooled the authorities in Tasmania into believing he was a man of considerable importance who deserved special treatment.

As often as the law baffled commoners, there were odd occasions when even a judge found himself frustrated. At Perth in 1822 John Miller and William Storier were accused of 'assault with intent to rape'. Their victim was a girl of fourteen who they had dragged into a wood and brutally abused. If ever a pair deserved to hang, here they were. But the judge, Lord Hermand, was forced to admit that because the indictment was one of intent to rape rather than rape he could not order their execution. The law, he said, needed to be changed. The *Caledonian Mercury* noted that the crime was 'a very atrocious' one and as if to assuage his annoyance Lord Hermand ruled that Miller and Storier should be whipped through Dundee and then transported. In a case that followed, middle-aged family man William Robertson had a severe fright. He was convicted of raping a neighbour and sentenced to hang at Cupar, Fife, but later reprieved.

Sex was behind the killing in September 1826 of Catherine Alexander. She lived with her husband William, a mason, in Leith Wynd but when the marriage went sour after eight years she turned to drink. The situation worsened when her husband took a mistress, Janet Blackwood, eventually moving her in as a lodger. Catherine was regularly beaten by both her husband and Blackwood and was sometimes forced to watch the couple's antics in bed. Finally one of the attacks was so severe that she died. After a trial at Edinburgh Alexander was convicted of culpable homicide and sentenced to transportation for fourteen years. He left Scotland forever on the convict vessel *Champion* in May 1827 while his lover was cleared and freed. Had Blackwood been convicted she would inevitably have been banished to Australia.

Judges in Scotland did not think twice about parting wives or mothers from their families and sending them to the growing colonies on the other side of the world. At least brothers Duncan and Peter Barr could consider themselves fortunate to be alive, even though that was 12,000 miles from their Tobermory home, instead of swinging by their necks from a scaffold in 1833. They ran a mill but found themselves with money troubles and came up with a scheme to burn the mill and make inflated insurance claims, having first removed a lot of the contents. Arson and the swindling of insurance companies were capital offences; the pair initially denied wrongdoing, but eventually they were persuaded that by pleading guilty to an amended charge their lives would be spared. The judge at Inveraray sentenced them to transportation for life.

Widow Ann Reid and her daughter Agnes were also able to stay together after they were convicted in Edinburgh in 1838 on a number of charges of aggravated theft. Both were sentenced to transportation for fourteen years and left on the convict vessel *Mary Anne*, which sailed in July 1839 bound for New South Wales. Of 143 female convicts on board, seventy-five were from Scottish courts, some having spent well over a year in prison before a passage became available. Among them was nineteen-year-old Janet Anderson, found guilty at the Gorbals police court in Glasgow of housebreaking and sentenced to seven years beyond the seas. In Australia Janet became a housemaid and although she could have returned home in 1846 if she'd had the means, she stayed in New South Wales until her death at the age of seventy-four in 1894. Ironically, had she not broken the law and spent the rest of her life in Glasgow, it is highly unlikely because of the harsh conditions and high level of poverty in the city that she would have survived into her seventies.

One of the few who did return from enforced exile was Christian Munro Steele, who had been convicted of theft at Inverness in 1828 and sentenced to seven years' banishment. Back in Scotland she had quickly returned to her wicked ways and stolen from a house in Perth, the proceeds being reset by her soldier lover John Smart. In 1835 Steele found herself back in court with four months of her first sentence still to run, a fact not missed by the judge, Lord Medwyn. The *Caledonian Mercury* said that, 'In passing sentence Lord Medwyn alluded to the fact of her return from banishment, noticing that she must have been in some of the English Penitentiaries, from which, by influence, or affected reformation, or professions and promises of good behaviour, the Secretary of State had been induced to grant her liberation, which lenity her subsequent conduct had proved how ill it was merited.' He sent her back to New South Wales, this time for fourteen years and jailed Smart for a year. The authorities wasted no time in making sure Steele was on her way quickly because just a month later she was on board the *Hector* with 133 other women convicts, this time bound for Van Diemen's Land, where she arrived in October 1835.

Sometimes convict ships found themselves carrying children among hardened criminals. In 1835 Thomas Leckie and Peter

Miller, described by newspapers at the time as 'two little boys about twelve years of age', appeared before a court in Edinburgh accused of housebreaking. The case could almost have inspired Charles Dickens' *Oliver Twist* published two years later, only here Dickens' Fagan was a female, Robina Forrest, aged sixty, who was convicted of reset. All three were transported for seven years. In 1850, the year in which Western Australia opened itself up to receiving convicts, William Edwards, aged thirteen was transported for ten years from Edinburgh for being a regular thief.

Exile across the world would always be a popular and simple option for judges. The *Dundee Courier and Argus* summed up the feelings of many in 1866 when it commented, 'the criminal by profession does dread transportation. It takes him away from the organisation that helps him to live by crime. Besides, it gives us the best guarantee against any further trouble from him and, lastly, it gives the man himself an opportunity, not only of reformation, but of re-establishment in a fresh world.'

These were sentiments that would not have been appreciated by Catherine Ross, Rachel Wilson and Helen McNeil, who had been sentenced to fourteen years transportation by a High Court judge at Edinburgh in November 1838. The *Caledonian Mercury* reported that, 'On being removed from the dock these wretched beings uttered the most horrid imprecations against both the Court and the jury.'

The same newspaper could not have known it, but ports down under were about to be closed to convict vessels. Just as they had in America years earlier, the new Australians felt that taking care of thousands of hardened lawbreakers was too much trouble, and transportation finally ended in 1868 when the last convict ship, the *Hougoumont*, arrived at the Swan River Colony close to Freemantle, Western Australia, carrying 279 prisoners, including a number of Scots. Daniel Stewart, aged forty-seven, had been charged with murder after stabbing fellow seaman Robert Williams at Greenock, but was allowed to plead guilty to culpable homicide and sentenced to spend the next twenty-one years in Australia. James Stewart, forty, had almost faced the capital offence of murder for killing his wife but he too admitted culpable homicide and was told he would be transported for fifteen years. Others from north of the border included Alexander Gordon, twenty-eight, from Glasgow accused of starting a series of fires; Robert Black, thirty-nine, who stole a coat at Dundee; Alexander Carey, thirty-six, who stole jewellery from a shop in Edinburgh; and two men from Glasgow who had pleaded guilty to incest.

7

BODY SNATCHERS

The Body Snatcher, the 1945 black and white film starring masters of horror Boris Karloff and Bela Lugosi, was a gruesome portrayal of men cashing in by selling dead bodies to unscrupulous and over-ambitious medical men for dissection. Set in Edinburgh in 1831, the film was based on a story published in 1884 by Robert Louis Stevenson who may have gained ideas for his plot from the murderous atrocities in 1828 of William Burke and William Hare (see Chapter 24). But equally the film makers or Stevenson could have developed their versions from reading horrific reports of the activities of resurrectionists, men and very occasionally women who were paid by anatomists to exhume and supply recently-buried bodies. Anatomists constantly complained they could never get hold of sufficient fresh, raw material. Courts helped out occasionally by directing that the remains of murderers had to be handed over to them but at a time of great poverty and hardship the fact that doctors were willing to pay and ask no questions for a dead body was an attraction a handful found impossible to resist.

Most people were appalled by the thought of a dead family member being crudely dug up and taken away to be cut into pieces. The Anatomy Act of 1832, introduced largely as a result of this revulsion, allowed the dissection of bodies legitimately donated for science. But before then watchkeepers had to make nightly patrols of graveyards where there had been recent burials. In 1821 a minister had bemoaned, 'Few burial grounds in Scotland, it is believed, have escaped the ravaging hands of resurrection men; and it is reported with respect to a church-yard not far from Edinburgh that till within three years ago, when the inhabitants began to watch the graves, the persons interred did not remain in their graves above a night and that these depredations were successfully carried out for nine successive winters.' Not surprisingly, when culprits were caught, they expected no mercy either from courts or ordinary folk.

The *Caledonian Mercury* reported one of these outrages in September 1807. 'Early on Tuesday morning, a gentleman going home, observed a ladder with a man on it at the wall of Lady Yester's churchyard [then in Infirmary Street, Edinburgh]. He immediately gave an alarm to the first police officer he saw, who sprung his rattle, and, in a few moments, a number of people assembled. One man was apprehended on the spot and another at the head of College Wynd. They had raised the body of a woman who had been buried very recently, and were in the act of getting the corpse over the wall when they were detected. The men were committed to the city guard, along with their implements, a ladder, a spade, and a rope which had been about the neck of the woman when found. The body was carried into Lady Yester's church, and, after being examined by a surgeon, was again interred in the evening.

'At ten o'clock, on Tuesday, the prisoners were brought before the Judge of Police, and examined, when they proved to be Archibald Begg and Robert Phillip, both wrights, and strongly suspected of being guilty of this shocking crime on former occasions. The judge took a precognition, and afterwards committed them to the tolbooth till liberated in due course of law. In the course of the investigation, it turned out that Begg was formerly tried for raising dead bodies, and was under sentence of banishment by the High Court of Justiciary since 14 January 1803. In consequence of this, he was brought before the Sitting Magistrate, and an extract of the above sentence was read to him, ordaining him to be banished from Scotland for fourteen years, under the usual certification of being whipped through this city if he returned before the expiry of that period. He acknowledged he was the person the sentence applied to, and signed a declaration to that effect. He was then ordered to be whipped through the city yesterday, which was done accordingly. The horrid nature of the offence which this man had committed collected an immense multitude of spectators, who encouraged the executioner to do his duty, which he did to their satisfaction. Begg was afterwards committed to prison, to stand trial for this new offence.

'In bringing him up the streets to the jail, he was assailed with every kind of dirt and rubbish, and was four or five times knocked down, which all the exertions of the officers and guard were unable to prevent. Begg is an old grey-headed man and lame of one leg.'

The lure of money could lead resurrectionists to dream up at times unbelievably vile schemes aimed both at cashing in on demand and avoiding the executioner's whip or, worse still, being chained up for months in prison. In July 1823, the *Caledonian Mercury* and the *Glasgow Herald* reported on an astonishing discovery by customs officers at Greenock when they were checking a consignment of parcels sent from Belfast for contraband. 'They lighted upon a cask which being a questionable shape in the mind's eye of a revenue officer, and not unlikely to contain crystal ware or some similar commodity, they rashly poked it with their searching instrument. Their olfactory nerves, however, soon convinced them of their woeful mistake, and more minute investigation satisfied them that the contents of the cask had already yielded tribute, though to no mortal hand and was far beyond the pale of their authority, and was neither more nor less than the corpse of a fellow creature, thus unceremoniously packed up by the unhallowed hands of a resurrectionist and doomed, after having shuffled off this mortal coil to traverse the seas and become the inmate of the anatomical room instead of remaining quietly interred amidst the ashes of its sires.'

The cask had been addressed to 'Mr John Duff, grocer, Register Street, Edinburgh' and officers recalled previous casks being sent there but further investigations were unable to throw light on the identity of the sender or whether they had ever actually been delivered to Mr Duff. The body was quietly buried in a Greenock graveyard.

Body snatching was not restricted to Scotland, but the most remarkable discovery in the field of resurrectionism was down to Scots with the uncovering in Liverpool of a full-scale and organised trade in corpses. In October a carter arrived at Liverpool docks and handed over three casks to the skipper of a vessel bound for Scotland. They were simply addressed to 'Mr G H Ironside, Edinburgh' and paperwork stated they held 'bitter salts' but as they were being stowed below decks the crew noticed a strong, offensive smell and eventually the skipper opened one of the casks and realised a dead body was inside. Police were called and discovered bodies in the other casks.

The carter took police to the address from where he had collected them, a building in Hope Street, Liverpool, next to a school. In a cellar, to their horror, officers uncovered a resurrectionist factory. They found eleven empty casks, four containing salted human bodies, three sacks each containing a body, a syringe used by anatomists for injecting hot wax into the veins and arteries of dead bodies together with a pile of smock coats, jackets and trousers thought to have been used as disguises by the gang using the cellar. The smell was said to have been horrendous but a surgeon agreed to examine the cellar and reported there were a total of thirty-three bodies, male and female and including some children. He was in no doubt that all had been dug up from different graveyards and cemeteries and carried to the Hope Street cellar where they were 'put into a strong brine, and afterwards, when thoroughly pickled, packed in the casks with the dry salt' for export to Scotland. The bodies, some badly decomposed, were immediately reinterred.

Inquiries revealed that some of the schoolboys, aware of an increasingly strong smell from the cellar, had gone into it and found two men fixing iron belts to secure casks. Asked what the barrels contained the boys, before being ordered out, were told by one of the men, 'Pickled herrings' and asked by the other,

'What do you think?' It was clear the trade had been carried on for months because a woman neighbour told police her husband had seen, the previous Christmas, a gang of men each carrying a sack into the cellar in the early hours one morning. Her husband had been told the casks were filled with cod oil. The cellar had first been rented by a Scotsman calling himself John Henderson who had vanished owing rent but another Scot, William Gillespie, turned up promising the money would be paid. A third Scot, James Donaldson, suspected of being the gang leader, was arrested when he was recognised by some of the schoolboys and women living in the area.

The scandal of the body factory set Liverpudlians on edge and wondering what might be inside every barrel or package destined for Scotland. As a result Glaswegian Duncan McGregor, who used a variety of names including Rob Roy McGregor, Francis Osbaldistone and John Brown, was arrested after he tried leaving a box addressed to Edinburgh at a coaching stop. A corpse was later found inside. He was recognised as the same man who had, a few days earlier, left a similar box one night and it had been found after the smell alerted staff to contain a dead body. It was addressed to a 'Capt. Woolsdale, Royal Marines. Mitchell's-buildings, 12 Castle Street, Edinburgh' and McGregor asked for it to be taken on the next coach north. A doctor who examined the corpse said it was that of a young man who had died of fever; the deceased had been buried at nine o'clock in the morning and by nine that same night he had been dug up, his body put into the box and delivered to the coaching inn. McGregor denied claims by some witnesses that he was a close friend of Donaldson, and protested that he did not know what had been in the boxes.

Donaldson claimed others who he could not identify had organised the trade in corpses. He was indicted at Liverpool Michaelmas Sessions for the misdemeanour of disinterring dead bodies, sentenced to eighteen months' jail and told he would further stay in prison until he paid a £50 fine. McGregor was convicted of 'stealing immense numbers of dead bodies and sending them to Scotland'. He and an accomplice named John

Ross were jailed for twelve months and ordered to pay a £25 fine to the King. Court records show that before they were sentenced the two made a statement in which they claimed to be, 'poor and destitute; that they had been hired by anatomical students at various universities who offered them large rewards for corpses and that it was their necessity not their will that led them to traffic in dead bodies'.

In Edinburgh, the clamour for bodies continued but suppliers were becoming more wary after the prison sentences given in Liverpool and a further banishment and whipping for Begg and Phillips. In late December three crates containing six corpses were landed at Glasgow Broomielaw from a Belfast steamer and the following day workers noticed a peculiar smell coming from two boxes unloaded off a steamer from Dublin. Inside were four more dead bodies. All had been addressed to a fictitious company in Edinburgh.

Resurrectionists searching for cadavers to sell to the enthusiastic anatomists had spread their nets far and wide. In February 1820 at Northumberland Assizes details emerged of how keen Scotsman Henry Gillies was to get a crate to Edinburgh after the discovery that three graves in a Tynemouth churchyard had been dug up and the bodies stolen. Gillies was happy to pay more than the normal fare for his box to be taken to Newcastle to meet the Edinburgh-bound coach. The crate was marked 'For Mr Dixon, left at Mr Allen's, philosophical instrument maker, Lothian Street, Edinburgh' and it was the eighth in a series sent to the same address. Gillies' eagerness to get his crate on the coach aroused suspicion and it was opened. Inside was the body of a seventy-eight-year-old woman.

His landlady told police that from time to time her lodger had gone out late at night. Once he'd come back with a sack over his shoulder and later that day a large red box he'd bought was fastened up and taken away. Gillies was found guilty of stealing bodies for the purpose of gain or profit. He was jailed for twelve months, fined £20 and told he would stay in jail until it was paid.

The following year new graves at Lanark were found to have been dug up and a search of the area revealed local men Andrew

Miller and Thomas Hodge driving a cart with two corpses in it. Both were jailed for six months.

As the clamour for action to stop the resurrectionists grew, the *Dumfries Courier* advocated filling coffins with lime to disintegrate corpses making them useless to anatomists. There was also a feeling that while it was right to punish those who desecrated graves, others who encouraged the robbers by enticing them with money should also be penalised. In a rare case, brought in 1823 at Stirling, John Forrest, described as a 'student of medicine', former gravedigger James McNab and David Mitchell were accused of having in the early hours crept into the churchyard where widow Mary Stevenson had been buried a few hours earlier and stolen her body. Forrest knew he would be in trouble and didn't hang about to hear the inevitable prison sentence; instead he disappeared and the court heard he had vanished to the continent. He was sentenced to 'fugitation', meaning he was outlawed and liable to arrest if he ever again set foot in Scotland; in addition all his property was to be handed over to the Crown. Because he had literally escaped jail the judge took pity on his accomplices who had been in prison awaiting the trial and set them free. However, that was not the end of the story.

Ill feeling and revulsion about the attack on the widow's grave had been building throughout Stirling and as crowds began gathering, demanding stiff punishment for McNab and Mitchell who were by now back in their homes, the town's provost obtained an order allowing him to take them back to jail for their own safety. By the time he had it though, matters were already out of hand. A mob, led by a group of furious women, marched on the home of McNab. An attempt to smash down his door failed, but a stone thrown through his window smashed on his head. He fell unconscious while the crowd cheered. By now police had arrived to rescue him but as officers dragged him away he was pelted with stones. It was now a race to reach Mitchell, whose home in St John's Street was close to Stirling prison.

An officer managed to get there first, but journalists were on hand to describe what happened next. 'No sooner had the police officer got him out than a parcel of fellows laid hold of him and instantly knocked him down, and dreadfully kicked and beat him whilst down; his clothes were torn off his back and flung out among the crowd.' Somehow Mitchell managed to escape, running into a nearby house and barricading the door against a series of attempts to ram it down only for the windows to be smashed in. As the rioters climbed in, Mitchell fled through a back door and then took shelter in another house, where he was finally rescued by the police but not before stones and bricks had smashed through its windows.

The *Caledonian Mercury* reported that, 'The crowd by this time assembled prodigiously, and became quite infuriated at the idea of their victim escaping out of their hands. There is not the slightest doubt but they would have torn him to pieces.' Most of the mob acceded to pleas by the police to clear a path so they could take Mitchell to jail, but once again raging women demanded the grave robber was handed over to them. And when they refused to disperse, troops armed with muskets, some with fixed bayonets and others carrying halberds were called. That ought to have ended the trouble; in fact even worse pandemonium was to follow.

Some of the soldiers were drunk and one fell down among the crowd. As he was being helped to his feet the mob pushed nearer to the troops, one of whom, thinking they were about to be attacked, began laying into the rioters with the butt of his musket. Another thrust at the crowd with his bayonet, stabbing a youngster in the chest while more civilians were cut by halberds. Furious at seeing their friends bleeding and wounded, men in the mob tried snatching the musket away from the man who had fired. In the confusion another of the troops fired a shot which inflamed the situation even more. Now further shots were fired by drunken soldiers who came under fire from stones and anything else the rioters could find to throw at them. Two of the troops who had hold of Mitchell thought that if they handed him over to the mob they would leave but as they were about to do this the police grabbed him and ran him into the nearby prison where he was later joined by five of the soldiers who were arrested for firing their muskets.

Two days later the judge who had originally freed Mitchell and McNab, who were now still in jail for their own safety, had harsh words to say about the riot. Describing it as a 'misguided and disgraceful outrage' Lord Gillies said stealing bodies was, 'Doubtless a crime of a heinous nature, and one which the law viewed with detestation.' But he wanted to know, 'Where was the independence of a British judge and jury if a mob was to be the judge of their conduct or if a rabble was to dispute the purity of their decisions?'

He wasn't the only judge to make his feelings towards grave robbers public. In 1829 John Kerr, James Barclay and George Cameron from Lasswade were convicted of grave robbing and jailed, Kerr for nine months and the others for six, all with hard labour. The Lord Advocate told them that what they had done was, 'The most disgraceful and disgusting violation of the sepulchres of the dead to be found in the annals of this or any other country.' And in April 1832 at Inveraray, John McLean admitted violating the sepulchres of the dead and carrying away the dead bodies of a woman and child from the little burial ground at Bellochantuy, a few miles north of Campbeltown in Argyll. Jailing him for twelve months, Lord Medwyn told McLean, 'One of the strongest instincts in our nature is a regard even for the lifeless body which was once animated by a living soul, and to respect the spot where it is laid to moulder.'

8

STRIPES

Until it was restricted to taking place within prisons, flogging was both a popular public entertainment and for the recipient an extremely painful punishment. Floggings were usually carried out by the local hangman, who made no distinction between males or females; both were stripped to the waist to receive on their bare back the number of lashes stipulated by a court. Floggings attracted huge crowds who would follow the hangman and his victim through the streets, cheering each lash or stripe, baying for blood and screaming insults at both when the little procession stopped for another section of the punishment.

Typical was the whipping ordered on English-born family man Edward Hand, forty-four, in September 1822. He had been convicted at Glasgow Circuit Court of committing an assault on a girl aged twelve at Greenock with the intention of raping her. He was fortunate to escape with a sentence of being whipped through the streets of Glasgow during which he would suffer eighty lashes before being returned to prison to await transportation for the remainder of his life. The trial judge, Lord Meadowbank, pointed out that had his victim been a few weeks younger Hand, a glassblower, would have hanged and added that, 'If every lash that is laid on your body does not atone for your crime, I hope it will at least bring repentance.' A broadside dramatically reported the judge's advice to Hand and then described what happened when the first part of the sentence was carried out.

'Glasgow, 25th Sept. This being the day on which he was to undergo the whipping, about 12 o'clock a detachment of the 7th Dragoons drew up before the east door of the prison, a cart soon after arrived, and the prisoner was immediately brought out, when the executioner tied his hands to the cart, which was surrounded by a numerous posse of peace officers, police officers, constable, the whole guarded by the dragoons. The cavalcade then proceeded to the front of the jail where he received twenty lashes, which he seemed to feel very keenly; it then proceeded west to the foot of Stockwell where the punishment was again repeated; and also at the head of Stockwell, and at the Cross, making eighty stripes in all. His back was much lacerated and bleeding profusely. Although the day was very wet, an immense crowd attended; and all the windows of the shops in the streets through which the cavalcade passed were shut up.'

In March the following year Hand, by now shipped south and held in the Thames hulks, was transported to Van Diemen's Land on board the *Competitor*, which arrived at Tasmania in August.

While they were stripped, women at least were not like males made to trudge behind the hangman's cart bare to the waist but permitted to have their breasts covered although their backs were naked. While frequent, the flogging of females was opposed by many. In 1817 the *Inverness Journal* reported that, 'A woman of the name of Grant, was flogged through the streets of Inverness, we understand for the third time, (once the previous week), for intoxication and bad behaviour in the streets. No doubt example if necessary, and was here made with the best intention; yet public and repeated flagellation on the naked body of a woman, is revolting to our general ideas of decency and humanity; it is to be regretted that some equally effectual punishment could not be fallen upon. It may be well to consider the effect of familiarising the public to such sights; and whether hard labour and solitary confinement, would not be a more successful punishment.'

It was a view echoed by one of its readers, who described the public flagellation of females as, 'A spectacle with which we have of late been so frequently disgusted.' These views gained increasing support, the result being the abolition of female flagellation in 1820.

Clearly Ms Grant had become immune, possibly through drink, to the pain of a lashing. Other hardened criminals managed to all but laugh off a whipping. In 1801 an old man known only as 'My Hearty' was whipped for the thirty-seventh time and on being untied from the whipping post calmly asked the beadle who had flogged him, 'Give me a quid of tobacco.' Those who argued that to the majority of felons whipping was an ineffective form of punishment pointed to cases like that of James Wilson from Glasgow who, having been publicly whipped twice at Glasgow prison on 1 and 13 January 1823 for returning early from banishment, simply ignored the order for a third time and on 29 January was given another fifty stripes. He then calmly put his shirt back on and was escorted by the hangman to the city boundaries and told not to come back.

Sometimes whippings seemed to have been dished out almost as an afterthought when judges were wondering what to do with offenders. In 1803 brothers John and William Williamson and John McCoull, coal hewers from Airdrie, were accused of murdering the wife of a merchant when celebrations following the town's annual fair got out of hand. The three faced being hanged but were eventually convicted of culpable homicide, still a serious offence and one for which they were told they would be transported for life, the judge adding that before they departed Scotland they were each to be given ninety lashes by the hangman.

Courts wanted flogging to act as a deterrent to lawbreakers. At the end of March 1815 while Napoleon was exhorting his soldiers to a final fatal effort, inmates of Edinburgh Bridewell on Calton Hill had been called into the yard to watch the flogging of James Kelly after hearing the jailer read out a statement giving the reason for his punishment. While serving a sentence at the jail for sheep stealing Kelly had tried escaping, bashing one of the turnkeys over the head before he was caught. For that he was ordered to be whipped in front of all the other prisoners, suffering thirty lashes from the city hangman.

Even youngsters were not exempt from the executioner's lash. In August 1852 five young boys were given between twenty and thirty-six stripes for pinching fruit from a garden in Falkirk, the *Caledonian Mercury* pointing out that, 'The gardens in the immediate neighbourhood of the town are peculiarly exposed to depredations of the above kind, but it is to be hoped that the vigilance of the county police, and the salutary warning contained in the sentence may have a wholesome effect in checking the reprehensible practice.' Needless to say hungry boys continued to steal apples.

In Edinburgh in 1858 Lawrence Milligan, aged thirteen, and his friend John Fraser, fourteen, stole four haddocks from the city fish market. The judge regretted there was no reformatory in the city to which he could send them. He realised whipping was a lesson lost on Fraser, who had been flogged just six weeks earlier, and so sent the boy to prison, ordering Milligan to be given twenty stripes on his bare back.

9

LAUNCHED INTO ETERNITY

It has been called the oldest profession in the world – the sale of sex. The main reason why a woman undertakes this work today is inevitably money, or the lack of it, or the desire for it. It was no different in 1800, when poverty drove so many to sell themselves, to try drinking away their miserable existence, to steal, or even murder. At her home in Smeiton's Close, Leith, Anne Bruce, struggling to feed three children, ran what was nothing more than a brothel. Prostitutes could take clients back there, sleep with them and while they were in bed Anne would steal. She operated a honeytrap in which sex was the lure.

She was a regular in the city courts, a person described by magistrates as being of 'bad character, much given to drink and quarrelsome'. According to the *Caledonian Mercury* she had 'often been before the courts for riots and petty thefts'. But her greed was about to cost two lives, her own and that of twenty-four-year-old seaman Griffith Williams. When his ship berthed at Leith the Welshman was eager to get into the city to enjoy drink, food and women; and he could afford all of them. In his pockets were a dozen golden guineas, a fortune at a time when a farm worker needed to work nearly a fortnight to earn a pound.

Very soon in a dockside inn Williams had picked up teenage prostitute Janet Mathie, who took him back to Bruce's home.

Before the couple clambered into bed the trusting seaman, taken in by his host's gentle smile and the sight of her dandling a baby on her knee, asked her to take care of his money. She put it into his trousers and carefully folded them beneath his pillow. But when he woke up most of the money was missing and Bruce denied being the culprit. 'I'll just have the life in her,' a witness at his trial later claimed the enraged seaman had threatened. Neighbours heard her being given a terrible beating from which she died the next morning and a passing naval press gang, on the lookout for young men to kidnap into navy service, hauled Williams off to the Leith guard house. He was convicted of murder and in March 1800 hanged outside the Edinburgh Tolbooth on a day when the rain was so heavy that final prayers on his behalf were cut short.

He was neither the first nor the last to fall victim to a honeytrap. In 1826 Belfast-born Andrew Stewart was sentenced to hang at Glasgow for a crime of robbery. Described in a broadside of the day: 'Stewart was convicted of having, along with several others, in the beginning of August last, knocked down and robbed in the Gallowgate, an Italian of the name of Filippo Testi, of a gold repeater watch, with chain, seals and key attached, two one-pound notes and a guinea one, ten or twelve shillings in silver, a pair of black, kid gloves, some tobacco with five or six segars [cigars] in a segar-holder. It appeared that the poor foreigner had been betrayed by a woman of the town, who gave information to a gang of ruffians that he had money upon him. After he had been knocked down, the villains were so numerous that they frightened away every person who wished to interfere and actually kept rifling him for several minutes and under the eyes of several spectators till the police came up when they ran off.'

Unfortunately for the gang a furious fight broke out among them when they started dividing the spoils and they were still battling when police arrived on the scene and arrested Stewart.

Alongside him on the scaffold that November day stood another Irishman, Edward Kelly, aged twenty-one, who had robbed James Fleming of £100 he had been carrying for his businessman son but who had also clearly dallied with a city prostitute. 'The circumstances of this case are nearly similar to the last and should be a warning to people who have money on them, to beware of the company they go into, for it appears that Fleming had imprudently allowed himself to be decoyed into a house with a woman whom he had picked up in the street and while in his company she had no doubt discovered that he had money in his possession, and after parting, had given information to some of her abandoned associates, for he was soon after waylaid by several fellows and dragged into a close, and robbed of his money and considerably hurt,' said the same broadside.

Kelly was quickly arrested and sentenced for assault and robbery. In a short speech to a huge crowd before the pair having been given a glass of wine were hanged, Stewart pleaded for the spectators to 'live honestly, obey the laws of their country, respect the Sabbath Day, and above all to beware of drunkenness', blaming drink 'as the sole cause of his unhappy fate'.

He was said to have been 'cool and collected', while Stewart trembled.

If it was felt that the women who instigated these tragedies were allowed to escape justice then that was remedied with the dramatic case in 1828 of Thomas Connor and Bell McMenemy, one in which they as good as pronounced their own death sentences by pleading guilty to the capital offences of assault and robbery. The case was remarkable for the efforts made by the judge, Lord Meadowbank, to persuade Connor and McMenemy to change their pleas. Sometimes even when they faced a capital charge defendants pleaded guilty in the hope that by making a clean breast of matters Crown prosecutors would not press for the death penalty but agree to what was termed 'arbitrary punishment', allowing judges discretion when it came to sentencing.

In this case Connor in particular was on a sticky wicket because only six years earlier he had been sentenced to death for theft but then reprieved. The *Caledonian Mercury* reported that after hearing their initial pleas, 'Lord Meadowbank again put the question to the two prisoners, if they were guilty or not guilty; they knew the consequences of adhering to their pleas, and they had an opportunity of retracting it if they thought proper. On hearing this announcement, both prisoners burst into tears. Connor called out several times, "Give me my life – do anything with me you please – but only give me my life for God's sake." The question was again put. Connor said, "Not Guilty my Lord if it will save my life." McMenemy stuck to her plea and said, with a firm voice, "Guilty my Lord."

'Well then,' replied Lord Meadowbank, 'you know the consequences.'

The evidence was overwhelming. Boatman Alexander McKinnon had arrived in Glasgow from Tralee to sell eggs and hid the money he made in one of his stockings. Then he met twenty-three-year-old McMenemy, strikingly good looking with a mop of flaming red hair, who like Connor had been born in County Tyrone, Ireland. She took him first for a drink and then lured him on with the promise of sex. On the way they met Connor, who bashed the Irishman over the head with a stone near the Broomielaw Bridge knocking him out. When McKinnon came to, one of his stockings was off and his money gone, but a watchman saw the attack and shouted for police. An officer tried grabbing McMenemy and although she squirmed away from him both were discovered in their lodgings, she hiding in a chest and he covered in blood and blaming her for the attack. McMenemy claimed she stole nothing because she said she took down the wrong stocking from the Irishman.

Connor was convicted and both were sentenced to die. A recommendation by the jury for mercy to be shown to Connor fell on deaf ears and Lord Meadowbank told McMenemy, 'I hold you to be the most guilty. It is seldom that the sentence of the law is executed on females if one of the other sex was found to be implicated, but in this case it is clear you were the principal in devising and executing the assault or the robbery.' The couple were reunited on the scaffold in front of Glasgow courthouse just after eight o'clock on the morning of Wednesday 22 October before a crowd estimated at 50,000. The *Aberdeen Journal* reported, 'After the executioner had drawn the caps over their faces, prayers were continued until one of the clergymen gave Connor the signal to let go the handkerchief, which was instantly done and the drop fell. The female once or twice after this slowly raised her hands as if still engaged in supplication. Although some complaints were made amongst the spectators that the executioner did not give the female enough of rope her sufferings appeared to be as speedily at an end as those of her companion who received a much greater fall.'

A one-penny broadside describing the execution included the three words so frequently used to round off reports of executions. 'The signal was dropt and they were instantly *launched into eternity.*'

Even more sensational and depraved was the 1853 case that became known as the New Vennel murder, after the narrow alleyway in the centre of Glasgow (now off Argyle Street between McDonald's bakers and Mrs Mitchell's sweet shop) which was the scene of a horrific murder. The circumstances were bad enough, but the decision to reprieve one of the killers caused nationwide outrage.

Gorbals-born Helen Blackwood, aged thirty, was a typical product of the poverty and deprivation that ravaged so many Scottish towns and cities. Abandoned by a worthless father and drunken mother she turned to prostitution and quickly degenerated even further into crime. Her home in the New Vennel became a curious mix between a brothel frequented by prostitutes and their customers and a home for abandoned children. She fell in love with wastrel Hans Smith Macfarlane, born twenty years earlier in Partick to Irish parents. Up the filth-strewn stairway to her third-floor flat stumbled a succession of men, mostly drunks, who were drugged, robbed and kicked out on to the street. Ship's carpenter Alexander Boyd, aged thirty-nine, celebrating his return to his native city after years of living in Valparaíso, Chile, was the thirteenth to follow that dreadful route in a single week in June 1853. Boyd and a friend, James Law, had spent a day in a succession of bars in Glasgow and by night were drink sodden and easy meat for prostitutes Mary Hamilton and Ann Marshall who enticed them with promises of sex to the flat where Blackwood and Macfarlane waited for prey.

Blackwood's kindness was her undoing. She had taken in and

cared for the young brothers of a close widowed relative who, unable to pay her rent, had been made homeless. The boys, John and James Shillinglaw, were lying beneath the bed where they slept when the group arrived and the youngsters would later give graphic accounts of what happened. John, aged eleven, told how Boyd was given a drink heavily drugged with snuff; it was the equivalent of a modern-day Mickey Finn and within moments he was reeling around helpless while Law passed out, only coming to in a police station the next day. As the youngsters watched, Boyd was smashed over the head with a chamber pot, stripped of most of his clothing and when Macfarlane told Blackwood and Marshall to 'haiv him over the window' he and Blackwood each took hold of an arm of the semi-conscious victim and Marshall his feet and Boyd was pushed out of the window, crashing into the New Vennel to die of multiple severe injuries. 'We'll get a shilling on his umbrella,' Blackwood was alleged to have said.

Macfarlane, Blackwood and Marshall, who had hurled Boyd to his death, were convicted of murder and sentenced to hang, the judge ordering, as was common in murder cases, that their only sustenance was to be bread and water.

However, the jury at the trial in Edinburgh had surprisingly recommended that mercy be shown to Marshall and days before she was due to die she was reprieved, a decision that caused outrage and considerable comment in a number of newspapers. Regardless of her fate, however, there was no way out for Blackwood and Macfarlane, who were refused permission to marry in prison. Shortly after eight o'clock on the morning of Thursday, 11 August, the pair were launched into eternity by executioner Thomas Calcraft before a 40,000-strong crowd. *Reynolds Newspaper* described how 'the struggles of the wretched creatures were painful and protracted especially in the case of the woman with whom life appeared to remain for four minutes after the drop'.

Visiting brothels and using prostitutes cost money. Michael McIntyre, William Kidston and William Dyer were regulars who haunted the inns and houses of ill repute in Glasgow even though Kidston was only seventeen, and the trio easily fell prey to the lures of women of the night, who cared not how clients had come about their money so long as they paid up. The three took to housebreaking and theft to pay for their women and were inevitably caught.

Irishman McIntyre had been a soldier, frequently whipped – he boasted of having suffered more than 2,000 lashes – before being booted out for stealing from his comrades; immature Kidston, a rope maker, was awestruck by the ex-soldier's reputation as a womaniser and despite his youth had already served a prison sentence and one of banishment. When twenty-two-year-old weaver Dyer was arrested, police found an astonishing hoard of fake keys, capable of opening almost any lock, hidden under his floor. All three were condemned, but as they waited for death in front of the Glasgow jail in October 1821 guarded by a strong contingent of dragoons, they were forced to listen as a clergyman told the crowd they were about to see 'a proof of the excellence of our constitution, which protects us from bad men, who lie in wait to rob our persons, or break into our houses, and plunder us of our property. It is necessary to cut off such persons.'

10

UNFAIR SEX

The sheer horror of the New Vennel case meant reports of it were eagerly read throughout Britain. Once Scottish newspapers arrived at major cities in England, other editors took the opportunity to repeat their accounts but it was the announcement by the then Home Secretary, Lord Palmerston, of a reprieve for Marshall that attracted more than usual passion. The *London Times* newspaper angrily demanded to know why women received reprieves when they 'seem to have been as proper subjects for the extreme penalty of the law as it is possible to find', while the *Glasgow Herald* pointed out that nobody in the city where the murder was committed petitioned on Marshall's behalf. 'If this woman is respired why is Blackwood hanged?' it protested, pointing out Marshall had 'worked as cordially up to the elbows in blood as any of them'.

In the condemned cell, despite continuing to protest her innocence, Blackwood entertained no possibility of being saved. As they awaited a date with the hangman, so many others before her, mainly men, had their hopes raised then dashed. In 1800 Peter Gray had been told the sentence of death against him was being respited for a fortnight to allow the London authorities to examine his claims of innocence. Gray had been arrested following a break-in at Ross Lodge, the home in Dunbartonshire of a Lieutenant Colonel Colquhoun not long after the officer had returned from collecting rents from his father's estate. Two men with their faces blackened had been watching and knew he had a sizeable sum but when they broke in expecting to quietly burgle the Lodge they made so much noise that servants, Colquhoun and two visitors intervened. The burglars were armed with clubs and badly beat most of the occupants, leaving two unconscious before disappearing towards Luss.

After a one hundred guinea reward was offered for information that would lead to the capture of the villains, Gray was arrested but denied being involved, saying he was elsewhere, although the evidence against him was strong. After he was condemned for the crime of 'hamesucken' – housebreaking with assault – it was decided his claims merited further examination and he was told his sentence would be respited – delayed – for a fortnight. Respite sometimes led to reprieve and possible transportation, and Gray's hopes of surviving rose. It was also a sly move on the part of the authorities, who wondered whether during the two weeks he might try to save himself by admitting he'd been there, name his accomplice and plead for mercy. But he maintained his innocence and at the end of the fortnight the forty-five-year-old was told no evidence had been found to support his story and he was hanged at Glasgow.

Thomas McNair too had high hopes of avoiding the drop but extraordinary measures were taken to make sure his death sentence was put into effect. When the *Resolution of Danzig* berthed at Falkirk, the skipper, Captain Luder Jantzen, discovered he had been robbed of fifteen guineas. A number of men were arrested, one of whom to save himself pointed the finger of guilt at McNair, who was convicted of robbery and sentenced to hang at Falkirk despite insisting he was blameless – even the jury signed a letter pleading for mercy for him.

McNair waited and prayed for a reprieve while the protests of his angry friends aroused official concern. So strong was the support for McNair that in the days leading up to his execution the authorities became convinced an attempt would be made to rescue him from the scaffold. Some Falkirk residents were said to have joined themselves into a form of neighbourhood watch, patrolling the streets and demanding the right to inspect public houses and brothels for signs of troublemakers; official handbills were distributed indicating a number of 'suspicious persons' would arrive in town and asking for anyone spotting a stranger to report this. More than 500 infantry soldiers and three cavalry troops were ordered to Falkirk, one-third of them being stationed around the scaffold while the others were held in reserve on the town outskirts.

The military presence was too strong and deterred a rescue effort. McNair's friends and acquaintances did manage to get their hands on him, but only after he was pronounced dead as they carried his body, accompanied by a military guard, to the home of his father. However, feeling that McNair had been harshly treated continued to run high and troops had to remain in town to guard officials who conducted the hanging until they left the next day.

James Ferguson must have believed the grim reaper had no interest in him because he had appeared in court three times on capital charges of housebreaking and theft and on each occasion walked free. Even after his fourth appearance and a guilty verdict against him he was confident of yet again avoiding the Glasgow executioner. Ferguson was accused of robbing a man of £32 in the city's Old Wynd, and although he was convicted the jury was divided, giving him the idea that he could expect mercy from the judges, he still held out hope of being spared.

However, the judge, George Fergusson Lord Hermand, a founder of the Royal Society of Edinburgh, was a man with a long legal experience, though occasionally suspected of being tetchy from the effects of the previous night's heavy drinking. Perhaps Ferguson appeared before him on such a day because his Lordship made no bones about what he believed lay in store, telling the culprit, whose shoulders may well have dropped further with each word, 'You may, perhaps, delude yourself with hoping, that as you were found guilty only by a plurality of the jury, consequently some of them may have misconceived your guilt, and that you may obtain mercy. Entertain no such idea. While I therefore feel no more can be done, or will be done, for you in this world, let me call forward your thoughts to the eternal future state, for which you ought zealously to prepare. Be once more assured, the hope of pardon is vain.' Ferguson was hanged in April 1813.

Often it was the age of a defendant that persuaded a jury while returning a guilty verdict to recommend mercy. Judges mostly had their hands tied by law when it came to fixing sentences and had no alternative but to pronounce death, although they also had a duty to forward the views of the jury to the government – technically to the monarch of the day – to decide if there were grounds for a rethink, in which case a respite of the sentence would be ordered until a decision was reached.

In January 1815, Thomas Pennycook and Alexander Knight, both in their late teens, who worked as carters, were accused of attacking two men, a gardener and his servant, on the outskirts of Edinburgh, seeing them in a public house in the Canongate receive just under £5 for selling a horse. When man and master left, Pennycook and Knight followed and once clear of the city on the road to Musselburgh near Wheatfield launched a vicious attack, threatening to kill them if the money was not handed over.

What followed was a comedy of errors. They also stole the gardener's hat and first had a fight over who should have it, then further on, after visiting public houses, argued over what had happened to the money they stole; Pennycook even forced Knight to strip to show he was not hiding it. They then had yet another row about ownership of the hat that ended when Pennycook stuck it on his head, a fatal decision because he was still wearing it when the gardener identified it as his after the attackers were arrested.

The jury found both guilty and because of their ages asked for mercy for them, a plea that gave hope to Knight and Pennycook, and to many in Edinburgh who felt the inevitable sentence of execution was too harsh; but the government refused to intervene and they were hanged.

From the day he was born in the large family home in Glasgow

High Street, William Campbell had a comfortable life mapped out for him. He paid attention to his teachers, was polite and studious, and when old enough joined the family calendar publishing business that he was due to inherit one day. But when he was eighteen it all went wrong. He fell in with some of his old school pals, criminals and wastrels who led him into trouble. A sheriff banished him from Glasgow and warned him he would be whipped if he returned. When he ignored the threat, he was thrashed. Within days he and a gang of cronies had broken into a business dyeing clothing and made off with a huge haul that they sold to a notorious female fence. Campbell was convicted of housebreaking, and the fence and her daughter of reset and theft, and both given prison sentences. If Campbell was buoyed by hearing the leniency shown to them, his hopes of similar treatment were short-lived. The judge, Lord Succoth, told him, 'Your days are numbered on earth. I beseech you to prostrate yourself before Almighty God for mercy for there are no hopes for you from man as you have seriously offended the laws of God and man. No pardon can be expected.' Then he was ordered to die for stealing clothes.

The severity of the sentence horrified Campbell's fellow gang members, who had been accused with him but were freed when the jury returned not proven and not guilty verdicts. His family, who were well connected in Glasgow, was especially horrified. Influential businessmen made representations to the government requesting a mitigation of the sentence. Due to his friends in high places and their frantic efforts to save his life, Campbell, in irons and shackled to a huge bar in the condemned cell, retained hopes of salvation. His father was a daily visitor to the prison, but it was all in vain. In May 1822 Campbell had to sit in the city courthouse, his arms pinioned, his family and friends around him, while the spectators sang a hymn beginning with the words, 'The hour of my departure'. His devoted father, distraught, stayed with him up to the moment he was led to the scaffold.

A week later it was the turn of Thomas Donachy to stand on the same ghastly spot. Like Campbell he too could count himself unlucky. He had been a member of a gang that broke into a cellar in Oxford Street, Glasgow, and carried off wine and spirits. However, as they were being arrested they made the mistake of arguing with police and trying to resist arrest. At the High Court, while the rest of the gang admitted their guilt, Donachy brazened it out, forcing a trial at the end of which he was convicted. All this, said the *Glasgow Herald*, tended to make the Crown 'select him as a fit person to make a public example of'.

Donachy didn't help himself by deciding to make a speech as Lord Meadowbank, after ordering his accomplices to be transported, was about to pronounce his own fate. 'My Lord, I just wish to say a word or two. I don't care for the value of what I get if I had got justice, but two of the witnesses have committed perjury.' At this point Donachy stopped to take a drink of water but didn't get the chance to finish what he wanted to say because by the time he put his glass down the judge, not bothering to wait for him to finish, had told him he was to be hanged.

11

FALL FROM GRACE

Most Scottish banks, even the smallest, produced their own notes and these were often crudely designed and printed with the result that even the lowliest criminals saw through forgery and uttering – passing forgeries – a means of making easy money. In England, juries in some forgery cases were told how accused men mainly from the middle classes made tens and in a couple of cases hundreds of thousands of pounds before they were caught. In Scotland the forgers and utterers pocketed considerably less, sometimes only a few pounds, but no matter how much the take, the cost of being caught was the same – death. Such was the fate of John McKana and Joseph Richardson at Dumfries in May 1823; but a terrible mistake would make their execution even more dreadful than should have been the case.

At their trial the previous month the two, together with Richardson's brother Joseph, had denied an allegation of 'uttering as genuine, false, forged and counterfeit notes on the Ship Bank of Glasgow knowing the same to be false and forged'. According to confessions they made after their arrest, thirty-nine-year-old McKana was an old hand at the forgery racket. In 1818 he had bought 500 fake British Linen Bank notes from a forger in Ireland but by August 1822, short of money, he had travelled back with Joseph, a thirty-two-year-old farmer, to meet the same forger, who took them to see an engraver at King's Court, west of Dublin. They were there almost three weeks, by the end of which the engraver had produced plates and arranged for them to print off 300 fake notes that were divided equally between McKana and the Richardsons. The total cost was under £27. But back in Scotland after passing a handful of the counterfeits in Dumfriesshire and near Carlisle they were caught. Investigators discovered seventy-two notes at McKana's home and another 163 hidden in a bush on a turf dyke. All three men were found guilty and sentenced to death, Joseph fainting in the dock when his fate was announced.

Because these were family men and very few notes had been passed there was considerable local sympathy for them and appeals for reprieves were made on their behalf to King George IV. Then days before they were due to die a letter arrived from the government in London announcing a reprieve for one of the three. As they lay together in chains in their condemned cell at Dumfries jail a note was handed to Joseph telling him he was the lucky brother who had been spared. For a few moments he was unable to speak, his emotions torn between what he saw as his own good fortune and the despair now facing his brother. But the joy on his face was enough for one of the lawyers present to realise he was the victim of an appalling bungle and had to relay the news that it was William and not he who had been reprieved. A broadside published after their execution revealed that after he was told the awful truth, Joseph 'expressed satisfaction that his brother's life was spared, since, to use his own words, "the idea of two brothers going out of life in the same awful way was painful to be thought on". McKana, meantime, admitted he had never held out any hope of being saved.'

They were executed together in Buccleuch Street before a huge sympathetic crowd, scores of whom, too distressed to watch, ran off before the hanging. The men's corpses were taken away by their heartbroken families for burial. The *Caledonian Mercury* described particularly distressing scenes when father-of-seven McKana was interred that evening in the town's St Michael's churchyard, 'in the presence of a numerous crowd of men, women and children. This unhappy man, it appears, had requested his wife to attend his funeral and see his head laid decently in the grave. This task she was enabled to perform but in place of accompanying the crowd she retired privately to the churchyard where she was seen seated on a tombstone amidst a torrent of rain and in a state of mind not to be described. When the funeral neared, an opening was made for her approach and the cord of the coffin slipped into her hand. This she grasped as one in convulsions and as the earth sounded on the coffin lid she stood, the very picture of despair.'

Just as the desire for easy money had devastated two brothers, so it ripped apart a father and his daughter when in 1824 as penal reformers pressed for forgery and uttering to cease being capital offences, William and Margaret McTeague faced the awful prospect of being hanged. The pair were accused at Glasgow of passing just two fake notes each on the Royal Bank and Sir William Forbes and Company Bank, the jury taking only twelve minutes to decide they were guilty. However, the Crown did not press for the death penalty in the case of nineteen-year-old Margaret, who protested she did not know the notes she passed were fake; she was told she would be transported spending the next fourteen years 'Beyond the Seas'. But there was little if any sympathy for her father. William, aged forty-three, ran an inn in Hutchesontown beside the Glasgow Gorbals but had a dangerous sideline in that he was known to make regular trips to Ireland where he bought counterfeit bank notes. He usually passed the notes himself but then recruited his daughter to help with the racket. The sentence of death on him was inevitable, but a petition for mercy on his behalf stated grounds that were remarkable in the light of what the authorities knew about him. This claimed he was a man of previous good character but because he was illiterate and uneducated he had not recognised that the notes, passed to him at his business when he and Margaret, who worked as a muslin sewer, were drunk were fakes. The petition went on to allege that, 'There was a lack of sympathy for the prisoner on the part of jury members because he was clearly a member of the poor Irish Catholic community who suffer much prejudice in Glasgow.' The mercy plea was rejected and William was executed on the city's Common in May 1824.

The news of his death was broken to Margaret while she waited in jail for a vessel to take her from Scotland, but it was five months later before she was shipped from Leith to the London hulks and in October she finally boarded the convict ship *Henry* along with seventy-eight other women, ten of them convicted in Scottish courts. It arrived at Van Diemen's Land the following February, where she married and raised a family before her early death at the age of thirty-four.

Just as William McTeague was said to be ignorant, Malcolm Gillespie was astute, clever and ambitious. His is a truly astonishing story. Born in Dunblane, Perthshire, he was determined to make for himself a career in the military and as soon as he was old enough enlisted. Eager to obtain a commission Gillespie waited and waited, finally falling in love, marrying, raising a family and as a result getting into debt. An army officer needed money; Gillespie had none and so, needing an income, he joined the Excise where his zeal and enthusiasm won widespread praise from superiors. He pursued crafty salt manufacturers at Prestonpans who tried to dodge paying taxes and became known as a terror to anyone trying to evade duty. Having been transferred to the north-east coast to hunt smugglers, it was said that he once single-handedly took on an armed mob after spotting them smuggling spirits. Fearless and courageous he was often badly injured in encounters with men trying to rob the King of his lawful income; yet always within days of being patched up he was back at work.

However, not everyone was in favour of methods that at times bordered on the brutal, especially when he targeted local fishermen whose small time smuggling was known to authorities content to turn a blind eye in exchange for getting information about major gangs. When he moved to Stonehaven he introduced the idea of using dogs to sniff out and track smugglers; but throughout nearly thirty years in the poorly paid Excise service, promotion had passed him by. And because he had paid most of his own expenses he was severely in debt. Gillespie's solution was to forge the signatures of farmers and businessmen to make it appear to banks they were settling his bills. He also set fire to his home and made inflated insurance claims. Inevitably the forgeries were uncovered and Gillespie was convicted on seven charges of forging and uttering the fake bills, and sentenced to death. His clerk, George Skene Edwards, found guilty of forgery, was sentenced to transportation for seven years.

Gillespie was convinced he would be pardoned. Strenuous efforts were made to get him a reprieve. William Gordon, MP for Aberdeen, wrote a petition asking for clemency in which he said, 'The local Distillers here look to his known exertions for protection to the trade and are particularly desirous for the continuance of his valuable services in this district.' Sir Alexander Keith, Knight Marischal of Scotland, appealed, 'Having applied to me to state what I know of his exertions in the execution of his duty in the suppression of illicit distillation, I can truly say that from a long knowledge of his services, I look upon him as one of the most active, enterprising and useful men in that line.'

But these and other entreaties were rejected, and when he was told all hope of a reprieve was lost horror-struck Gillespie broke down and cried. The man who fell from grace with a noose about his neck was hanged before a huge crowd at Aberdeen in November 1827 and his body buried at Skene.

Just as Gillespie had been confident of cheating death, William Harries fell into the trap that entices so many criminals; the belief they will never be caught. In 1770, having lain in prison at Edinburgh for fifteen months awaiting his trial, accused of forging twenty shilling notes of the Thistle Bank of Glasgow, he escaped. Most criminals either fled across the border to lose themselves in England or begged passage on a ship to London, but Harries hung around Edinburgh, a decision that cast doubt on his sanity because he was recaptured. Back in jail he tried strangling himself with a handkerchief and his garters but was saved by a doctor. When the time came for his trial he attempted but failed to convince a jury he was insane. A second jury then had to be sworn to try him on the forgery charge and he was convicted and sentenced to hang at Edinburgh Grassmarket in May 1770. According to the *Scots Magazine,* Harries 'continued the farce of playing the madman even when sentence was pronouncing and on the way from the court to the prison'.

In fact Harries was no fool. Before his arrest he had managed to pass more than 450 of the forged £20 banknotes and had another 9,677 ready to exchange. Realising the game was up and his act convinced nobody, Harries spent the rest of his short life in jail writing his life story before his meeting with the executioner. At least he had given his life for a fortune.

Samuel Bell sacrificed his for a guinea in 1800. And yet he was described by witnesses at his trial for forgery in July that year as being a man of 'considerable property, sober and industrious'. The case gave a fascinating insight into travel in those times when innkeeper John Inglis told how an escaped prisoner named Mason had written from London to him at his Edinburgh home suggesting a meeting in Newcastle-upon-Tyne to which he was to bring 'a certain person' – Bell – and promising to show him, 'something new that would suit Edinburgh.' Inglis went on horseback to Ayton then walked to the home of Bell in Spittal near Berwick-upon-Tweed. Next day the two walked to Belford in Northumberland to catch the coach to Newcastle and on the way Bell revealed Mason was in London having one guinea notes forged on the Ship Bank and Brown, Carrick and Company banks of Glasgow. The counterfeits would not arouse suspicion because they had never been passed in Scotland, and Mason would also be bringing Bank of England notes said to be so perfectly forged that it was impossible to detect them from the real thing.

At the meeting with Mason in Newcastle, Bell took some of the Brown, Carrick and Company forged notes and when back in Scotland a friend asked him for a loan, he gave him one of these. The friend used it to buy a pair of boot garters costing a few pence from a shop in Stirling; the note was discovered to be a forgery and when the friend was arrested he named Bell as having given it to him. It was tantamount to a death sentence which was formally pronounced by the judge after the jury convicted Bell of forgery. He was executed at Edinburgh in September 1800.

For decades penal reformers such as Samuel Romilly urged the government to drastically reduce the number of capital crimes. There was much support for campaigns to remove forgery and uttering from the list of offences for which death was the penalty. However, horrific cases such as that of John Henderson in 1830 endangered the arguments put forward by the reformers that killing someone for a crime such as handing over a fake one guinea note did not justify legal execution.

Henderson worked as a live-in lowly paid damask weaver for elderly James Millie, who ran the business from his home at Whinny Park near Monimail in Fife. When he had not been seen for some time, Henderson was asked whether he knew where Millie was and he said his employer was in Edinburgh dealing with a legal matter. Henderson began attracting attention because he suddenly seemed to have come into money, spending freely in public houses, hiring gigs to get about and buying a new suit. Around a month after he was last seen, a group of men had been at Millie's home to look over one of the weaving looms with a view to buying it but became alarmed when they saw what appeared to be bloodstains. In the garden they noticed a patch of earth that had been disturbed and asked passing workmen to dig at the spot. Soon the remains of a corpse began appearing. Police were called and after the body was exhumed it was found to be that of Millie, who had been battered to death about a month earlier apparently with a hammer; his body had then been burned and an attempt made to bury it in the loom shop, but because the soil was too shallow it had been interred in the garden.

When he was detained Henderson insisted his master was in Edinburgh but inquiries showed he had already forged Millie's signature on a money order to get £40 cash from a bank as a result of which he was arrested and charged at Perth Circuit Court in September 1830 with murder, theft and forgery. He pleaded not guilty but after hearing the evidence the jury took only four minutes to find him guilty and he was sentenced to be hanged at Cupar at the end of the month. The judge, Lord Meadowbank, told him, 'This has been a dreadful case. An unfortunate man was basely and cruelly murdered by an assassin while sitting at his own honest trade by his companion, his only companion who was bound to defend him even at the risk of your own life. It was a crime committed for the sake of base lucre and the determination to attain that end was followed up with a degree of coolness and perseverance unexampled. You remained in the house at the door of which the mangled body of your master had been buried and you continued living in it day by day and sleeping in it night by night and all the while committed a series of more crimes and carried on a continued system of plunder.'

As he lay in jail waiting to die Henderson tried to commit suicide but after that failed he was said to have slept well, not even being awakened by the sound outside of workmen building the scaffold. Yet after he had climbed to the gibbet there was more drama. With the noose around his neck and the executioner about to pull the bolt that would launch him into eternity Henderson called back one of the clergymen who, seconds before, had given him a last handshake, and asked if the hanging could be held up for a few minutes longer. 'I'm frightened to go,' he admitted, but was told his time on earth was at an end. Resigned to his fate he dropped the handkerchief, the signal that opened the floor beneath him.

Henderson had committed two capital crimes – murder and forgery. But just two years later, the 1832 Punishment of Death Act abolished execution for a series of crimes including forgery, uttering, stealing a horse, sheep or cattle, and theft from a house. Lord Dacre told the House of Lords, 'In this enlightened age the frowning aspect of a barbarous and bloody code, whatever might have been its effect formerly, has lost all its terrors.'

12

NEVER ON SUNDAY

Watching a hanging was one of the few entertainments available to the poor living in the squalor of Scotland's towns and cities. True, Glasgow, Edinburgh and Aberdeen had their theatres, but then these cost money to enter and were continually coming under threat from religious groups who believed acting in general to be a form of the worship of graven images and that of women in particular to be scandalous and a vice on a par with prostitution. One of these groups even burned down Glasgow's first theatre, built on the site of what is now Central Station. There were occasional travelling fairs and sporting events – bare-knuckle boxing matches between men and women were an especial favourite of the rich – while alehouses were becoming more numerous. But these too cost money. However, a hanging was free and it was hardly surprising that spectators would walk many miles to attend one.

Religion dominated life. While working classes all too frequently looked on an execution as a day out, the chance to meet up with friends, chat and even sing, priests, clergy and ministers frowned on such levity. A hanging was a serious affair where the victim might well be only moments from coming face to face with God and the last words from the scaffold of men or women about to be launched into eternity were often worth waiting many hours to hear.

Sunday was a day for kirk, church or chapel, a time of reflection. John Malloch made the mistake of treating it as an opportunity not just to commit crime but to despoil God's law by dressing himself as a woman. The crafty villain had spent some time watching the remote home in the village of Meigle, a few miles north-west of Dundee, of an elderly woman who lived with a maidservant. Malloch lived in the area but was heavily in debt and as he mooched about the village he noticed how on Sunday mornings the maidservant religiously went to church, leaving her mistress alone in the house for a few hours. He knew the old woman was vulnerable and suspected she kept money, but his problem was that villagers knew him and he needed to avoid being recognised. His answer was to dress up as a woman and once he heard the bells summoning the worshippers to Sunday service he crept along to the unsuspecting woman's home.

His victim heard him enter and at first thought a woman friend had called to visit, but suddenly she was knocked to the floor. While she lay too terrified to move Malloch began rifling through her property, smashing open chests and drawers and finally running off with money, bills, papers, linen and ornaments. By the time the old woman plucked up courage to scream for help he had vanished. But news of the theft coupled with Malloch suddenly appearing to have come into funds was enough to have him arrested, and when female clothing matching that of the burglar was found hidden at his home his days were as good as numbered. At Perth Circuit Court in October 1801 he was accused of 'disguising himself in women's clothes on a Sunday in the forenoon during Divine Service' to carry out the raid. He was convicted of robbery and theft. The judges, Lords Dunfinnan and Cullen, told Malloch he had committed an 'atrocious' crime and sentenced him to death. He was put to death at Perth on 18 December – a Friday.

Sinning on the Sabbath cost Malloch his life; the message from William Cunningham two years later was simply, 'Never on a Sunday'. He had been convicted at Glasgow for theft and reset but on the scaffold in front of the tolbooth, Cunningham had a message for others who might tread the same path into crime. The *Aberdeen Journal* said he had 'lamented that, disregard in the advice of parents, desertion from public worship, profanation of the Lord's Day, and associating with improper company, had rendered him callous to the warnings he had received and at length led him to an untimely end. The unhappy man behaved with becoming decency and considerable firmness, cautioning young persons against frequenting low public houses and bad company, which present temptations to deviate from truth and honesty.'

Cunningham ought to have listened to the words of James Dick, who was hanged at Glasgow in May 1792 for murdering his wife Mabel. The *Glasgow Mercury* reported, 'This unhappy man's fate furnishes an additional instance to the many which are daily occurring of the fatal effects of drunkenness. He confessed that on the night on which the murder was committed he had gone to bed somewhat intoxicated, that his wife who for some time had been much addicted to drunkenness soon after came in showing a state of intoxication and that a quarrel ensued when he started up from his bed and seized a knife which was lying on a work stool beside him and in the height of his passion plunged it into her bosom. In a short address to the spectators he admonished them to take warning by his untimely end and in a particular manner to guard against the vice of drunkenness, especially on Sundays.'

His words were echoed by Richard Broxup, hanged at Edinburgh a few months before Malloch, for picking locks and theft. A broadside detailing his 'Confession and Dying Declaration' said the thirty-three-year-old Yorkshireman pleaded with spectators, 'I earnestly hope, that all those who shall see or hear of my untimely end, will take warning and avoid the paths which have brought me to be a public spectacle to the world, especially those who are or may be addicted to such crimes as I have been guilty of; and I beg to let all such know, that though they may escape the laws of their country, they cannot escape the eyes of an all-seeing God.'

His words and those of Cunningham were intended to bring home the consequences of being reckless because hanging was a miserable, sordid, painful affair in which the awful wait for the dreadful event was meant to be part of the criminal's punishment. If the whole process from indictment to dangling was intended to be a lesson to others not to follow the same path, then Mark Devlin would have gained praise from his teachers. According to the *Caledonian Mercury*, in his last hours of life in the condemned cell before his meeting with the executioner at Dundee in May 1835 Devlin had told clergymen, 'He was quite prepared to meet his fate, trusting for pardon through the merits of our Saviour and expressed thankfulness to God for arresting him in the midst of his career of crime.' Remarkably Devlin had appeared quite perky to those who arrived to take him to the gibbet because others in jail around him had been awakened in the early hours by the arrival of workmen who began assembling the scaffold in the front of Dundee Town House and yet he had slept soundly through the din.

Devlin, a Roman Catholic, continued his contrition as the noose was being placed around his neck, telling the crowd, 'Brethren, this is a disgraceful death in the eyes of the public, but I hope the Lord will have mercy on me.' As far as the public were concerned it wasn't his death that was disgraceful but the reason for it. Married with a family and in his twenties, he had been condemned for rape, which was regarded as an especially revolting crime. Had he managed to convince the jury he was innocent of that offence then he would have needed even more luck the very next day when he was once again due in court accused, along with two other men, of theft by means of housebreaking. But because he was already doomed it was not even thought necessary to bother with a trial and simply assumed he was guilty. His absence gave his accomplices the chance to blame him of being the ringleader in a series of thefts from warehouses and as a result they were spared the death penalty but sentenced to be transported. So when with his final words Devlin said, 'I forgive all my enemies from the bottom of my heart,' those close to him knew to whom he was referring.

Devlin's appearance on the scaffold was brief; that of Allan Mair, the oldest man to be hanged in Scotland, went on so long that the crowd, waiting in drizzle to see him launched into eternity, lost patience. Mair, eighty-four, had been convicted of murdering his eighty-five-year-old bedridden wife Mary by beating her to death in their Muiravonside, Stirling, home. He had been particularly cruel, starving the old woman and often hitting her until neighbours intervened to stop him and feed her. 'Oh, Allan, we could live like the King on the throne, although we are poor, if you were good to me,' she was said to have often told him. But her words were ignored; he even locked the food cupboard to prevent her eating. At his trial in September 1843 his counsel suggested he should be spared the death penalty because he was clearly insane, a defence that was instantly rejected. But what happened on the scaffold the following month gave weight to the madness argument, although it was too late to save the old miser.

According to the *Stirling Observer*, Mair had already talked at great length earlier in the courthouse where the formalities were being gone through but now, 'Being placed upon the drop, he was accommodated with a chair, upon which he was no sooner placed than he began a speech, which continued for nearly ten minutes. We were apprehensive that not a word of what he said would have been understood by the people; but we were mistaken, for when he got to the fresh air and felt himself at ease upon the chair, and saw the immense crowd gathered thick together, he assumed a courage greater than we thought his advanced age alone could have allowed to remain. As he advanced in his harangue, he got more and more animated, hurling fire and brimstone, death and damnation, both temporal and eternal upon all, with the exception of the judge and jury, who had any part in his apprehension, examination and trial. He called upon the whole assembly, great as it was, and more especially those who came from his own parish and neighbourhood, to listen to what he had to say, as they had not given him a single opportunity ever since his apprehension, to prove that innocence which was clear as noon-day. The minister of the parish had invented lies against him, had taken these lies to the pulpit, had brought them into his examination and had even brought them with him into his cell, after he was condemned and upbraided him with them.'

And so it went on, with Mair spitting venom against the police constable who arrested him, the fiscal and sheriff who 'had brought a Roman Catholic man and woman, people who worshipped sticks and stones, to witness against him.' His next-door neighbours were next to be verbally slaughtered followed by witnesses and people in Muiravonside. While the diatribe continued the executioner began fixing the noose about Muir's neck, but neither that nor the mutterings of the now soaked crowd could stop him and Mair was still talking when he dropped to his death.

Another whose final speech was only halted by the sudden plunge into space was Edward McCrory, convicted of assaulting and robbing a labourer between Gatehouse of Fleet and Cree-town in Kirkcudbrightshire in 1820. The victim said he'd been attacked by two men on a lonely road and the pair took all his money. As they were about to run off one had shouted to the other that the victim was 'not half done yet' and that unless they did something more to him, 'He would be able to follow them and get them both hanged.' So they had given him another savage beating, his life only being saved when he managed to crawl to a nearby house for help and a doctor was called. Word of the attack spread and McCrory was arrested, but denied being the attacker; however, he was convicted and sentenced to hang at Dumfries in October.

While he was in prison McCrory, a thirty-two-year-old Irishman from Ballybrack, said that both his father and brother had been executed in his homeland. But remarkable as that was, an even greater sensation was to come. On the scaffold McCrory was said to have spoken at length to explain why he was inno-cent, but as if to hammer that message home even after the execu-tioner had put the noose around his neck and fixed a white cap over his head to hide his face from the crowd, McCrory, despite having his arms pinioned, suddenly lifted them up pulled up the cap and once again protested he was innocent. The startled hangman pulled the cap back down and returned to his position by the bolt only for McCrory to once more lift it and shout out he was being wronged. At last having had his say he pulled the cap back over his face, allowing the bolt to be drawn and his protests finally silenced.

When he arrived on the scaffold at Greenlaw, the village sitting on Blackadder Water in the Scottish Borders in 1853, American-born John Williams was greeted by boos and catcalls. He ought not to have been surprised. Williams had brutally attacked and murdered a toll keeper in the Lauder area and many of the dead man's friends had travelled the dozen or so miles to watch his execution. The unusual and relatively remote location had combined with a cold, gloomy early spring morning to keep the number of spectators down to about 500 but at times their shouts drowned out the prayers of clergymen attending the doomed man.

The murder had been callous and vicious. When toll keeper Andrew Mather, aged sixty-one, failed to return home late one night his daughters Agnes and Isabella went looking for him and discovered his dead body lying on a blood-spattered road. Stretched over him was Williams, who suddenly leapt up, but he was caught as others hearing the shouts of the women ran to the scene. In Williams' pockets were the dead man's tobacco, pipe and pouch. 'The Devil tempted me,' he said, and then made a statement saying he had fallen asleep on the road after finding Mather's body. He had words too for the watching crowd at Greenlaw that morning, like McCrory lifting up the white cap, only in his case to angrily tell them off for shouting, hooting and booing at him before he was hanged.

13

WILD, WILD, WEST

Stealing a horse in the American Wild West was to gamble on facing rough justice, with the culprit most probably being strung up from the nearest tree without the formality of a trial. Years earlier in Britain it wasn't just the theft of a horse that was liable to end in hanging; until the 1832 legislation that greatly reduced the number of capital offences, pinching a cow, bull or sheep very often saw an offender climbing the steps to the scaffold. In the two decades leading up to that major revision of hanging crimes, judges tended to show far more compassion although there was still a heavy penalty to be paid through transportation to Australia. Horses then were much more valuable than the motor cars of today: farmers needed them to plough and produce food; industry to move and sell its goods, while to deprive a man of a cow or his sheep was to rob him of his food. Harsh as it might seem to put a man or woman to death for taking away a beast, until the development of engines and the gradual mechanisation of life in general, Britons survived on the backs of animals and would sometimes go to remarkable lengths to protect their ownership.

No better demonstrations of that were the capital cases of George Walker in 1801 and of father and son George Watson, senior and junior, ten years later that showed the extraordinary lengths to which owners would go to recoup their livestock. As the spring sunshine of 1801 broke through the darkness of night to melt the early morning frost farmer John Henderson was horrified to discover that while he and his family and workers had slept a thief had broken into his stables at Longcraig on the southern outskirts of Stirling. A valuable gelding and mare were missing. Henderson immediately sprang into action, saddling up other horses to begin a search for the animals. He and his son would scour roads to the north, and farm worker Robert Wilson was ordered to take the southern routes. By midday the despondent Hendersons were back at the stables, having seen and heard nothing; but Wilson was by then proving to be the hero of the day, showing remarkable brightness for a young man in such a lowly role.

Wilson began by calling on keepers at toll bars, who collected small fees for the use of various sections of roads, bridges or tracks, and after a number of fruitless enquiries hit lucky when a keeper told him a man and boy shepherding two horses had passed through in the middle of the night. Encouraged, Wilson rode on, enquiring at more toll gates where keepers remembered the man with the boy and horses until it became evident his quarry had turned south. Close to Carnwath in Lanarkshire he was told his pursuit was almost at an end because he learned the man he was seeking was George Walker, who lived a dozen miles away outside the village of Newhouse. Not knowing what he might face when he confronted the thief, Wilson called on other farmers, who agreed to join him, and when they arrived at Walker's smallholding the stolen beasts were discovered in a stable to the rear of his home. A further search revealed Walker hiding in a ditch and after being questioned by a magistrate he was committed to Peebles prison, twice trying to escape on the way there by running away from his escorts but soon being recaptured. Wilson meanwhile went back to Henderson with the horses. His search had taken two days.

In a desperate effort to save his skin Walker claimed he had bought the horses not knowing they were stolen and then said he had been sleeping at the home of a woman; but her account suggested he and the boy seen with him had been in the area earlier to spy out possible targets. At the High Court in Edinburgh in July Walker was convicted of horse stealing and hanged in the city the following month.

An even more extraordinary pursuit saw George Watson senior dangling on the gallows at Ayr ten years later. He and his son, also George, were tinkers who travelled about Scotland taking on any work that might be available but mostly mending pots and pans and scrounging board and a bed from farms and big houses. It was a hard and, at times, miserable life and few people trusted tinkers, who had a reputation, often unfairly so, for being thieves. One man willing to trust them was John Kerr, who allowed the Watsons to shelter in outhouses at his farm at Knockburnie, close to New Cumnock in Ayrshire. Kerr had a reputation for kindness but his generosity was repaid with treachery because when he woke up and checked his farm the next morning he found to his distress and anger that not only had the two tinkers already left but they had taken a valuable Clydesdale mare with them. The horse was much admired in the area because of its immense size and strength, and for its outstanding grey coat. Kerr needed the horse; it was a vital cog in the running of his farm and there was no way he was going to let the thieves get away. There was another reason why he needed the mare back at his farm; one of her shoes was broken; if it was not mended it could damage her hoof and so he had arranged to visit a local blacksmith.

He immediately set off to seek help from his brother William, who owned a farm a short distance away, but when he arrived he found him in a state of turmoil. During the night he too had been robbed of a horse. And when the brothers inspected the building from which it had been taken they discovered the marks left by a broken shoe. Whoever had taken the Clydesdale had then led it to William's farm to steal from him and disappear into the night. Furious, the brothers set off in pursuit. Fortunately, days of wet weather had left the ground muddy and to an experienced eye it was a simple enough matter although a slow one to follow the Clydesdale's tracks. And soon there were people on the roads who remembered the grey mare and the two tinkers, one younger than the other. However, two farms were now without their owners and at Kilmarnock the brothers agreed that William would go back and keep an eye on both, leaving John to carry on, encouraged by his own disgust at having his kindness and generosity abused in such a way.

With his eyes to the ground and ears open for news of the Clydesdale, John pressed on to the north, occasionally calling in at other farms to beg news and a bite. Farmers were more than happy to help; the theft of animals was loathsome. Occasionally some would ride along with him to help find the tracks left by the Clydesdale. After heading up the side of Loch Lomond he reached Tarbet, where he was advised to make for Inveraray and ask at the jail for the whereabouts of a sheriff who could give him a warrant, making the chase and any arrest lawful. The seriousness of the theft encouraged the sheriff to appoint two police officers to accompany John in case of trouble and after resuming the tracking the trio, who had been joined by farm workers ordered by landowners to assist, continued further north and west. Finally, after almost a week and a trek of well over 150 miles, John spotted his grey mare in a glen north of Oban and close to the coast at Benderloch.

'I didn't expect to see you,' said an astonished Watson to the farmer, who told him, 'I didn't expect you would steal my horse.' With that both Watsons were arrested and the little band retraced its steps, the police and culprits to Inveraray, where they were locked up, John Kerr to a blacksmith to have his mare's broken shoe mended and then to return to Knockburnie and a delighted William.

The Watsons went on trial for their lives at Ayr in May, their agents arguing that because technically only one horse had been stolen from each farm that did not justify the death penalty, but judges dismissed the suggestion. Although his father was condemned, a distressed George junior was sentenced to transportation. Lord Meadowbank berated the father for what he described as the enormity of the crime and telling him, according to the *Glasgow Herald*, that he had not only committed a capital crime but had 'corrupted the mind of his own son in seducing him to prove an associate in crimes in forgetting every paternal duty and stifling every parental feeling'. He was 'guilty of a sin against nature'. The older man was hanged at Ayr the following month while his son waited in jail to be shipped south to the Thames hulks to await his voyage to the other side of the world.

Campaigners for an overhaul of the law might have pointed to the Watsons' case as one in which there was an apparent lack of consistency when it came to sentencing. On the same day and at the same court William Gillespie, indicted for horse stealing and other thefts, admitted he was guilty and must have expected to follow Watson senior into the condemned cell but was instead surprisingly only jailed for twelve months. Reporting on Gillespie's case, the *Scots Magazine* said, 'The appearance of the prisoner indicated extreme wretchedness. His meagre and squalid appearance and long beard and projecting teeth excited in the spectators a degree of horror mixed with compassion.' Supporters of Watson felt he had been treated unduly harshly when compared to the punishment meted out to Gillespie and others. The previous day in the High Court at Edinburgh, Thomas Stewart had been found guilty of horse stealing and sentenced to death only to be reprieved soon after. And just over a week later at Perth, Janet Gordon pleaded guilty to horse stealing but here again, like the younger Watson, instead of death was sentenced to transportation.

Inconsistency ravaged through the legal system in Scotland. Ten years previously, and not long after George Walker had met his doom, John Clark, a crofter from the Banchory area of Aberdeenshire, was convicted of stealing a mare from a local farm and ordered to be transported for seven years.

The cases involving Walker and the Watsons demonstrated just how valuable owners and thieves regarded livestock. Culprits were willing to travel considerable distances to steal and another example of this was that of Thomas Smith and George Stevenson in 1806. The pair were from Newcastle-upon-Tyne and had made their way well over 100 miles into Scotland with the intention of stealing livestock that they would shepherd back into England, perhaps selling it on their way to Tyneside or even returning there with it, claiming it had been legitimately bought. Certainly to be so far away from the scene of any crime gave a thief a huge advantage.

They found themselves at Livingston, west of Edinburgh, and noticed that the farm of the Reverend James Maitland Robertson was left unoccupied when he went off visiting parishioners. During one of these absences Smith and Stevenson made off with two of his horses and then took a third from a neighbouring farm. Two men speaking with strange accents and accompanying three horses was always likely to attract attention and they were quickly arrested before they could reach the border. They had not expected to be condemned and when they were sentenced to death at the High Court of Justiciary in Edinburgh in December desperately pleaded with the jury and the judges to ask the King to show them mercy. However, their pleadings were wasted and they were sentenced to die in January the following year.

A broadside published shortly after their deaths on the Edinburgh scaffold revealed their despair, shown in letters to their wives. In one, thirty-nine-year-old Smith, married with five children, three by a former marriage, had written to his second wife, 'Dear Wife, Do not merely read this and throw it in the fire, but save it and read it at different times, for this is my desire and I hope you will attend to it. Dear Wife, it is my desire from my heart that you will not part with my watch nor any of the seals, but keep them for my sake, till my own son William Humerston Smith, is old enough to take care of it; and I hope and trust you will give it to him and tell him it was his own dear Father's watch, and that it was my desire he should have it, and that he should keep it for my sake. Dear Wife, let you marry who you will, pray make this agreement with them that they are never to wear that watch but that you are to keep it yourself, till my son can take care of it. If you make this agreement before you marry; it will occasion no difference between you afterwards.

'Dear Wife, I think your best way to act after my death will be to go home, and sell off all you have, but your bed and bed clothes and take these by the wagon, or by water, which ever you may think best and go to the town where ---------- lives, and where everyone will caress you, and lament for you, and be glad to see you and they will help you into some way of doing that will be better for you than staying at ----------, to spend all you have or to marry a poor pitman or any other drunken men.

'You are worthy of yourself of a gentleman, or a good tradesman, who can maintain you as you ought to be. Never let it come into your mind, that any person of good sense will despise you, or think you unworthy of being a wife, if you behave yourself, as I hope, you will do. Now my dear Wife, believe this to be a truth, and that it is for your good both in this world and with a view to the next, that you let no man living overcome you by promises, nor by oaths, or ever such fair speeches. For depend upon it, a man that makes such oaths and promises, he only wants to satisfy his own lust; and any man that wishes to make a woman his whore I am sure he has no regard for her.'

Stevenson, aged thirty-two, wrote to his wife, who had moved to London, and she only found out he was dead when she received his letter after the execution. 'My Dear Wife, my God has granted me grace to write these few lines to you; and I hope you and my Dear Little Child are well. My dear Wife, I hope you will forgive me for the ill using of you, as I have my dear Wife. I send you these few lines to let you know, that I am dead. And I hope that you will always take care of my Dear Little Angel.'

Sadly hopes by Smith and Stevenson for a last-minute reprieve with the sentence being commuted to transportation were never realised.

Sheep, too, had been a frequent target for thieves. Long before Smith and Stevenson, labourer John Brown had ventured across the border from his Northumberland home and stolen a flock of seventy sheep from a farm to the south of Edinburgh. He was caught near Duns and according to the *Scots Magazine*, in his final speech before being hanged at Jedburgh on 5 June 1770, admitted to having led a 'very wicked life' but claimed this was his first attempt at stealing sheep. 'I owe the justice of my sentence to the laws of the land and earnestly pray that God may forgive my judges, jury and prosecutors. But one thing I cannot omit is this: the owners got all their own sheep again, a few miles travel and a little expense was all their loss. O then mercy give and mercy crave; O but life be sweet, and death be bitter, to an unregenerate soul. Might not I be condemned to slavery during life, rather than hurried into eternity in this sad case I am in, full of fears and doubts, shame and sin.'

Just as John Kerr and Robert Wilson had turned sleuths to track down stolen horses, so farmers at Blackford in Perthshire set about finding forty-five sheep that had vanished one night. It was difficult to hide such a number and the angry hunters were quickly on the trail looking for clues dropped by the animals and appealing for help from travellers who were only too eager to assist. Eventually the flock was traced to Glasgow but unfortunately the owners would not be taking their property back to Blackford; the sheep had been driven to a slaughterhouse and were now hanging in butchers' shops in the city. The slaughter men said the animals had been sold by William Crighton, who assured them they belonged to him after he had bought them from a farmer. But when he was confronted he admitted being the thief, saying he had fallen on hard times and needed money. He was hanged at Perth in November 1803.

At one time Crighton had been well off, owning property in the Highlands, where cattle thieving was rife, so much so that at the opening of the spring circuit at Inverness in 1819, Lord Reston had instructed local sheriffs to 'use their utmost exertions' to stamp down on what he said were the most prevalent crimes – illicit distillation and sheep-stealing. Perhaps the respected judge might have preferred a return to the days of a century earlier. In 1700 John Duncan, convicted of cattle theft and resetting the animals at local markets, was tied to another thief, John Reid, on their way to the gibbet at Dunnottar on the north-east coast. Reid was branded on his shoulder by the hangman; made to watch

Duncan hanged; told to dig the dead man's grave beneath the spot where he was executed and bury him, then ordered never again to return to the area on pain of death.

Lord Reston's concern was brought about by the almost total dependence of Highlanders on cattle and over the years the harshest punishments had failed to stop a thriving trade in stolen beasts. In 1767 John MacLeod from Drimrinie of Coigach, north of Ullapool, had been sentenced to death for cattle theft and reset. He begged for a reprieve but was not helped by having been long suspected of direct involvement in stolen cattle and then escaping from the Inverness Tolbooth following his arrest. After his recapture the Crown agent in London told the authorities at Inverness that MacLeod was, 'Not found, after the most mature deliberation any way entitled to the Royal mercy and that the law was to take place against that unhappy man.'

Escapes from the Inverness Tolbooth were frequent. In 1789 John Doo Kennedy, taken to the prison for stealing a horse, decided he was not going to hang about and wait for a judge to sentence him, the jailer recording that, 'The said John Doo Kennedy escaped by breach the prison.' The following year Donald Macdonald, alias Donald the Duke, and Donald Kennedy were both convicted of horse stealing and ordered to be whipped on their naked backs through Inverness , then returned to the tolbooth and held there until arrangements were made for their transportation for life. It was more than a year before the jailer recorded he had handed them over to a sheriff for the journey to the Thames.

John Doo Kennedy escaped the worst the law could throw at him and the idea of escape was in the mind of James Grant from Kincardineshire as he was being taken by a pair of sheriff's officers in April 1818 from Stonehaven to Aberdeen, where he would be tried for stealing sheep. Suddenly Grant sprang from between his escorts and hurled himself over the parapet of the Bridge of Dee. Was it an escape from custody or from what life held in store? No one would ever know because Grant's skull was smashed and he died on the spot. Perhaps had the tragic man waited he might have discovered that judges, conscious of the growing strength of opinion that stealing cattle did not merit the sentence of execution still open to them, were becoming more merciful. A year earlier at Glasgow Daniel O'Donnell, accused of stealing a sheep and some potatoes, was merely banished from Scotland for life.

14

ON THE SPOT

The sentence for murder, once execution, is now mandatory life imprisonment. But judges still retain considerable discretion, having the power to recommend how long an offender should serve before applying for parole. A degree of leeway was open to judges more than 200 years ago and it gave them the authority to heap even greater punishment and misery on a man and woman convicted of any of the then abundance of capital crimes. A culprit could be told he or she would hang in chains, or that their dead body was to be left hanging from the gibbet in chains so birds and beasts could feast on it and nature rot it. Judges had the right to decree that a body after hanging was to be handed to anatomists to be publicly dissected, a punishment that families and women offenders in particular found especially humiliating; some murderers might be told they would live only on bread and water from the time of their conviction until their execution, although here sympathetic jailers might add a smear of honey to their bread and quietly allow them an occasional drink of hot tea; and then their Lordships acting at their own discretion decided condemned persons could be put to death on, or as near as possible to, the spot where they had committed their offence.

It was a decision generally welcomed. Following the execution at Dundee in 1801 of weaver John Watt for housebreaking and theft, the *Aberdeen Journal* described it as, 'Certainly a wise and salutary measure and we have no doubt will be followed by the most beneficial consequences.' And so the hanging roadshow was born.

Of course it wasn't always practical to take the gibbet to some out-of-the-way places. In December that year John Young was put to death in front of the Aberdeen Tolbooth. He was suspected of being the leader of a gang of thieving Aberdeenshire tinkers and during a fallout over the division of the takings had stabbed dead his cousin Hugh Graham at Chapel of Garioch outside Inverurie. Judges occasionally delayed pronouncing a sentence to see whether there might be problems ordering a hanging on a particular spot and in this case there were real concerns, particularly when it came to security about performing the execution at such an out-of-the-way, remote hamlet. While he waited in prison he was visited by some of his associates whose behaviour gave the tolbooth jailer concerns and he ordered a search of Young's cell. It uncovered two lengths of steel rod with which he had managed to prise up part of the floor with the intention of escaping via the ceiling of the room below him. Despite his having carefully replaced the floorboards his plot was literally uncovered and from that moment it was decided not to risk taking him around eighteen miles through countryside.

If there was such a thing as a beautiful setting in which to hang a man, then that was the Crinan Canal. Three years after it was opened in 1801 to connect Loch Gilp with the Sound of Jura and thus reduce to nine miles what had been the tortuous shipping route between the Clyde and Inner Hebrides, its banks were the scene for two killings, one illicit and the other judicial. The double tragedy had begun innocently enough one evening when Duncan Macarthur and his wife Elizabeth were walking along the side of the canal, heading for Lochgilphead. But Elizabeth never reached her destination because the next morning a horrified boatman discovered her body lying on the bank with her feet in the canal. A doctor confirmed she had been strangled. Her husband denied being the murderer and there were no witnesses to tell what had actually happened, but after a long trial that lasted into the early hours the jury unanimously found him guilty and he was sentenced to live on bread and water until his execution at the murder scene after which his body was to be handed over for dissection.

Soon after realising he was doomed, Macarthur admitted he had killed Elizabeth during an argument and he spent the remainder of his time deep in prayer in Inveraray jail while workmen built a gibbet on the side of the canal from which he was executed on 31 October 1804, his body being put in a cart and taken to the home of his parents for them to bury him after surgeons turned down the offer of his corpse.

Two years later judges at Perth delayed sentence on John Westwater, found guilty of stabbing through the heart fellow flax dresser John Orr, until checks were made to ensure he could be hanged near the spot at Kinghorn on the Fife coast where the crime was committed. A sheriff gave the thumbs-up and the execution went ahead, attracting a huge crowd, many of whom had walked for hours for the unique experience, to those in that vicinity, of seeing a man hanged.

In July 1813 workmen were instructed to build a gibbet that had to be so precisely placed that the feet of the two doomed culprits would dangle exactly over the spot where they had committed a terrible murder. The killers were both young; James Williamson Black, aged eighteen, a slater, dark haired with thick lips and who walked with a limp, and painter John McDonald, slim and looking younger than his twenty years. Their victim had been seventy-three-year-old blacksmith William Muirhead, well respected by fellow businessmen and much loved by his family, who lived with him in the Calton area of Edinburgh. Muirhead had been doomed from the moment he decided to take an evening stroll into the country in May. Just over a week earlier Black and McDonald had gone into a hardware shop in the city's Royal Exchange and after a good deal of bartering handed over twenty shillings and went off with two pistols. They bought ammunition in the form of slugs at another nearby store and set about planning a robbery.

Muirhead's walk took him close to the hamlet of Coltbridge

on a road leading to the then village of Corstorphine and he had turned for home when two young men who minutes earlier had been drinking in a nearby inn approached and asked him for the time. He took out his silver pocket watch but found himself looking at the barrels of two pistols and pleaded, 'Oh no my man, you'll surely no do that.' They were the last words he ever spoke. Later that night as the Glasgow to Edinburgh Telegraph coach was nearing the last leg of its seven-hour journey the coachman halted on seeing the body of a man lying face down in the fading light before him and realising he and his passengers were looking at the victim of a shooting, went for help. By now Muirhead's family, worried that he had not yet returned home, had gone to look for him but were met by police who had to break the news that he was dead, shot three times through the heart. Witnesses, who included a girl who had earlier served the killers with drink, told of hearing the sound of shots and she remembered one of her visitors was Black, having known him some years earlier. She said she had seen him winking at his acquaintance while he tucked something into his waistband as they were leaving. Not far from the spot where Muirhead was killed police discovered two pistols pushed into the muddy ground. The dead man's watch had been taken and soon afterwards was sold, but was later returned to his family.

Black and McDonald were arrested and made statements detailing the murder but each accused the other of having fired the fatal shots. They were both convicted of highway robbery and murder. At their trial the judge had stern words for James Kyle, the apprentice who had sold them the pistols, formally admonishing him and warning, 'If in future you should deal in such dangerous weapons then you ought to be extremely careful how you sell them, especially to persons of the appearance of the prisoners.' And he pointed out that he was responsible for selling weapons that had resulted in murder. Black too was reminded that he had been a witness in a murder trial a few months earlier that resulted in the hanging of three of his friends, Hugh McIntosh, Hugh McDonald and Neil Sutherland (see Chapter 29) and according to the judge he ought to have learned a lesson from that experience.

The *Caledonian Mercury* said the conduct of McDonald during the trial was 'distinguished by the most atrocious insensibility having more than once interrupted both the witnesses and counsel. He exhibited the utmost indifference when sentence was pronounced frequently interrupting the judge in his exhortations to the proper employment of the short time he had to live; and, in conclusion, when his Lordship prayed Almighty God to have mercy on his soul, he loudly exclaimed – "He will have none on yours."'

The sentence was that they were, 'To be carried back to the Tolbooth of Edinburgh, therein to be detained and to be fed on bread and water only till Wednesday 14 July next; and upon that date to be delivered over to the sheriff of the county, or his substitute, who is ordained to transmit them, under a sure guard, to such place in the immediate vicinity of the spot where the deceased William Muirhead was murdered and robbed, as shall be appointed by the said sheriff-depute and then and there to be executed and their bodies thereafter to be delivered to the Professor of Anatomy for dissection.'

There was immense interest in the double hanging, even though it was out in the then countryside and the authorities were taking no chances, knowing Black in particular had numerous friends among the troublesome younger element who might, with a few glasses of porter inside them, rashly try a dramatic rescue. And so when the cart carrying the prisoners to Coltbridge left the Edinburgh Tolbooth at half-past twelve it was surrounded by more than 300 soldiers. Black and McDonald were tied with their backs to the horse drawing the cart and facing the hangman who fingered the ropes he would fashion into nooses and put about their necks. The procession led by high-ranking officials was joined by city guards and policemen and wound its way through the Lawnmarket, along Bank Street, the Mound and into Princes Street from the west end of which it continued to the spot, a quarter of a mile from Coltbridge, where the body of Muirhead had been found. It was now dominated by the scaffold and surrounded by a huge crowd, and shortly before three o'clock the hangman withdrew his bolt and, just as the judge had ordered, the feet of both dangled over the exact place where the old blacksmith had been slain. As if they had waited until the souls of the men were on their journey to eternity, the skies suddenly opened, drenching the spectators as they trudged back into the city.

It had been a good day for the families that enjoyed the games and entertainment at the annual Kilmarnock Fair. But now it was time to head for home. Tragically on the way evil waited. Irishman James Worthington was a pedlar and troublemaker convicted in the past of minor offences, mainly stealing, and at one time he was banished from Ayrshire. Now he was back and teamed up with three other riff-raff who had armed themselves with sticks and clubs. As Worthington reached Rosemount at Symington Toll apprentice upholsterer David Dickie, his coat pulled up about his neck to protect him from the rain, was suddenly confronted by the gang, dragged from his horse, which ran off, bundled into a ditch and robbed. He tried getting up to run off only to find a pistol being pointed at him and he was ordered to stay where he was. But soon the gang had spotted two more victims. Farmers James Ferguson and Alexander Paterson had left the fair together and were riding home when they were dragged from their horses near Rosemount, beaten and robbed. All three victims remembered that one of the attackers had been bearded and wore a blue coat with yellow buttons.

Dickie and the farmers went for help and police looked for the gang who had disappeared. But the villains were about to be undone by a woman's curiosity. Earlier in the day the gang's scruffy and sinister appearance had drawn the interest of drinkers at an inn, one of whom had commented that he, 'would not be surprised if some robbery was committed before the people came home from the fair'. Now the four had gone with their booty along the road to Glasgow and as midnight approached knocked up innkeeper David Taylor and his wife Jean at the village of Rose Fenwick. The couple weren't happy when the visitors more or less demanded to be allowed inside, given whisky and then an upstairs room. Jean in particular sensed something was wrong and she would tell Worthington's trial for highway robbery at Edinburgh in January 1815 that she did something she had never done before, which was to take off her shoes, quietly creep up the staircase and put her eye to a hole in the plaster wall. She saw seated around a table the four, one of them bearded wearing a blue coat with yellow buttons, sharing out money, one of them complaining he had been given too little and Worthington telling him he had received too much. Jean was just in time to silently return downstairs when the group said they had decided to leave.

Worthington, a widower in his late forties with a daughter aged seventeen and a son of twelve, was arrested in Glasgow after newspaper appeals for witnesses described him and the others. He claimed that on the day of the fair he had been in Lochgilphead, but the jury convicted him and he was sentenced to be hanged on 17 February 'on the highway between Symington toll-bar and Monkton as near as possible to the place where the robberies were committed'.

The spot chosen as the site for the gibbet was in a field on the south side of the road and he arrived there handcuffed, tied to a cart and surrounded by police constables and a troop of cavalry after rumours that Irish friends might help him make an escape attempt. He asked that his hat be given to his son and as he was mounting the scaffold heard a bystander among the immense crowd comment, 'Poor man' at which Worthington turned and responded, 'I am not poor now.'

Fears there might be trouble at the execution of Worthington proved unfounded. There were concerns too when Robert Scott was hanged in October 1823 but the worry was due to there being so much anger over what he had done that attempts might be made to kill him before the hangman got to work. Also, the remote location chosen by the judges made life easier for a would-be assassin. Widower Scott, aged thirty-six, who was bringing up five children was a remarkable character. A native of Berwickshire he was noted for his immense strength and athleticism. He was once reputed to have kept up with a stagecoach travelling at seven miles an hour on a thirty-four mile journey from Edinburgh to Gordon in the Scottish Borders; but at the same time others found him short tempered and vindictive. The indictment to which he pleaded not guilty at his trial in the High Court at Jedburgh in September demonstrated the full horror of what Scott was accused of doing and revealed why there was so much hatred of him. It alleged that he, 'Upon the road leading from Earlstown to Greenlaw and at or near to a plantation in the immediate vicinity of the hamlet of Henlees did wickedly, maliciously and feloniously attack and assault the deceased James Aitcheson, cooper in Greenlaw, and county of Berwick, and the deceased Robert Simm, horse-dealer in Greenlaw aforesaid, and did, with a sheep stake, or bludgeon, or stone, or some other unlawful weapon, cruelly and barbarously inflict various severe blows and wounds upon the person of the said James Aitcheson and Robert Simm, whereby the head and left leg of the said Robert Simm were fractured and broken, and the head of the said James Aitcheson was severely wounded; and did likewise, with a knife, or other sharp instrument; in a cruel and barbarous manner, cut and slit the noses of the said James Aitcheson and Robert Simm; in consequence of all which they were both or each or one or other of them bereaved of life.'

News of the murders spread through the Borders like wildfire. Aitcheson and Simm were popular members of Greenlaw society; the fact they had been killed was hard enough to take but the intensity of the fury against Scott was deepened by the fact that they had also been mutilated. One rumour suggested he had actually cut off their noses, another that he had inflicted the terrible wounds while they were still alive, something authenticated by a witness claiming he heard screams for mercy from the victims. As he was being transferred to Jedburgh from Greenlaw for his trial Scott was booed and insulted and there were frequent shouts of 'Hang him!' It was little wonder that the courtroom was packed, with scores waiting outside to hear the outcome, but they did not have long to wait once the final speeches were made because the jury took just eight minutes to find Scott guilty. The judge ruled that he should be taken to 'the most convenient place for execution, near to the spot where the murders were committed, and there hanged by the neck till he be dead'. His body was to be handed over for dissection, at which Scott said, 'They might make pye-meat of my flesh, and whistle of my bones for anything I care when my life is gone.'

He was held overnight in the prison at Jedburgh and after having his shackles struck off taken through the crowded streets of the town in a chaise for his own protection. However, on reaching Earlston he was tied to a chair in a cart guarded by a detachment of yeomanry who kept the vast crowd away. The site where workmen had erected the scaffold was known as Fan's Farm and on it with death only moments away the doomed man pleaded for his wife and children to be cared for before untying his neckcloth, placing it into his hat and dropping both over the side of the scaffold, then plunging into eternity.

15

SUFFER LITTLE CHILDREN

Life was tough for children in the years before campaigners successfully argued for legislation to protect youngsters. The first United Kingdom Census in 1801 showed some infants just four years old registered as workers helping make shoes, work on farms or sweep chimneys. In Scottish towns and cities children began work on average before they had reached their ninth birthday and it was not until the passing of the 1833 Factory Act that the minimum starting age was laid down as nine. Campaigners fought for decades to improve the lot of those forced to climb up and down chimneys; the Chimney Sweeps Act of 1834 made it illegal for an employee to use anyone aged fourteen or under to sweep a chimney, a limit raised to sixteen in 1840.

Just how risky a job this was for youngsters was shown by a case in 1817 at the High Court in Edinburgh in which chimney sweeps Robert Reid and Joseph Rae were accused of murdering their apprentice John Fraser aged eleven. According to the prosecution the boy had been sent up a very narrow chimney at a house in the New Town but became stuck fast. The *Liverpool Mercury* reported, 'One of the witnesses was a master sweep, he offered to ascend the chimney himself; Rae however pushed him away and continued bullying the boy. Reid, in a little time, ordered another boy to ascend the chimney with a rope which he was to fasten round the boy's feet. Having fastened the rope, Reid desired him to come down; Reid took the rope and pulled but did not bring down the boy. The rope broke. The boy was sent up again with the other end of the rope that he fastened to the boy's feet. When Reid was pulling the rope, Rae said, "Damn you, you have not the strength of a cat"; he took the rope into his own hands, pulling as strongly as he could. Having pulled about a quarter of an hour Rae and Reid fastened the rope round a crowbar and both pulled with all their strength for a quarter of an hour, when it broke. During this time the trapped boy was heard screaming in agony and crying, "My God Almighty" to which Rae yelled back, "If I had you here I would God Almighty you."'

After an attempt to fasten a new rope failed, a hole was smashed in the wall of the house to get to the boy but by the time he was finally recovered he was dead, his head having been trapped in a turn of the chimney. Rae and Reid were cleared of murder but convicted of culpable homicide and transported, the former for fourteen years and the latter for seven, the judge telling them, 'This case approaches the nearest to murder of any I can remember.'

Just as child workers had little if any protection from unscrupulous employers, when it came to dishing out punishment the law itself made no distinction as far as the age of an offender was concerned. Children of twelve were hanged; those even younger whipped or jailed along with hardened adults and it was not until 1847 that anyone under the age of fourteen had to be tried in a special juvenile court and a further seven years elapsed before the first reform schools opened.

The hanging of teenagers was a regular occurrence. Juries and occasionally judges could plead for mercy for a young offender but it was up to Crown agents in London acting on behalf of the monarch to decide whether a death sentence should be replaced by prison or more usually transportation. No such relief was afforded Andrew Macghie, aged eighteen, in 1770 after he was convicted of street robbery in Edinburgh. The *Scots Magazine* said he 'acknowledged the justice of his sentence but did not behave with the decency and concern that might have been expected'.

Simon Ross and James Boyd, convicted of housebreaking and theft at Rutherglen, were both sentenced to be hanged after their conviction at Glasgow in 1818, an outcome that was especially horrifying to the family of Boyd because he was only fourteen. Ross, six years his senior, was a hardened lawbreaker, having seen the inside of the tolbooth several times even though he was just twenty. Following their verdict the jury, conscious of the youthful appearance of Boyd, put forward a plea for mercy on his behalf but he had to endure an agonising wait shackled in irons in the condemned cell before, just four days prior to the hanging of his friend, word came from London that he was being spared a similar ordeal. It was unlikely the pair could read and perhaps as well if they did not; otherwise they might have seen in newspapers of the time reports that in the case of Ross in particular hopes of a reprieve were highly unlikely.

Several newspapers had carried reports of the case of seventeen-year-old James Ritchie accused of stealing thirty sheep from the parks of Gordon Castle, Aberdeenshire. All but one of the same jury that found him guilty pleaded for mercy because of his age. It was likely the dissenting voice was that of a farmer, because they and estate owners throughout Scotland were determined to put cattle thieves to the hangman. Ritchie was a first offender and it was anticipated he would be spared, probably ending his days on a sheep farm somewhere in Australia. But as the days ticked by nothing was heard from the Crown and to the disgust of so many in Aberdeen the youngster was executed in June watched by a huge crowd, many of them in tears, impressed by the courage with which he met his fate. On the scaffold Ritchie made a moving plea to other young people to 'avoid Sabbath breaking and bad company'. The hanging was widely reviled, the *Caledonian Mercury* describing it as a 'revolting spectacle', but criticism would not halt the execution of young people.

There were many other youngsters who were glad to be shipped off in convict transports knowing the alternative was to dangle on a gibbet. At the same time as Ritchie was being condemned thirteen-year-old Alexander Story was convicted at Jedburgh of theft aggravated by breaking open lockfast places, a capital crime. Story was saved from death by pleading guilty, and because of his age he was transported for seven years. A few days later at Glasgow three youngsters were said to have laughed as Lord Pitmilly sentenced them to transportation for life for theft and being known thieves. They were followed into the dock by Walter Turnbull, aged ten, and nine-year-old Hill Boyd Hay, who pleaded guilty to housebreaking.

The *Caledonian Mercury* reported that the children 'presented a most afflicting spectacle, for they were so little that they were mounted on the dock seat and were bathed in tears. The Advocate Depute observed that some persons might consider apology from him for bringing such infants to the bar of their country. He was well aware of the tender years of the prisoners at the time he raised the indictment against them.' The case, the Advocate Depute went on, 'demonstrated that there was among the lower orders a looseness of principle and a tendency to commit crime'. He concluded by saying, 'God only knows what is the cause of this deterioration of character and what can be its cure. The present conviction will teach young persons, if they know right from wrong, that if they commit a crime it matters nothing in the eyes of the law whether the prisoner is nine or sixty years of age.' It was an uncompromising view shared by Lord Pitmilly who, after pleading for the opening in Glasgow of an institute in which juvenile offenders could be confined, sent them to prison for twelve months.

Even such a savage sentence failed to scare off the young from crime. At the start of June 1820, sixteen-year-old Richard Smith, found guilty of housebreaking and theft, was strung up at Glasgow despite a unanimous plea by the jury for him to be shown mercy, one that left him hopeful he would be spared, but he waited in vain for news of a reprieve. He was said to be so small that gangs used him to crawl through the tiniest openings to let in burglars. The execution of such a little boy was the cause of considerable anger in the city and the scaffold was protected by contingents of riflemen and hussars. His youthfulness was made all the more obvious when he appeared at the gallows dressed in black clothing made for a child.

It could be argued that Smith had only himself to blame. The previous year he had gone on trial in Edinburgh with a man who was subsequently executed while he was cleared, but it seemed he had not learned a lesson from his narrow escape because soon after walking free he had been caught burgling the home of a candle maker. When told he was to hang, he had burst into tears.

A year later in Edinburgh twenty-year-old David Haggart was hanged and a most remarkable story of evil combined with bad luck was brought to an end. Haggart had started his adolescence as a drummer in the Norfolk Militia, although after two years was discharged and went to work in a mill. However, when the firm went broke he found himself without a job or means of income and developed aspirations of being a major criminal. His entry into the underworld was not successful and he was able to commit nothing more serious than petty thefts, one of which landed him in Leith jail, where security was lax and as a result the teenager, son of a gamekeeper, escaped. He headed south but was soon back in prison, this time in Dumfries, where he now committed the crime that was to bring his young life to a premature end. In October 1820 he broke out by smashing the turnkey over the head with a heavy stone concealed inside a stocking, killing the prison official, and fled to Ireland where he was arrested for picking pockets, gave the false name of Daniel O'Brien and was sentenced to life transportation.

But an Irish magistrate reading *Hue and Cry*, the early version of the *Police Gazette*, realised O'Brien matched the description of the man wanted for the Dumfries murder and wrote to the authorities in Scotland suggesting someone who knew their quarry should travel to Ireland. A police officer from Dumfries arrived at Kilmainham Gaol, where Haggart was awaiting the arrival of a vessel to transport him to Australia – and safety – and accompanied by a heavy guard returned with him to Scotland to face a murder charge.

Sentenced to die on 18 July 1821 he spent his twentieth birthday in the Edinburgh Tolbooth in irons, yet still managed to write what he claimed to be his autobiography, a highly colourful account of crime and prison escapes and which was published in book form after his death as *The Life of David Haggart, alias John Wilson, alias John Morrison, alias Barney Maccoull, alias John MacColgan, alias Daniel O'Brien, alias the Switcher*. It was said to contain an 'Account of his Robberies, Burglaries, Murders, Trials, Escapes and other remarkable adventures'. Haggart gained a minor cult following as a result of the book, but there were many who felt it to be a tissue of lies and exaggeration.

In contrast to Haggart, luck was indeed on the side of fifteen-year-olds Hugh Hosey and Alexander Mackay in December 1825. They were convicted separately at the High Court in Edinburgh: Hosey of stealing clothing from a house in Argyle Square and of being an habitual thief; Mackay of housebreaking and also being an habitual thief. In between a series of thefts the latter had made a living by travelling Scotland selling religious tracts and, despite his age, already had a lengthy police record, having been convicted eight times. The jury pleaded for mercy for him because of his youth. However, Lord Gillies pointed out he had no alternative but to condemn him, and Mackay was told he would be executed the following month. His counsel had urged him to plead guilty, a move that would improve the chances of saving his life, but the youngster had rejected this idea. Hosey on the other hand had pleaded guilty and was ordered to be transported for fourteen years. Then Lady Luck in the form of youth smiled. As the pair languished in jail it was discovered that a member of the jury had been under the age of twenty-one and therefore too young to have served, making the convictions invalid. Both were pardoned and given their immediate freedom. But it would not last for long and they were later transported after again being caught stealing.

The same good fortune did not extend to William Adams, aged twenty, in 1830. Convicted of robbery aggravated by assault Adams was sentenced to die at Edinburgh. From the moment of the awful pronouncement of doom many respectable citizens in the city campaigned for mercy for him, arguing that he was too young to die; he also came from a highly respectable family and the jury had recommended he should be shown mercy. It was all to no avail. His execution was a remarkable example of a young man, well brought up, determined to die with dignity. Wanting to appear on the scaffold neat and tidy, after having his arms pinioned, he asked one of the officials to wipe dust from his shoes. Having climbed to stand under the noose, he looked about the crowd for friends to whom he smiled and nodded acknowledgement while they fought back tears. His voice failing he pleaded with the young men and women watching not to make the same mistakes that had led him to the gibbet. Adams was known to have an at times vicious and uncontrollable temper and before his death told friends that while his father had been firm and strict his guidance had been wasted by a grandmother who too often had mollycoddled him.

16

THE BABY KILLERS

Few crimes excited such anger and disgust as that of child murder, an offence made prevalent almost exclusively by poverty. Yet when it came to punishing those who took the lives of helpless innocents, the law showed a strange contradictory mix of cruelty, sympathy and mercy. There seemed to be no consistency in the way it was applied to child killers and this would ultimately lead to a unique public challenge to the authority of the state. While child murders are among the most horrific in the story of crime and punishment in Scotland, demonstrating extreme barbarity and inflicting scarcely believable degrees of pain on the most vulnerable members of society, it is at times difficult not to feel an equal level of pity for the perpetrators.

At Inverness in October 1749 servant Marjory McEanduy, found guilty of murdering her illegitimate baby, was ordered to be held in the town's tolbooth then, taken to the Gallows Muir and hanged on a gibbet. After giving birth the terrified young woman had fled and was tracked by the equivalent of a local bounty hunter who, as the town treasurer's records showed, was paid for bringing her in. She was then kept in solitude for five months before her execution brought an end to her misery.

Three years later at Aberdeen the townspeople watched in appalled silence as Christian Phren, who had killed her newly born baby then tried to conceal its very existence by throwing the corpse on a fire only to be discovered in the act, was hung in chains and then her body dissected. Both were victims of laws intended to humiliate and punish unmarried women who found themselves pregnant. It wasn't just a capital offence to kill a baby but the mere act of trying to avoid shame by hiding a pregnancy or a birth could result in execution and by its severity and lack of sympathy or understanding the law was the direct cause of the majority of infant killings.

In 1765 a jury at Inverness brought in by a majority decision a verdict of guilty against Helen Preston of Raigbeg in the Parish of Moy for the murder of a child. The court ruled she should be kept in the town tolbooth for a month then hanged and her body publicly dissected. Papers held at the Highland Archive Centre paint a terrible story of suffering and humiliation inflicted on this young mother. These reveal that as a consequence of information that 'the body of an infant had been found buried in the hill above and about an English mile distant from Raigbeg, Helen Preston was suspected of being the mother or at least to have brought forth a child lately.' After Helen's arrest the authorities appointed crofter's wife Anne McLister, local housewife Bessie McGilvray and widow Elspet McQueen, 'all of them practising midwives to examine the breast and body of the said Helen Preston and report their opinion of her according to the best of their skills and judgement'. The trio reported back that they had found 'fresh milk in her breasts' and were of the view that she had 'lately brought forth a child'. How recently she had given birth they were unable to say. Their findings resulted in Helen being taken to prison under suspicion of child murder, 'Or at least of concealing her pregnancy until after the birth and that the child was afterwards found dead.' And that was good enough to condemn her.

While she waited for death Helen was not without support. The authorities at Inverness received a letter from the Provost of Jedburgh saying the town's officers had read about the sentence imposed upon her and that a young woman of that name had left Jedburgh five or six years ago to travel to near Inverness to visit her mother Christine Preston. The letter continued: 'The apprehension that it may be her who is condemned gives her relations here the utmost concern especially that while she was in the town she behaved herself with the greatest honesty and decency. We therefore beg leave to trouble you with this. Desiring to know if she be the same person that came from this place with the circumstances of the crime for which she is to suffer.'

Helen was reprieved before her execution and banished – it was believed to have returned to Jedburgh.

Barely a High Court sitting did not hear a case in which a woman, and rarely a man, was accused of child murder. Very often an accused woman would admit her guilt and plead to be simply banished overseas, thus avoiding the expense of a trial. Around the time Helen Preston was arrested Catherine Finlay, daughter of weaver Robert Finlay from Falkirk, appealed to the Court of Justiciary for banishment and was sent to the American plantations for life, being warned that if she ever returned to Scotland she would face being hanged.

Not everyone was so fortunate. Newspapers regularly carried reports of the discovery of newborn babies and children, mostly dead, abandoned at roadsides, dumped in ditches or rivers, or hidden in woods.

After a baby girl aged five or six weeks was found lying at the entry to a house in Cambuslang, Glasgow, a reward of twenty shillings was offered by the local Parish Session to anybody who identified the 'unnatural' mother.

Was it reading about the disposal of the bodies of children that gave cruel Agnes Dougal the idea of how to get rid of the corpse of her daughter in 1767? Sadly for her there was neither mercy nor salvation, as the *Scots Magazine* recorded following her execution at Glasgow. 'She died penitent, confessing that she had lived a very lewd life, born four children in adultery with married men; and that the reason of her murdering her child, a girl of about eight years of age, was that one of her libidinous customers pretended he would marry her, but that the chattering child informed the neighbourhood of all that was said or done in the house. She then felt a contriving how to destroy the poor innocent child. "My first design was," says she in her speech, "to have strangled her in bed when asleep; then I thought to have drowned her in the Clyde, and was taking her away that fatal morning to throw her in, when it came to my mind, as I went out of the door, to turn and take with me a large, sharp knife, being resolved that she should never return. And so by the side of a hedge between Anderston and the water-side, where I thought none could see me, I took her head close to my left breast, and with one fatal stroke across the neck I cut her throat almost from ear to ear."

"Her last words were, *Oh mother! Oh Mother! Do not kill me. I'll never do it again*, which words of hers I think I hear almost sound loud in my ears, but far louder in my conscience. She then fell on her face, and spurned with her feet, gripping the ground with both her hands. I turned her over upon her back, and looked upon her mangled neck, where the blood was belshing and spouting out. O then was I struck with remorse, anguish, fear and confusion, trembling seized every joint of my body and flesh and had I been mistress of the whole world, I would with a thousand goodwills have given it all to have had her alive again."'

The death of the little girl must have been high up the table of evil, but also near the top was surely the gruesome killing of the daughter of Agnes McCallum from Paisley in 1793. A broadside detailed the horror written on the indictment at the High Court in Glasgow which stated she was accused, 'Of the murder of her own bastard child, about five or six months of age, by pouring into the mouth of the child vitriol or some acid liquor mixed with milk, by which the child died in a short time afterwards.'

One feature of the trial was that some of the witnesses having been born in the Highlands did not speak English and an interpreter who understood Gaelic had to be found and sworn in. After hearing from them the jury unanimously found her guilty of murder and she was told she would go back to prison to be allowed only bread and water until her execution. Hearing the dread sentence, she fainted. Yet at the same court Hannah Main from the Glasgow Calton also indicted for murdering her child was saved from the death penalty by admitting the offence and putting forward a petition pleading to be banished for the rest of her life.

Agnes was hanged along with highway robber James Mackenzie, who had been followed into the dock that day by his brother James, who was transported for seven years for stealing a horse.

While Agnes starved in the Glasgow Tolbooth, in Inverness Jean Bisset was hearing a judge pronounce on her a similar fate after she too was convicted of child murder by drowning her baby. However, the eventual outcome had a vastly different ending compared to that of the others. Pleas for mercy on her behalf to King George III on grounds there were mitigating circumstances surrounding the death of the baby resulted in a Royal Pardon, the formal document giving Jean the good news telling her that His Majesty did, 'Pardon and Truly Forgive' her of the crime of murder and ordered that she was in future to be free from, 'Troubling, apprehending, imprisoning, prosecuting' over the 'said crime of murder'.

Just as the country was increasingly being gripped by the announcement of another nationwide Lottery, with prizes between £1,000 and £50 – sizeable fortunes then – so the law in regard to the penalties for child murder seemed to some to work on a pot-luck basis. In 1778 Isabella Perston, daughter of a Cambuslang weaver, was accused at the High Court in Glasgow of murdering her baby. Her 'not guilty' plea was accompanied by an appeal for banishment, something the judge agreed to but with a condition that if she ever again returned to Scotland she would be publicly whipped through the streets and once again banished. Her case attracted vast interest from the publishers of broadsides, one of which stated, 'The public are ever anxious to hear of the character of any unhappy wretch who, by a wicked course of life, becomes amenable to the law; but when murder happens to be the crime imputed, curiosity becomes still greater; and from the moment the law lays hold of the person suspected, rumour is ever ready to relate a thousand circumstances that perhaps never happened. Being fully aware that this is but too often the case.'

According to the broadside account Isabella had, 'much to the distress of her disconsolate parents, for a long time past, led a very irregular life, despising all advice, and indulging, even to excess, those passions, which, when not kept in due bounds, inevitably prove the destruction of the weaker sex'. She had set up home with a young man to whom she bore up to seven children and was pregnant so often that neighbours were used to seeing her in the condition. Two months after she had evidently given birth again there was no sign of a baby and rumour spread she had murdered the infant. When questioned she at first claimed she could not afford to support another youngster and had given the baby to a beggar woman; but her story was not believed and finally she was accused of murder.

That a mother being deserted by the father and unable to maintain a child had taken a murderous way out was a story that had been, and would continue to be heard up and down the land. And so the banishments went on but in between were cases so appalling that prosecutors felt they had no alternative than to seek the ultimate penalty. In 1807 Scotland was gripped by accounts of a ghastly killing in Paisley involving Alexander Taylor, aged sixteen, apprentice to surgeon James Kerr, and twenty-six-year-old gardener Matthew Smith. According to the indictment Smith had 'taken or received from Agnes Kelly on the streets of Paisley a female child of between two and three months old,' and then 'immediately carried the child to a garden and left it lying on the ground while he went in the shop and called on Taylor'. It was alleged that they then returned to the garden and, finding the child still alive, murdered the infant, 'By squeezing its neck with their hands and putting its head under water.' Taylor was cleared after his counsel argued he had no hand in the killing but the jury unanimously found Smith guilty and he was executed at Edinburgh on 11 March.

Two months later at Glasgow, father of three Adam Cox, an Irishman, was launched into eternity after being convicted of murdering his infant son by throwing the child into a clay hole near the Tradeston area of the city.

The following year the sheer horror of the case of Barbara

Malcolm resulted in it being reported in newspapers circulating throughout Britain. According to the *Morning Post* she had sat her eighteen-month-old daughter Margaret on her knee at her lodgings in Lady Lawson's Wynd, Edinburgh, and poured oil of vitriol into the infant's mouth, pretending to watchers she was feeding the waif raw sugar to clear its throat. Little Margaret quickly began struggling and choking with her cries of agony alerting others but even the prompt appearance of a doctor could not save her from a ghastly death. The *Ipswich Journal* reported that at Malcolm's execution at Edinburgh, before her body was handed over for public dissection, 'She appeared very penitent and resigned but so feeble that two men were obliged to support her.'

In 1809 following considerable campaigning by reformers new legislation made concealing a pregnancy no longer a statutory capital crime and replaced hanging by prison of up to two years, although most judges usually limited a sentence to not more than six months. But there was still nothing on the statute books to force the father of a baby to take responsibility for the main-tenance of his offspring. And it was the issue of fatherhood that led to a revolting atrocity at Kirkwall in Orkney in the spring of 1813. It began when Jean Petrie gave birth to a baby daughter in August the previous year. She said the father was her lover, married man Thomas Sinclair, who was terrified that if it became public knowledge he had committed adultery he would be casti-gated in front of the entire community – 'feared at standing in the Kirk'. His brother George was persuaded to write to the local minister confessing to be the father, but Jean was adamant this was not the case and wanted regular maintenance from Thomas, something that was not forthcoming.

As the months passed Jean persisted in her demands until one day when the child was nine months old, healthy and lively, she was visited by the Sinclairs' sister Christina, aged sixty, who ordered Jean to go out and buy her a bottle of ale, promising to look after the infant. Jean told a murder trial at Edinburgh in November 1813 that she didn't want to go, but was afraid to refuse because according to her Christina was 'a very violent tempered woman'. She said she left the house for no more than four minutes but when she returned her daughter was 'roaring as if in pain'. The youngster's condition worsened and, despite a doctor being called, she died hours later. Tests revealed the little girl had been fed arsenic and poisoned. Christina was convicted of murder and, after being carried to the scaffold in a chair, was launched into eternity at Edinburgh on 29 December 1813 and her body publicly dissected.

A mother's demand for maintenance was the cause of yet another child killing, resulting in carter James Glen being hanged at Glasgow in December 1827 for what a broadside described as the 'inhuman murder' of his own son, named James after him. The child was the result of intimacy between Margaret McComb and Glen, her lodger, and when the boy was eighteen months old penniless Margaret had begged the carter for money. He refused, at which Margaret threatened to simply leave her son with him. Glen's response was to tell her that if she did he would 'drown him before two hours'. Tragically both did as they threatened, the child's body being found floating in the Forth and Clyde Canal.

'I was under the influence of the Devil,' Glen said just before he was executed. The terrible manner of the murder caused fury among the huge crowd surrounding the scaffold and the *Caledonian Mercury* reported, 'The greatest order prevailed during the execution, but a disturbance was afterwards excited. The carter who conveyed the body to the college (for dissection) was, on his return, shamefully maltreated by the crowd who had followed the cart. He was several times thrown down, and severely struck, while the police were in the college and had it not been for the interference of some individuals, the consequences might have been serious. A boy who led the horse was also much abused and even the horse received many severe blows.'

Farm worker James Robertson paid the highest of prices for his lovemaking. Although he was only twenty-five, he had three illegitimate children to one mistress and a fourth, aged five, to his latest lover, Jean Duguid, who broke the news to him in the spring of 1847 that she was once again pregnant. Jean gave birth to a baby girl in December and three weeks later Robertson arrived at her farm home at Unthank near Brechin in Angus after she had asked him for maintenance. He pleaded he could not support all the children but said a couple he knew had agreed to look after the little girl and he would take the baby to them. Jean never saw her daughter alive again. Shortly afterwards Robertson suffocated the tiny girl by pulling her clothes over her head and dumping the little body in a field, where it was found. The jury at Perth who convicted him of murder begged for mercy to be shown Robertson because he had made a full confession, but the plea fell on stony ground. As he was climbing to the scaffold at Forfar on a fine spring morning in May 1848 he told one of his jailors, 'When you see any of my friends tell them this is the happiest morning of my life.' A crowd of 5,000 watched as he was launched into eternity, most of them women and children.

To many it seemed that while men who killed children were executed, even when as in the case of Robertson juries asked for mercy, women who murdered their children were regularly reprieved, too regularly as far as many newspapers were concerned. A number of cases prompted anger, in particular that of Celestina Somner, who had cut the throat of her ten-year-old daughter in London in 1856 claiming she and her husband frequently quarrelled about the child's upkeep. She and Elizabeth Anne Harris, who drowned her two illegitimate children Ellen and Angus, in a canal had both been sentenced to death but were reprieved, a decision which brought 'public disgust', according to the *Liverpool Mercury*.

Around this time two other women were sentenced to death in Devon and Suffolk for murdering their children but, like Somner and Harris, were reprieved and their sentences commuted to life transportation. The *Glasgow Herald* complained, 'After the respite of Celestina Somner, we do not see why anybody should be hanged at all. She was a Lady Macbeth of a butcheress.'

Needless to say these complaints failed to sway judges.

Elizabeth McIntosh was sentenced to death at Perth for murdering her five-month-old baby, then reprieved and transported for life, while days after the *Herald* article baby killer Mary Wood was condemned and almost immediately reprieved at Edinburgh.

17

KIDNAPPED

On a warm Friday evening in July 1808 Flora Amos, aged three, played happily at the door of the close leading to her home in King Street, a narrow, heavily populated lane leading to the River Clyde in the centre of Glasgow. Her mother had been gossiping with neighbours and, needing to pop along to an adjoining close, warned her daughter not to stray. When she returned ten minutes later, the little girl had vanished. At first her mother wondered whether she had wandered into another close but finding no trace of Flora and with her fears rising begged help from friends and neighbours to search for the child. One immediate fear was that the toddler had fallen into the Clyde, but the riverbank was busy that day and nobody had seen a little girl on her own. Frantic with worry her parents called in help from city guards. By the following day the entire area had been scoured and on Sunday morning ministers in Glasgow appealed from their pulpits for anyone who might have seen Flora to come forward. Their pleas hit gold. A woman worshipper in one of the congregations said she remembered seeing a woman carrying a child on the road from Glasgow to Kilmarnock and suspected from the cries and struggles of the infant the youngster was not her own.

The news was immediately given to Flora's father, sparking a remarkable and determined hunt. The description of the infant matched that of his daughter and he was sure the woman with her would be making slow progress. It was long before the age of engines and the family was too poor to afford the hire of a gig or even a horse and so he set off on foot asking toll keepers, travellers and innkeepers for news. There had been sightings, a lone woman carrying a crying girl was unusual, but then the father, by now certain he was on the trail of the missing Flora, learned the kidnapper had changed course and was heading for Irvine. Distraught, exhausted and desperate he hurried on, meeting a rider who was so upset at hearing his story that he loaned him his horse. Flora's dad had never ridden before but after a series of falls met up with a soldier who mounted the horse and near Prestwick discovered the woman with Flora.

He ordered her to stop and hand over the child, which she did without protest, being, according to the *Scots Magazine*, 'fixed to the spot and speechless'. The woman gave her name as Rachel Wright, a native of Ireland, and said she was making for Portpatrick in Dumfries and Galloway. She was arrested by passing soldiers and Flora was returned to her family. Wright eventually found herself in the High Court at Glasgow convicted on her own confession of the rare offence of child stealing.

In fact, it was such an unusual crime that for many months judges were baffled as to whether the penalty for the offence, hanging in England, also applied to Scotland. The case ended up at the Court of Justiciary in Edinburgh, where records of trials dating back decades had been searched for any precedents. In 1752 two men had been tried and executed at Edinburgh for stealing a boy and selling his body to surgeons, while in 1784 Margaret Irvine had been condemned at Aberdeen for taking a little boy but was later reprieved. Based on these, Rachel was sentenced to be hanged at Edinburgh, but after appeals for mercy on her behalf was reprieved and ordered to be transported, sailing with 100 other women convicts from the Thames in April 1811 and arriving in New South Wales six months later.

The fact that the earlier precedents had been confirmed made life easier for the judges when sentencing Janet Douglas in 1817 for kidnapping Margaret Reach, aged three, from her parents' home at King's Stables in the St Cuthbert's area of Edinburgh. When her father James arrived home from work one Monday in May his wife gave the shattering news that the little girl was missing. He immediately went off to seek help from the police and then to see the Town Crier, who strode through the city's streets bawling out the news that a child had vanished and appealing for information as to her whereabouts, but nothing was forthcoming.

By the next morning the family was frantic. James was on the road by four o'clock, asking anyone he met if they had seen his daughter, but he had to return home to tell his wife and their other two children there had been no sightings. After a quick meal he set off again, this time heading towards Queensferry. Almost immediately there came hope at a farm when a group of workers recalled seeing a woman and child hurrying past the day before. Further on, nearing the Firth of Forth, a Miss Marshall said she had felt sorry for this woman and had given her a penny to pay for her ferry crossing. James followed over the water and in Fife was given news of more sightings, and these led him to Halbeath near Dunfermline and eventually to his daughter and then Janet, who had an astonishing story to tell.

She had been a coal bearer at Gilmerton Colliery, Edinburgh, but was paid off and with no money she had neither a home nor anything to eat. Desperate and starving she hit on the idea that if she went to a prospective employer with a child in her arms and pleaded that she needed work to feed the youngster it might elicit enough sympathy for her to be offered work. And so on seeing Margaret had taken her. The ruse worked because when twenty-year-old Janet applied for work at Halbeath Colliery she had been employed. She said she was about to take Margaret back to her parents when she was arrested.

At the High Court of Justiciary in Edinburgh in September the indictment alleged Janet had committed plagium – man stealing – and said she did 'wickedly steal and barbarously carry away' Margaret. She was found guilty and sentenced to death but a month later reprieved and ordered to be transported for life to New South Wales.

After being shipped south from Leith she was held in a hulk

prison vessel at Deptford from where she and 125 other women offenders sailed in the convict ship *Maria* in May 1818. They were seen off by reformer Elizabeth Fry, often called the 'Angel of Prisons' for her determination to improve conditions for convicts. In his log Thomas Prosser, surgeon on the *Maria*, said Janet and the other women received three meals a day, breakfast at eight o'clock and dinner at noon and supper at four o'clock, while in between they were given a daily allowance of wine and lime juice. He said the prison in which they were held was kept clean and fumigated with vinegar but the female convicts were said to be continually stealing from one another and the only form of punishment was to separate them from each other.

18

WAS IT WORTH IT?

The issue on which judges at the High Court of Justiciary in Edinburgh had to decide in January 1817 was a tricky one: when was a banknote a banknote, and what was the value of a forged banknote? John Larg and Thomas Mitchell together with an accomplice, Alexander Steel, had burst into the home of toll keeper William McRitchie on the high road between Perth and Kinross not long after he had counted the day's takings and gone to bed beside his wife Emilia. As he was trying to get off to sleep McRitchie heard a shout from outside; a man wanted beer, and when he was told there was none asked for water instead. The toll keeper had called back that there was plenty of water on the roadside. Because it was so late he was determined not to open his door. It was soon obvious there was more than one visitor and, finally, their persistence led to McRitchie getting up and looking out of a window only to find himself staring down the barrel of a pistol. It was a clear, moonlit November night and he saw two men wearing red jackets, one with a gun. Still, McRitchie refused to let them in but when they began battering at the door and then smashed a widow with the gun he relented.

As soon as the pair entered one of them ran to the bedroom and threatened to kill Emilia if the takings were not handed over, and as if to emphasise the menace he warned he would shoot their children. Hoping it would satisfy the attackers, she handed over her own savings of a few shillings. The racket had awoken the family serving girl, who managed to jump out of a window and run for help. McRitchie, meanwhile, began fumbling in a drawer from which he took the bag containing the takings and while the robbers were distracted hid it in his pocket. He then handed over a couple of banknotes. The crafty toll keeper knew they were forged, but Larg and Mitchell seemed satisfied with their haul and, seeing the girl running off, fled themselves.

Next day Mitchell's wife Lydia tried getting change for one of the notes but a merchant instantly recognised it as a forgery and police were called. By the time they searched Mitchell's home he had disappeared but he was later arrested at Torryburn in Fife. Larg, a private in the Royal Perth Militia, was discovered hiding in a coal hole. Both denied having been the robbers, Larg claiming he had pocked money as a result of smuggling whisky while Mitchell blamed his accomplice as being behind the hold-up.

The fact that they had stolen two forged notes led to their counsel arguing that they could hardly be accused of robbery when they went on trial for that offence because by being fake the banknotes were worthless. Therefore all Larg and Mitchell had done was to steal two pieces of waste paper. But after a legal debate the judges ruled it was not the value of what was stolen but the act of taking it that constituted the crime.

However, should two men hang for stealing waste paper? The jury, while finding both guilty, felt justified in pleading for the lives of the accused men, pointing out neither of the McRitchies had been hurt, a move that clearly upset the judge, Lord Hermand. According to a report in the *Caledonian Mercury*, 'He was at a loss to conceive why the majority had recommended them to mercy. If it was, as they said, on account of no personal violence having been done to McRitchie and his wife, they were grossly mistaken. A man's home is his castle and to say that attacking and forcibly entering his house, holding a loaded pistol to his head, demanding his money, and threatening to murder himself, his wife and children, is not offering personal violence then, observed his Lordship, "I am at a loss to know what personal violence means. That pistol might have gone off by intention or accident."'

And so two scraps of useless paper led to Mitchell and Larg climbing the scaffold at Perth in March, from where Larg pleaded with the crowd 'to abstain from drinking, gambling and night rioting which had seduced him to the commission of the crimes for which he was to suffer'.

Just as the doomed men must have wondered, 'Was it worth it?', that same question probably taxed the mind of John Sherry, a Houdini character, as he had lain manacled in the Glasgow Tolbooth waiting for the arrival of the executioner two years earlier. In his case the cause of his downfall had been a mere handkerchief. In May 1815 as manufacturer Robert McCulloch was walking home on a moonlit night from Glasgow to Paisley he found himself joined at Cardonald Toll by two men, one of whom suddenly grabbed him by the arm while the other threatened to blow his brains out if he uttered a word and demanded his money. The victim was pushed violently to the ground and his pockets rifled of money, his watch, hat and a silk handkerchief. Following a search Sherry and a gang of men were arrested and one of them, Barney Nilas, was found to have McCulloch's silk handkerchief about his neck. Nilas knew that was enough to hang him and in a desperate attempt to save his own skin turned King's evidence, claiming the robbery had been organised by Sherry, who was sentenced to be executed.

As he awaited his date with death the authorities were taking no chances with twenty-nine-year-old father-of-five Sherry, a remarkable character who was expected to make an attempt to break out of prison. Born in Ireland he had begun work virtually from the day he learned to walk but soon chose a career in petty crime and on the run from the Irish authorities moved to Scotland in his late teens. Eventually at Carlisle he was arrested on suspicion of housebreaking, a capital offence, but before he could be tried he escaped from the town's prison. Recaptured a few weeks later his adventures were not over as a broadside sold by a publisher in Glasgow's Saltmarket soon after his hanging revealed. 'He was, however, apprehended at Glasgow, and remained in jail a week, when he was sent off to Carlisle, under the care of a messenger. The mode of conveyance was the top of the coach, the inside being full; but, on the road to Carlisle, Sherry complained that he was in great pain, on account of his arms being too hard bound, and requested the messenger to ease the cords, in order that he might travel a little more comfortably. This request being humanely complied with and Sherry now finding he could use his arms with considerable freedom, watched an opportunity, sprung from the top of the coach, and, before the astonished messenger could get down, was out of sight, and succeeded in making his escape. He was no more heard of till he committed the robbery on the Paisley road.'

In the prison, Sherry had, for a time, shared the condemned cell with Robert White, who had been tried on the same day for breaking into a shop. However, White had been quickly reprieved, sentenced to transportation for seven years and moved to an ordinary cell where he waited for a ship to carry him to the Thames. White heard the executioner arrive to pinion his friend and then he and Sherry were allowed a final embrace as the doomed man told him, 'Farewell Bob,' White responding with a tearful, 'Farewell.'

Sherry even tried putting at ease hangman Tam Young from the Glasgow Calton who, as an out-of-work labourer, had applied for the post the previous year after seeing a newspaper advertisement offering £52 a year plus a guinea for each execution, a small fee for every whipping and a house within the jail grounds. There was the added bonus of two new pairs of shoes every year as well as free coal and candles. Sherry would be Young's second victim and the hangman was anxious for the young man before him to know he was simply carrying out his job, asking him if he felt any sense of malice towards him. 'No, you are doing nothing but your duty. I bear ill will to no man living,' said Sherry. This time there would be no escape and minutes later Young launched him into eternity.

Cat burglar David Thomson couldn't resist the dainty petticoat he came across after breaking into an inn at Burdiehouse on the outskirts of Edinburgh. There was plenty of other loot, but it was the pretty garment that attracted him and he knew it would make an unexpected but most welcome gift for his wife. It went into a sack together with many other items and when he arrived home, while most of the rest of the haul was sold off to pawnbrokers, his wife, to her joy, was given the petticoat to wear.

Thomson was an adept burglar, his method of entry being to climb to upper windows and either force them open or carefully cut out a pane of glass to get inside. His takings were prodigious; anything from silver-crested spoons to a basket of eggs, but the petticoat would be his undoing. Police had alerted pawnbrokers in Edinburgh to be on the lookout for property stolen during the raids and after his wife sold the petticoat for sixpence she was traced and a search of the Thomas home uncovered incriminating evidence. He was later hanged after being convicted of five housebreakings and thefts.

In the famous horror story by Edgar Allan Poe, 'The Cask of Amontillado', published in 1846, a victim is lured to a gruesome death by being bricked up while still alive through the promise of sampling from a cask of rare Amontillado wine. More than thirty years earlier it was a cask of brandy that cost Robert Brown Anderson and James Menzies their lives and at the same time devastated those of innkeeper John Burns and his wife Elizabeth. Yet again greed was the seducer and, for a comparative crumb, lives were lost. After breaking into a warehouse at Grahamstown near Falkirk and stealing a cask of brandy as well as some tea, copper coins and sugar, Anderson and Menzies sold the cask to Burns, who ran a nearby inn. It wasn't long before a tip-off led the authorities to the Burns, who knew they were in serious trouble, and to try easing their predicament gave the names of the thieves as the men from whom they bought the brandy. The outcome was devastating. Anderson and Menzies were executed at Stirling in October 1811 despite the jury that convicted them having had an impassioned plea for them to be shown mercy.

The day after their launch into eternity an earthquake rocked the area, shaking houses and leaving women and children screaming in fear. The Burns couple meantime lost their home and inn, having been ordered to be transported, John being shipped off in chains in May 1813 to New South Wales and his wife to the same destination three months later.

Brothers Michael and Peter Scanlan brutally slaughtered a helpless old woman and took her copy of the New Testament. Perhaps it was the shame of such a vile crime that made them wish life to be over quickly. Whatever it was they literally ran to their own hanging. Evidence at their trial at Edinburgh in June 1852 for murder and stouthrief horrified and disgusted those in the packed courtroom. The pair originally from County Mayo, Ireland, had been employed at a lime works and for a time lodged next door to Margaret Maxwell, who ran a small shop in the tiny hamlet of Hilton of Forthar in Fife. The brothers harboured a longing to emigrate to America but had no money and often spoke to a workmate about 'sloping' Margaret, which they explained meant borrowing from her then running away. As they became more desperate they began openly boasting of how they not only knew she had enough money to cover their voyage but they had even worked out a way of breaking into her home and robbing her.

One night they had crept in by breaking a back window as Margaret lay in her bed and then taken off their shoes so as to make no noise. A third man, Thomas McManus, had waited outside. He had been granted immunity from prosecution in exchange for being the main Crown witness against them and told of hearing the old woman scream 'O my God' after the brothers went inside. They emerged not long afterwards with Michael carrying a watch and a copy of the New Testament, muttering he hadn't found any money but had given Margaret 'a knock or two'. The next day Margaret's blood-spattered body was discovered; she had been viciously smashed about the head with a three legged stool. Inquiries and a search at the nearby lime works turned up the watch, which led police to McManus, who pointed the finger of guilt at the Scanlans. They denied being the killers but were convicted and sentenced to death, the *Dundee Courier* reporting that, 'Both prisoners appeared to be quite indifferent to their fate and on leaving the dock denounced both judges and jury, exclaiming, on leaving the bar, that they were damned asses, and expressing a hope that they would be dead and damned before the execution.'

They persisted in their claims of innocence right up to their hanging at Cupar, Fife, and there was little sympathy for them. Hardly anyone signed either of two petitions seeking a reprieve, a move rejected by Home Secretary Spencer Horatio Walpole. Their executioner was hangman William Calcraft, who had travelled from London to put them to death, and because of fears that they might be attacked the scaffold was surrounded by troops from the 42nd Regiment from Dundee, a contingent of the 7th Hussars, Edinburgh, and a large body of special constables. When the cart carrying them arrived at the foot of the scaffold the brothers ran up steps to the gibbet and as they were launched into eternity Michael Scanlon's lover, who had stood among a huge watching crowd, screamed out 'Oh Mike, Mike' before breaking down in tears and being led away. Almost as soon as they dangled, a heavy thunderstorm drove the spectators home and the bodies dripped rain as they were taken down, put into coffins and buried within the precincts of Cupar county prison.

19

MAD OR BAD?

The defence of madness was rarely used simply because judges were inclined not to believe the argument that a defendant was deranged at the time he or she committed a crime. Even in cases where it appeared the sanity of an accused was clearly doubtful the inevitable verdict was one of death. Once before a High Court judge on a capital charge there was little if any hope of escape. An obvious example was that of John Barclay in 1833, aged twenty-one. He was alleged to have beaten to death with a hammer or part of a cartwheel cattle dealer Samuel Neilson in a house at Cambusnethan in North Lanarkshire. When he appeared before the High Court at Glasgow and the charge of murder was put to him, Barclay's reply was, 'By necessity going to take my life yet, Sir?'

The *Caledonian Mercury* had already made up its mind, describing weaver's son Barclay as 'a stupid looking, stout young fellow'. His counsel tried to persuade the bench that at the time of the murder Barclay was deranged, calling a succession of witnesses who described instances of bizarre behaviour. The young man's mother said he was in the habit of going out, tearing his clothes to pieces and throwing them away; the minister at Cambusnethan Kirk said Barclay was considered an idiot; another witness told how he was known locally as 'Daft

Jock Barclay' while a doctor who examined him said he had a mental age of thirteen, telling the jury that when he asked Barclay how many days there were in a year the reply had been '700' and in answer to questions about the number of months in a year, number of days in a week and number of days in a month had been told, respectively, '6', '6' and '20'.

However, the judge and prosecution would have none of it, insisting not sufficient evidence of lunacy had been produced and when the jury convicted him of murder there could only be one sentence, that of death, even though jurors 'strongly recommended him to mercy on account of the weakness of his intellect'. Their plea on his behalf was, it was felt, enough to persuade the Crown in London to save Barclay but to considerable surprise no reprieve was granted and he went to his death on a gibbet at the end of Saltmarket Street, Glasgow, in May 1833.

Courts were faced with the problem of deciding whether an accused was genuinely mad or simply bad and determining the truth was never easy. In 1802 James Clark and Robert Brown, both former members of the Coldstream Guards, denied holding up and robbing a mail coach three miles west of Linlithgow, a serious charge and one carrying the death penalty. In a series of often conflicting statements made after his arrest Clark claimed he was innocent and that the incriminating money he was known to have come into after the holdup had been given to him by Brown. Counsel for his co-accused on the other hand said Brown was weak-minded and under Clark's influence. As proof of this he said that when both were in the Coldstream Guards friends of Brown in Scotland had written offering to buy him out of the regiment but it was Clark who had replied rejecting the suggestion. The lawyer produced an engraver to confirm Clark was the writer and show Brown was easily led by him. A friend of Brown said he had been 'weaker in the mind' since falling off a horse he was trying to ride up a staircase, while another told the court he had been weak-minded following a severe fever. Brown's defence was that because he was weak-minded and prone to imbecility he was 'subject to be imposed upon and easily persuaded to engage in the most foolish or dangerous

147

enterprises'. The prosecution, however, insisted that being easily led was no excuse for committing a major crime and both men were convicted and later hanged at Edinburgh in December.

Five years later the case of Maitland Smith was one that aroused considerable sympathy among the middle classes, while the poor argued that simply because he had become depressed at finding himself in the same situation as millions of others he had no excuse for committing crime. Nevertheless it was a distressing saga of a man put to death even though he was a victim of severe melancholia. Born in Penpont, Dumfriesshire, Smith was well educated but from an early age resented discipline and at one time tried to stab his boss, a former sea captain who had predicted, 'I am sure you will not die in your bed. You are a hot brained fool.' He followed the sad path of so many after moving north to the Glasgow area, becoming involved with young petty criminals and narrowly avoiding transportation after being caught running an illicit distillery by enlisting in the army.

He was highly regarded by officers and according to the *Scots Magazine* was hailed a hero in 1798 after snatching an infant girl from under the hooves of a runaway horse. Marriage and the start of a family seemed to settle him but after leaving the army and opening a business as a spirit dealer his world began crumbling and finally it collapsed. He was an incompetent businessman. Money troubles, bankruptcy, the winding up of his dealership, a marriage under strain and then stealing money from a savings society resulted in a series of suicide attempts. Desperate to return the missing money to the society, he had happened to meet cattle dealer foreman Alexander Williamson, who was returning on horseback from a business meeting in England. Smith shot the kindly old man and after being seen rifling through his pockets was arrested.

The evidence suggested Smith had been insane at the time, his mind driven awry by the pressures of being penniless, but this was dismissed and he was convicted of murder and robbery and condemned. In a letter written to his parents shortly before he was hanged he told them, 'You got me from the Lord and to him I would have you deliver me again, by prayer, on Wednesday about three o'clock.' That was the time in October when he was due to be put to death. On the scaffold he told the crowd, 'There are, no doubt, many here witnessing my disgraceful end, who were formerly the companions of my drunken revels. You pity me, perhaps, but I solemnly assure you, that I feel more comfort at this moment than I ever did sitting with any of you, in an ale-house, in my life.' He was thirty-two when he was launched into eternity, leaving behind his faithful wife and four children.

Jealously has driven many a man and woman mad. It has destroyed lives, families and relationships; punished inno-cents; turned sweet love to acid; caused pain, intolerable misery and led to countless murders. All of these were the barbs that cut, wounded, drove to madness and killed nailer John Gibson at Hawick in 1814. And it was all the fault of Napoleon Bonaparte.

Crazy for power the French tyrant had caused mayhem all over Europe. As his armies were gradually taken apart thousands of his soldiers were captured and shipped across the Channel to Britain, some finding themselves at Hawick, where most gave their parole, promising not to escape in exchange for being allowed generous freedom. Their presence caused few problems but trouble brewed when an officer began paying regular visits to the Gibson home. Gibson had been a soldier before marrying handsome Janet Renwick and settling with her in Hawick. She bore him eleven children, three of whom were still living, but Gibson began suspecting that he was not the father of the youngest, a boy of seven months, and that the Frenchman had turned her affections from him. Slowly, thoughts of his wife and the beautifully uniformed foreigner naked together making love dominated his mind and began loosening sanity from reality. He started beating Janet, one inevitable result of which was that her love for him waned to a point where he imagined an innocent look to be a sneer, a mere word an intention to begin an argu-ment; even if she innocently made him a cup of tea he saw that as an attempt to poison him.

Finally he snapped and launched a frenzied attack on Janet, murderously beating, kicking and punching her, then slashing her throat wide open with a penknife. Her screams for help subsided into silence and she fell among blood-soaked bedding. Gibson said to a horrified neighbour, 'Yes, I have murdered her and meant to have done the same to myself, but I will now let that alone, yet I will have to die for it,' while he told the local Sheriff, 'I have sold her to the Frenchman now.' In a coach carrying him to jail, Gibson said that at his trial he would plead to be banished, but that was a crazy hope and even though a doctor said he was suffering from 'a considerable degree of melancholy' he was still sentenced to death having been found guilty.

To the very end of his life in May 1814 on the scaffold at Hawick Heugh, specially built opposite the house where he had killed Janet, Gibson maintained he had not used a weapon on her. He told a huge crowd, 'I now warn all who hear me to beware of any excess in drink or passion. To these causes I owe my unhappy fate.'

On a rare occasion in January 1811 a court accepted that an accused man facing a capital charge was not fit to plead even though the allegation was that he and his brother had committed a violent and frightening robbery in broad daylight on cattle dealer Matthew Boyd near Sheriffmuir in Perthshire, scene of a famous battle in 1715 during the Jacobite rising. Boyd told the High Court in Edinburgh that as he rode home from a market two armed men suddenly appeared and pointed pistols at him, ordering him to hand over his money. He gave them just under £30 but they told him that if he did not produce more they would blow his brains out and he was forced to part with £100 in large-value notes that had been hidden in a wallet. They ordered him to ride off, which he did, but then he stopped and thought it strange that anyone should rob him in the middle of the day. He was angry and, according to newspaper reports, determined to have the robbers caught, so after riding on for about 300 yards to make sure he was out of their sight he dismounted, climbed over a dyke and looked to see in which direction they had gone. He spotted one of the men, with a pistol in his hand, but then noticed they had left behind two bundles which Boyd took, ran back to his horse and galloped to the nearby home of a farmer to get help.

There began a remarkable hunt, with Boyd and a police officer following the thieves to Alloa, where they were told the culprits had hired a chaise to take them to the ferry at North Queens-ferry. Next day Boyd and the officer continued the pursuit, finally tracking their quarry to a hotel in Princes Street in the centre of Edinburgh where Boyd grabbed one of the men by the collar. The other ran off but was quickly caught. The miscreants suggested going to a public house, where they would hand over what remained of Boyd's money but instead were hauled off to prison. The robbers were Adam Lyall and his brother John, the latter being stood down after the court heard evidence about his mental state.

The *Caledonian Mercury* said two doctors told of examining John and concluded, 'He laboured under a state of idiotism and that he was totally incapable of knowing the right hand from the left.' But while doctors were often vague, susceptible and reluc-tant to commit to outright statements of madness or badness the same could not be said of Captain Sibbald, the man in charge of Edinburgh jail. He was no fool and had been suspicious of John who, when he was first incarcerated, was sulky and uncom-municative, symptoms easy to fake for a man wanting to escape the death penalty by demonstrating he was mad. Even the fact that John then began talking incoherently, saying his brother had been murdered and how he had even seen his wraith did not convince the jailer he was looking after a lunatic. But then one day Sibbald had crept up the stairs of the jail in his stockinged feet to John's cell and, looking through a hole in the door, discov-ered him sitting fixedly in the same posture as he had been in when he saw him hours earlier, his eyes staring unblinkingly at a point above him. Sibbald told the court that as a result of this he had no doubt his prisoner was not feigning madness and so John avoided the same fate as Adam, hanged at Edinburgh on 27 March.

A few days after the execution an appalling tragedy more than

300 miles away at Bath in Gloucestershire showed just how fine a line there was between life and death. William Townley had been condemned for burglary and sentenced to die on Saturday, 6 April at Gloucester. However, on the Friday night of 5 April a formal notice that he had been reprieved, sent from London, was put into the post office at Hereford addressed by mistake to the Under Sheriff of Herefordshire instead of Gloucestershire. It was opened the next morning by the Under Sheriff of Herefordshire, who realised a terrible mistake had been made and, with a man's life in the balance, a horseman immediately set off on a frantic twenty-eight-mile gallop to try to reach the gallows before Townley was put to death. The rider arrived at the scaffold to see the body of Townley still swaying in a light breeze, having been hanged only minutes earlier.

Mad or bad? That was the question jurors had to decide when father-of-two porter William McFeat appeared before them at Glasgow in 1830 accused of the brutal murder by kicking and stabbing of his wife Maxwell at their home in Simpson's Island, Shuttle Street, Glasgow. He pleaded not guilty but the evidence seemed to conclusively prove that he slew her following a bitter row over her excessive drinking that often resulted in her spending short terms in prison, periods which, he confided to neighbours, at least gave him some peace. Her addiction to alcohol had, according to witnesses, driven McFeat out of his mind. He was often agitated – neighbours were sure he was 'unsound of mind'; he regularly talked to his wife when she wasn't there, thought he was a soldier and would sometimes wander about half naked, as though deranged. A former boss told of him taking fits, said he was deranged and not in his right mind.

All of this resulted in the jury, while having no alternative but to find him guilty, pleading in the strongest possible terms for him to be shown mercy, not least because it was felt he had for years been the victim of provocation by his wife. The *Aberdeen Journal* reported that as a result of the jury's view, 'It was the opinion of many persons that there would be a commutation of the sentence.' It was wrong. There was no mercy for McFeat, who was hanged, leaving two now orphaned children to be raised in a kirk-run home.

Just how bizarre had a man's behaviour to be for him to be classed crazy and spared a meeting with the hangman? Malcolm Macleod was an intelligent, good-natured family man who lived happily with his wife Henrietta on the Isle of Lewis. There was nothing to suggest that life held anything but years of peaceable joy in the company of one another. He hoped to become a teacher of Gaelic and for a time studied at a kirk school in Knockbain on the Black Isle on the mainland to help his qualification by learning English. Teachers there thought him mild and gentle but then out of the blue after he left came a letter to the school hinting he had made a remarkable discovery, the secret of perpetual motion and he wanted to know where he could buy fourteen to twenty-eight pounds of lodestone, a mineral used to magnetise. What was astonishing was that the letter was written in blood.

Something had snapped in the mind of Malcolm Macleod. Henrietta had given him three healthy, loving boys but gradually from an ordinary crofter his moods alternated between being some days lazy, indolent and disinterested and on others working joyfully and hard at harvesting and fishing. Had he gone mad? It was suspected there had been insanity in other members of his family but for most of his life his behaviour had been normal. Now his actions were increasingly bizarre. In woods near his home he erected a round, wooden structure inside which he would climb to pray. On one memorable Sunday morning in church the congregation had been shocked when he stood up and told the minister, 'I am tired of you, you Devil.' He stopped attending church but so highly regarded had Macleod been that others in the congregation preferred going to him for religious instruction. He became obsessed with the idea of manufacturing a perpetual motion machine and told his brother Roderick he had devised an invention for propelling ships without the need for tide or wind and even tested it out on a small boat.

Life in the Macleod house deteriorated. He complained his

wife nagged him for not working hard enough and had even threatened to stab or suffocate him. Finally, on a morning in February 1838 while the children were out he suddenly seized Henrietta, pushed her to the floor and strangled her. Then he gently and calmly picked her up, laid her on a bed, carefully washed the dust from her face and took to his heels. While a huge manhunt for him got under way he slept rough on moors, praying hard for guidance as to what he should do. The *Caledonian Mercury*, reporting his trial for murder at Edinburgh, said that in a declaration after his capture Macleod told how while at prayer, 'Something struck him that it would be better for him to give himself up whatever the consequences might be.' The jury found him guilty, leaving the judge, Lord Cockburn, who had dismissed defence claims Macleod was insane, with no option other than to order his execution. But following appeals for further investigations into his mental state Macleod was confined in an asylum, finally reprieved and transported for life to New South Wales in November 1839.

Does a man lose his senses as he is about to face eternity? John Howison's antics on the eve of his death at Edinburgh in January 1832 sent many home wondering just what to make of what the forty-five-year-old did and said. As the day of his hanging neared for viciously battering to death widow Martha Geddes in her home at Long Row, Cramond – a crime he denied – he suddenly developed a ravenous appetite, especially for potatoes. And on his last morning, as he left his cell to head for the scaffold he took with him an armful of bread rolls.

With the fatal moment drawing ever nearer Howison then made an astonishing declaration, claiming that in 1829 he had murdered a labourer named Jameson near Lauder in the Borders; the following year in a wood near the village of Whittingham in Northumberland he killed a man with a stick after a quarrel; in the West Port he killed two boys and a girl; in the Cowgate two boys, and at the head of the Canongate another boy. Was any of this true? The *Caledonian Mercury* commented, 'From the extraordinary and incredible confession of Howison, and his obstinacy in refusing to confess the crime of which he was so clearly found guilty, it would appear that he wished to impress people's minds with a notion of his being insane.'

Even though police in the Borders and Northumberland were made aware of the claims no evidence confirming the murders was ever found.

20

DEMON DRINK

'This unhappy case adds another to the many melancholy proofs we daily witness of the dreadful effects of intoxication operating upon a mind not, at all times, perhaps, under the best regulation,' commented the *Aberdeen Journal* in April 1822 after reporting that fishing-tackle maker William Gordon had been condemned for the murder of his wife, a heavy drinker. The demon called drink had claimed yet another victim. The case was typical of dozens of others in which working-class families were ripped apart by drink as men, women and even children sought through alcohol an escape from misery and hopelessness.

The Gordons had been drinking at an inn near their Aberdeen home and trouble began as they were leaving when they quarrelled after she refused to give him the key to their front door. She then fell over and soon after disappearing inside she was heard shouting, 'Murder, murder, let me be.'

Neighbours called the watchman, who broke in to find the woman on the floor bleeding heavily from a wound to her abdomen that proved fatal and it was found to have been made with a sharpened poker. Gordon's counsel pleaded for a culpable homicide verdict, but the tackle-maker was convicted and told he would die. The judge, Lord Gillies, warned him, 'There is no hope of a pardon for you on this side of the grave.' He was hanged in the city in May. A petty squabble over a key had taken two lives, and so often drink was the catalyst that turned mole-hills into mountains.

In 1802, John Allan, aged twenty-four, a soldier in the 23rd Dragoons, had been on leave staying with his family in Glasgow. Returning from a night out, he encountered a drunken neighbour, George Lindsay, who stumbled into him, knocking him over. When he got to his feet Allan realised the smart white trousers of his uniform had been muddied and rebuked the drunkard, whose response was to fatally stab him in the stomach and chest, the consequence of which was his being hanged for murder in April that year.

Equally trifling was the motive for the murder in 1832 of William Mason near Shotts in Lanarkshire by William Lindsay. The pair had been drinking and a mere joke about the Reform Bill flared into violence, ending when millwright Lindsay fatally stabbed Mason and was hanged in Glasgow.

Regularly, juries, while convicting a man of murder, would plead for mercy, usually on grounds that he had been provoked by a drunken wife. So it was in 1836 with Charles Donaldson, who killed his wife Margaret at their Edinburgh home by smashing her over the head with a frying pan and whisky bottle; and then with Thomas Templeton four years later after he beat his wife, also named Margaret, in their College Street, Glasgow, home. But in each case the pleas by jurors were ignored. Ironi-cally, on his way to the scaffold and the flames of hell Donaldson complained of the cold.

Part-time policeman John Cowie was arrested by colleagues at Edinburgh in 1804 after a brutal attack on his intoxicated wife Bella in their home at Borthwick's Close with the defence objecting to witness Mary Galbraith giving evidence because she was a prostitute with a grudge against him. The protests were overruled and she told the High Court she was present when Cowie discovered his wife lying drunk on the floor and began battering her with a stick, screaming he would murder her. She claimed he then, 'danced on her body and breast and took her by the hair and clashed her head against the hearth'. He was found guilty of murder, the *Newcastle Courant* reporting, 'It appeared in evidence that the deceased had been subject to intoxication and lost her life in one of the barbarous instances of correction which she received from her husband.' Once again the jury recommended he should be shown mercy, and the execution was respited while investigations into the background of the couple were made. But the Crown ultimately decided it could find no reason to spare him and he was hanged in January.

Jurors also did their best for hatter John Boyd, who dragged his boozed-up wife by the hair along the floor of their home in Harvie's Close, Greenock, in July 1834 before choking her. After finding him guilty they asked for a recommendation for mercy to be forwarded to the Crown on the grounds of his own previous good character and the 'irregular habits' of his wife. Boyd was confident of being reprieved even though that meant transportation for the remainder of his life, but after his execution newspapers such as the *Morning Chronicle* were critical of the Crown decision not to save him. It reported, 'The deep sympathy which the public felt for the peculiar situation of poor Boyd when, after having been respited for a while, he was ordered after all for execution renders any apology on our part unnecessary for describing the manner in which he received the announcement that he had not another week to live. As might have been expected Boyd was much stunned at the news but conducted himself with great manliness and firmness.' As a result of the delay he was not hanged in Cathcart Square, Greenock, until October.

Virtually every prison at some time or other held men or women convicted of crimes that were caused by drink. In just over a fortnight in December 1831 at Edinburgh, three men were hanged for killing their wives and in each case drunkenness was involved. Shoemaker James Gow and Thomas Beveridge, a blacksmith, were executed together for murders committed according to the *Morning Post*, 'while in a state of infuriated passion, superinduced by excessive intoxication'.

The details of Gow's tragedy are told in full in Chapter 30. Beveridge was described by the *Belfast Newsletter* as a 'sober, inoffensive man but dreadfully harassed by the misconduct and drunken habits of his wife' and he had complained he often came home to breakfast, dinner or supper to find 'nothing but a black fire, starving children and a drunken wife', but he himself was no pillar of temperance and his grouse was probably a case of the kettle calling the pot black. He was often found in public houses and immediately after brutally attacking his wife Janet on the head, face, hands, arms, legs and thighs with a poker, shovel and knife, leaving her to bleed to death from multiple injuries, he ran away and was later found drinking in a public house. Even after being convicted of murder, he was certain he would be reprieved and the news that he had to hang came as a shock.

The third of the trio was John McCourt. His was an especially heartrending story and yet so typical of the age of just how devastating could be the effects of drink. The *Caledonian Mercury* described it as a 'truly melancholy case' and this was no exaggeration. McCourt's wife Catherine had given birth to eleven children, three of whom – Dennis, Henry and John – had survived, but around three years before her death she became addicted to drink. There were frequent quarrels and Catherine regularly complained to neighbours she had been beaten at their home in Rattray's Close, Cowgate, Edinburgh. But that was not the only source of her unhappiness; she would never again see her surviving sons. Even though he was not yet ten years old Dennis had been transported to Australia in July 1831 after stealing three shillings and sixpence from the till of an Edinburgh baker's shop, while both Henry, aged twelve, and John were in prison waiting to follow him Beyond the Seas; the former for stealing a lady's side saddle and even at that tender age already in police records as a common thief, while John too had been convicted of stealing.

Their absence and plummet into disgrace had doubtless preyed on the minds of their parents, aggravating Catherine's addiction and leading her husband along a similar path with an almost inevitable outcome. On the morning of her murder she had staggered into the street after being severely kicked. As she was dying she not only accused her husband and knew he was doomed to hang but told friends news of his fate would 'be a source of gratification and amusement to her banished children'. McCourt denied murder and said it was Catherine's drunken behaviour that had driven him to drink. However, in his summing up the judge commented, 'It cannot be tolerated in a civilised country that because the deceased had become a public nuisance the prisoner was to be the avenger of public wrongs.' After that there was little doubt of the outcome. On his way to the Edinburgh scaffold McCourt twice stopped to drink beer and on his journey to eternity might have been comforted by the words of the *Morning Post* which stated, 'We never recollect of any criminal whose untimely end excited such a general commiseration, it being generally known that his deceased wife was one of the very worst of characters and although there is no doubt that he inflicted injuries on her person which led to her death, he was exposed to such daily sufferings as human nature could not bear.'

Occasionally a condemned man simply got on with the ordeal of being hanged. Edward Moore, aged thirty-three, had murdered his wife Mary in Bridgeton in 1829 and on the scaffold protested his innocence. Then with the noose about his neck he gave the executioner the signal to put him to death. Much to the annoyance of the crowd the hangman wasn't ready and Moore was forced to wait for several minutes before being launched into eternity.

Sail maker John Kerr, aged fifty-four, was anxious before his execution to put at rest the minds of two women witnesses who gave vital evidence against him when he went on trial at Greenock in 1827 for murdering his wife of thirty years, also named Mary, while drunk. He asked for the two to visit him in the condemned cell and when they both arrived said he knew they had told the truth and were in no way to blame for his death.

Four years earlier many of the spectators who attended a High Court trial in Edinburgh were astonished that all four accused, two men and two women, did not hang on the same scaffold because the evidence appeared to suggest all were equally guilty of a brutal and cowardly murder. The victim was weaver John McClure; the accused James Anderson, a collier, weaver David Glen, Margaret Frew and Margaret Anderson, who were all from Ayr. The victim, accompanied by divinity student Thomas Young, had been driving home in a gig after attending the ancient Ochiltree Sacrament near Cumnock, Ayrshire. As they jogged along the two chatted happily but about a mile from Ayr they were confronted by the four accused, who were drunk and had been thrown out of a public house along the road. The men grabbed the horse and when Young fell out of the gig and tried to run away he was brutally beaten and kicked by all four and hit with a stone by Margaret Anderson, the result being that he died a few hours later from his injuries.

The packed court heard the two men convicted but the women were found not guilty and allowed to go free. An appeal by Anderson and Glen to the Crown for a pardon was rejected and the men were taken to Ayr in December and, amidst a rainstorm, hanged, their bodies then returned to the capital for dissection.

Was there an intentional irony in the hanging in May 1843 of ham curer Charles McKay at Glasgow for murdering his wife in their home in the Old Wynd? Both liked a drink and may have been suffering hangovers when he launched a vicious attack after finding she had not cooked his breakfast, first threatening to throw her out of a window then stabbing her as she pleaded, 'Oh Charlie dear, what is this you have done to me?' McKay was hanged minutes after eight o'clock in the morning – breakfast time.

21

ORANGE AND GREEN

Sectarianism is nothing new. Just as twenty-first-century society seeks to eradicate it, so it was equally a problem 200 years ago, especially in the west of Scotland, where huge numbers of Irish families had settled. Famine in 1740 decimated the population of Ireland, leading to mass emigration principally to Scotland but also the Americas to escape starvation, poverty and hopelessness. In the decades that followed, the trail east in the hunt for work and survival continued. A further severe famine in the years after 1845 led to another major exodus to Scotland where newcomers, mainly Roman Catholics, were often met with suspicion that they had arrived to take jobs from natives. Trouble motivated by religious differences was inevitable.

The majority of incomers settled in Ayrshire and they brought with them long-held customs and celebrations including the annual 12th of July parade, a Protestant tradition remembering the victory by Prince William of Orange over Catholic King James II at the Battle of the Boyne in 1690. The parade and build-up to it caused much resentment among Roman Catholics, ill feeling that soured the atmosphere with Protestants. Marches by members of Orange groups or Lodges loyal to Protestant beliefs on 12th July had been held through the streets of Girvan where the town's baillies became increasingly concerned at the level of violence surrounding the parades. In the past some marchers had been spotted openly carrying swords and as a result it was announced that the procession planned for 1831 would not be allowed. Orange Lodge members in the town agreed to abstain, but word reached the authorities that lodges based in surrounding villages were determined to go ahead regardless and so on 9 July an officer went through Girvan announcing a formal Proclamation against the procession while on the morning of the 12th an extra 100 special constables were sworn in to keep the peace. Additionally townspeople were urged to stay away from the proposed route of the march. Senior Baillie Andrew Hunter later said he and his colleagues knew, 'People of the opposite parties daily insulted each other – in short there was a greater degree of hostility between them than on any former occasion.'

That hostility would end in tragedy when one of the special constables, Alexander Ross, was shot dead and two of the Orangemen found themselves in the dock of the High Court at Edinburgh in late December. Samuel Waugh and publican John Ramsey were charged with murdering Ross and according to the indictment, 'In having along with disorderly persons banded together as clubs or associations known by the name of Orange Lodges resolved to walk in procession into or through the town of Girvan notwithstanding they had been prohibited by the magistrates of that town from entering it in procession.'

Ramsey was also charged with, 'Exercising a command and role over the Lodges that he took an active and leading part in directing their proceedings, and did instigate and encourage to advance against the will of the magistrates and that he commanded and ordered those in the Lodges who had arms to fire and that it was in consequence of his instigation or command and order that the prisoner Waugh fired his gun by which Alexander Ross was mortally wounded in the lower part of the body.'

Both pleaded not guilty and gave special defences denying being engaged in any illegal mob or having used firearms, 'until attacked while peaceably proceeding along the road'.

George McDend, a drummer in the New Lodge which met at Ramsey's home in Masons Row, Maybole, said he saw men there armed with pistols and guns. He said that as the procession neared Girvan it was told not to come on and it was then said among the 100 marchers that they would still go forward 'and fight their way'. However, after an appeal from a town official the Orangemen agreed to go into the town via a back road. Even so, tension on both sides was rapidly rising and a growing crowd on both sides of the route, mainly comprised of youngsters, began bombarding the procession with stones. Some of the marchers retaliated by throwing stones back into the spectators. McDend said an order was a given for men carrying weapons to go to the front of the procession, an instruction that not everyone agreed with, most believing these men should be held back to protect the various Lodge flags. When he heard the sound of firing, he became afraid and ran off.

Ayr shoemaker John Coffin was a drummer in the Crosshill Lodge and said that as they neared Girvan ammunition was handed out and James Farrell, a weaver from Crosshill, badly injured his hand when his gun blew up as he was loading it. Robert McMillan, a piper in the Red Lion Lodge of Maybole, said he saw men carrying firelocks, pistols, a bayonet and swords. Coming into Girvan a scuffle broke out and somebody shouted, 'Fire!'.

Other witnesses said Ross had merely been trying to keep back the crowd, the constables being armed only with batons. Ross pointed his stick at the man holding the gun and shouted, 'If you fire that gun I will apprehend you.' Waugh, a member of the Crosshill Lodge, was seen to step to the front of the parade, level his piece and fire. The gun went off and Ross collapsed, dying soon afterwards. Catholic Henry McKeatings said he was four yards from Waugh when he had pointed his gun at a number of the crowd before firing. McKeatings immediately picked up a stone and threw it at Waugh, slashing open his cheek and fracturing his jaw. After the shooting the crowd broke up and the Orangemen marched on into the town.

Some of the Girvan townspeople felt the march should have been stopped by force and that the policing had been poorly organised. Angry at the shooting of Ross a mob surrounded the house where the sheriff substitute had taken refuge and threatened to smash it down. He was unable to get out for four hours and when he fled he was stoned and his carriage destroyed. The trial ended at two o'clock in the morning with the jury finding the charges against Ramsey not proven, but by a majority Waugh guilty and he was sentenced to hang.

At his execution in Ayr in January 1832, three weeks after his trial, Waugh told spectators that his own blood, 'and the blood of Alexander Ross lay upon the people of Girvan because if they had not attacked and opposed the procession no violence would have been committed and no mischief would have been done'.

However, Ramsey did not escape scot-free. The following day he, Andrew Forsyth and three other Orangemen were accused of mobbing and rioting at the parade and assaulting some of the special constables. Ramsey and Forsyth were jailed for nine months and the other three for twelve months. In a further case of rioting three others, including a boy, were jailed.

Orangemen weren't the only offenders but some who felt the length of these sentences was unfairly harsh pointed to the case in May that year of Temple Annesley, son of a well-to-do businessman who was given just two months and a £100 fine for firing lead pellets through the window of a Wesleyan Chapel in Charlotte Street, Ayr, while a service was being conducted inside, the missiles narrowly missing minister Henry Turner and some of his congregation. Judges pointed out that some of those in church could have been badly hurt.

Some Irishmen felt they were the victims of discrimination, not from political or religious motives but simply for reasons of personal dislike. Normally ill feeling was settled with fists but in December 1840 matters ended in tragedy and the deaths of three men.

Dennis Doolan, Patrick Redding and James Hickie were among a large group of Irish labourers who were helping to build the Glasgow to Edinburgh railway line at Crosshill near Bishopbriggs. The three friends all lodged together. They were under the supervision of ganger John Green, an Englishman from Cheshire, and all the group believed he did not like Irishmen for a reason they could not understand. In fact what Green, a tough taskmaster, didn't like was slackness and he had gone to railway superintendent Francis Rooney and asked him to sack Doolan on grounds that the Irishman had been 'saucy' when told he was lazy. Doolan was dismissed, a move that angered his fellow lodgers and the six blamed Green. Then that night they plotted to beat him.

Two days later with Christmas approaching Green arrived for work at seven o'clock, giving a cheerful, despite the darkness, 'Men, this is going to be a nice morning,' as he passed the labourers. Moments later he was clutching his head, crying, 'Murder, murder,' as he was viciously battered by Redding and Doolan using an iron bar handed to them by Hickie.

According to the *Caledonian Mercury* Rooney later told the trial of the three for murder, 'I saw two men beating another. I called "Murder" and ran up. One of them had a weapon and was striking with that; I saw the other man once or twice leaping on the body of the man that was down. This leaping and beating continued for two or three minutes. I was terrified.' Plucking up courage Rooney went to the victim and recognised Green, who was still alive but died soon after. Police searched for the killers but Redding and Doolan had separated and fled, Doolan first to Greenock, then Liverpool, from where he planned to take a boat to America, Redding to Leeds then Huddersfield in Yorkshire. However, their descriptions had been circulated throughout Britain and both were arrested. When interrogated each blamed the other.

After they and Hickie were charged with Green's murder hundreds of Irishmen working on the building of the railway system voluntarily paid in a weekly levy to ensure the three could afford defence counsel. But the evidence against Doolan and Redding in particular was overwhelming. At their trial at Glasgow in April witnesses named them as responsible and in a statement to police Doolan, twenty-five, admitted attacking Green, saying it was meant only to hurt not kill him. All three were convicted and sentenced to death but the jury said it was felt Hickie was not directly responsible and guilty only of being 'art and part' and as a result he was reprieved and transported for life to Tasmania in July that year.

As he was being led to the condemned cell Redding told a jailer, 'Hanging is better than seven years transportation.' Massive security precautions were in place over fears there might be an attempt to rescue them at their execution at Crosshill in May, with extra troops being drafted in to guard the scaffold but the crowd estimated at 50,000 included few Irishmen who had vowed not to watch their countrymen put to death.

Sometimes a silly remark was enough to spark vicious violence but when that comment was made in drink it could have fearful consequences. So it was in mid-August 1851 when a group of men had spent several hours drinking at Blantyre in South Lanarkshire. As they emerged into the street dyer James Agnew heard one of them, Irish-born Archibald Hare, aged twenty-five, shouting, 'To hell with the Pope and popery and if there is any popish b***** let him turn out.'

Seeing Agnew, Hare went to him and asked if he was a Catholic. According to the *Glasgow Herald*, Agnew's version was, 'I said I was not. He replied, "If you were a Catholic, I would rip you up and let your puddings out." He put his hand to my belly but I did not see anything in it. Says he, "Are you an Orangeman?" and I said I was, "Anything." He then put up his hand to give the Orange grip, and I put up my hand also; but he said I was no Orangeman for I could not give the Orange grip.'

But Hare seemed set on trouble and wanted to pick a fight with a group of miners who had been drinking in the same inn. One of them was Ronald McGregor, who held back others from attacking Hare and then tried to pacify the troublemaker. Moments later, McGregor collapsed from a stab wound and although he fought to survive died two weeks later.

In October Hare, despite protesting his innocence, was convicted and condemned. The date proposed for his execution had to be delayed when it was discovered it fell on a Catholic holy day but it went ahead later at Glasgow with an eighty-four-year-old executioner in charge of proceedings. The *Glasgow Citizen* described the ceremony as a 'sickening spectacle' and said that following a last painful meeting with his parents and wife Hare said he had, 'Many sins to answer for, but that the murder of Ronald McGregor was not one of them.' On the scaffold he spoke briefly to the crowd, telling them, 'I am going to die for a crime of which I am innocent. All of you beware of dram drinking.'

The case had shown how drink and religious bickering were dangerous bedfellows and the mixture was repeated with an equally deadly outcome in November 1856. At one moment a group of miners and their friends had been drinking apparently happily together; shortly afterwards one of the miners was dying from a terrible stab wound, his brother was lying unconscious and a husband and wife and one of their friends were facing the death penalty. But during the trial of the three in the High Court at Edinburgh it became evident that an underlying current of religious hostility had lain dormant waiting to surface. It came into the open late one night when mining brothers Thomas and John Maxwell, their wages fresh in their pockets, had found themselves in the same Bathgate public house as Peter McLean, his wife Christina and their friend William Maxwell. Everything appeared normal because the brothers had often enjoyed the company of McLean but after a few drinks it became obvious all was not well.

McLean began muttering threats to attack the Maxwells while his wife hardly helped. Her attitude towards Catholics was to call them 'papist b******s'. In the street outside McLean struck first, trying to stab John, and when his blow was deflected he took out his rage on William, who bled to death, while John was hit on the back of the head by William Maxwell. Peter McLean was convicted of murder, the jury recommending he be shown mercy, a request backed by a petition from citizens in Linlithgow supporting him, but expecting a reprieve he was shocked when told none would be forthcoming. William Maxwell was cleared of murder but found guilty of assaulting John Maxwell and jailed for two years with hard labour while the jury decided a charge of murder against Christina, who had egged on her husband, was not proven.

The case caused considerable ill feeling in the area and McLean's fellow workers at Kinneil Ironworks in Bo'ness raised £100 to help pay for his defence. They also refused to work in protest at his condemnation on the day of his execution in February 1857. Fearing trouble, magistrates ordered the closure of public houses in the area on the day he was hanged and brought in troops to guard the scaffold on which McLean trembled so much he had to be supported. His final words before being launched into eternity were, according to the *Glasgow Citizen*, 'Avoid drinking and avoid evil company and keep the Sabbath day.'

22

REWARDS

Robert Ferguson decided army life was not for him. He had thought his job as a plasterer dull and unexciting and had listened to stories of old soldiers as they told of the thrill of battle, journeys to the far side of the world and how women were seduced by the mere sight of a man in his bright uniform. When a sergeant from the 35th Regiment of Foot appeared and promised glory and rewards to young men who joined up Ferguson threw down his tools, raised his hand, made his mark on a sheet of paper and marched off. The teenager soon discovered the picture painted by the recruiting sergeant was very different from reality. Discipline was harsh, training rigorous and never ceasing, while meals were dull, unreliable and the pay poor. His eight pence a day was not even half what he'd received as a plasterer although his uniform and keep were provided. After just over a year Ferguson had had enough, but getting out of the regiment would not be easy. Then out of the blue came the chance for freedom.

In 1767 he was ordered to march to Stirling as a member of a recruiting party who would spin the same stories as the sergeant who had convinced him his future lay in uniform. At the same time another unit, including twenty-four-year-old Private James Smith, was headed to Kilpatrick in Dunbartonshire and, like Ferguson, Smith wanted out. Two years earlier the regiment had returned from years of duty in America and there were rumours its officers and men were in line to head back over the Atlantic. For both soldiers it was a daunting prospect and each, unaware of the plans of the other, determined their days of soldiering were at an end. Being in a recruiting party gave them relative freedom and each took his chance to desert and vanished. They were desperate not to be caught because recapture would mean their being branded and whipped, and if they repeated the offence and were again discovered the punishment could be execution by a firing squad.

Always short of men the army wanted them back and it resorted to the only means available at the time of broadcasting that fact. Town criers could shout news locally and although broadsides were in limited circulation, their sale tended to be restricted to the town or city where they were published and Smith and Ferguson would certainly not be hanging about Stirling or Kilpatrick. In fact the latter had confided to comrades he intended making his way to Inverness and from there to lose himself in the Highlands until the fuss had died down.

So the military turned to the only means of widespread communication by advertising in newspapers. In October the *Glasgow Journal* carried an advertisement offering a two guineas reward for the recapture of either man. It was a sizeable inducement, the equivalent to almost three months' wages for a labourer, the modern-day equivalent of £650. The same advertisement appeared again later leading to suspicions that neither was apprehended. But the authorities had no alternative source of communicating to the masses and knew the offer of substantial rewards was the most likely method of paying dividends. Almost every issue of a newspaper carried among its advertisements details of a reward, mostly for the apprehension of fugitives.

In January 1792 the *Glasgow Mercury* carried an advertisement that, because of the huge sum on offer, attracted immense interest. 'TWO HUNDRED GUINEAS REWARD' it began – the modern-day equivalent of almost £30,000. It continued: 'Whereas Mr Archibald Young, Surgeon in this city was betwixt nine and ten o'clock of the evening of 24th of January accosted by two men near the head of Hutcheson Street who asked him if he was Doctor Young? Being answered in the affirmative each of them laid hold of one of his arms and one of them struck him in the side with a sharp instrument manifestly with the design of murdering him. The Lord Provosts and magistrates of Glasgow hereby offer a reward of fifty guineas to any person or persons who shall give such information as shall lead to the discovery and conviction of the offenders. The Faculty of Physicians and Surgeons of Glasgow eager to contribute to the detention and punishment of the perpetrators of so horrid an attempt on the life of one of their members offer on the same terms a reward of fifty guineas.'

Young himself doubled these enormous amounts and said his attackers had made off in the direction of Ingram Street. If they were caught the culprits faced certain execution while such a sum could guarantee a whole new life for an informant. For instance it would enable a claimant to make a substantial down payment for ownership of a public house, and such an opportunity was available. The following month the best known inn in Glasgow, the Saracen's Head in Gallowgate Street, was being auctioned along with stables and other buildings. And then there was always the prospect that one of the attackers might in exchange for a guarantee of not being prosecuted decide to inform on his accomplice. But had the two left the area? Shortly afterwards the advertisement was repeated but the pair were never found.

Just as police in the twenty-first century rely largely on the media to appeal for information, occasionally forces offered rewards normally donated by individuals or newspapers. So it was for instance in 1800 when the town council at St Andrews in Fife took space in the *Caledonian Mercury* to seek help in capturing those responsible for a break-in at the home of local golf ball maker George Robertson. It pledged twenty guineas to anyone helping nail the villain or villains while at the same time gave details of high-value bills – the equivalent of open cheques made out to cash – stolen in the raid and urged stores and banks to be on the lookout for them.

Of course just as potential informers were able to take note of reward advertisements so were those they were intended to catch. Typical was the appalling case of the murder in late February 1800 of Elspet Imlach, aged twenty, at her home near Banff, Aberdeenshire. Elspet had announced to her lover William Morrison that she was pregnant by him and had given up work as a housemaid to stay with a friend until the birth. The *Aberdeen Journal* revealed, 'Morrison had attempted formerly to entice her to meet after dark at the Bridge of Alva [Alvah] with intention, as now evidently appears, of murdering her but she was prevented from meeting him by some of her friends. However on the fatal day he enticed her to meet him at the Church of Alva on pretence of attending the Kirk Session and prevailed on her to accompany him through Lord Fife's woods of Mountcoffer [Montcoffer] and there murdered her by stabbing her in the neck with a knife and giving her many other horrid wounds with a large stick so her body was much disfigured.'

Almost immediately, advertisements began appearing offering a reward of twenty guineas (£2,100) for news of the whereabouts of Morrison and giving his description including the fact his hands were thought to be scratched and that he had hinted he intended escaping from Scotland by boat. Morrison in fact had headed south to Perth probably in an attempt to reach the ports at Leith or Greenock. In Perth a young man answering his description had bought gloves in a shop in George Street to cover his badly scratched hands. But by the time copies of newspapers carrying these advertisements reached the Fair City he had disappeared.

However, whether it was as a result of the advertisements or simply local vigilance, by August Morrison had been arrested after farm workers spotted him lurking in the hills and begging for food at farmhouses. He was arrested and held in prison at Elgin, but by the time he was called to his trial at Aberdeen for murder in April 1801 he had once again vanished.

Alleged murderers such as Morrison were frequently sought with the lure of generous rewards. In October 1800 Lieutenant Stewart Watson of the North British militia and twenty-nine-year-old ensign Godfrey Magarey fought a duel on the outskirts of Dundee in the course of which Watson was shot dead. Duels were not unusual but officially barred and while the winner was liable to be charged with murder this rarely happened in civilian cases. It tended to be a different matter in the case of soldiers and when Magarey and the two seconds, Edward O'Keefe and James Bryson, fled the scene the Crown Office insisted they had to be arrested and tried for murder. A fifty guineas reward was offered for their apprehension, which resulted in the capture of Magarey and O'Keefe, who went on trial but were eventually transported for life.

Double that amount went on offer in December 1800 after the murder at Mains of Skellater, Aberdeenshire, of farm worker Findlay Farquharson. The money would be paid for information that resulted in the arrest and conviction of suspect Paul Michie, but an advertisement giving details admitted it was thought that immediately after the killing Michie had fled south into England. Nothing further was heard of him.

Rewards meant that a wrongdoer was in constant fear of being caught as a result of a word from a friend or even a family member. Magistrates at Edinburgh promised fifteen guineas for information leading to the arrest of someone who threw a stone through the window of a house in Princes Street in 1801. It was a huge sum, the modern equivalent of £1,300, for what at first appeared a trivial offence but an advertisement offering the incentive pointed out that the stone had narrowly missed members of the owner's family and had smashed a valuable mirror. Even so, some may have thought it a strange reason for spending public money. Fifteen guineas for a broken mirror seemed even stranger when compared with the reward pledged for the return of seven inmates who broke out of the Edinburgh Tolbooth in May 1801. The bounty of each of them was a relatively niggardly ten guineas.

The previous month the *Glasgow Mercury* reported that an escape plan at the tolbooth involving a number of prisoners had been thwarted. It was suspected that a woman who regularly visited one of the men had somehow smuggled knives with hacked edges to him and the plotters used these to saw through grates covering the windows of the room where they were held. They had also managed to steal lengths of ropes used for pinioning offenders and planned to use these to lower themselves to the street below. The plan was uncovered and the culprits put in irons to prevent a repetition. However, laxity at the tolbooth was exposed by the escape of seven others who were awaiting transportation to Australia.

While elsewhere, fellow inmates were cutting through bars, the seven were hacking their way through floors before fleeing. An embarrassed tolbooth keeper, realising his job was on the line, had offered an extra two guineas per man out of his own pocket, making the price on each man's head twelve guineas. Among the escapers was Andrew Holmes who had been sentenced to hang for shop-breaking but given a reprieve. Lachlan Love, a former private in the Argyllshire Regiment of the North British militia had been convicted of breaking into a shoemaker's shop and stealing leather that was later discovered under his bed. James Stevens stole an ox from a farm and drove it to Edinburgh, where he slaughtered it and sold the meat. He had been lucky to escape execution. William Maxwell, a member of the Society of United Scotsmen and supporter of George Mealmaker, had been found guilty of seditious practices.

In November 1806 William Begbie, a porter at the British Linen Bank in Leith, was stabbed and murdered beside the bank's offices in Edinburgh and robbed of a yellow canvas bag containing more than £4,000. The killer had dropped his weapon, a breadknife, at the scene before disappearing. It would be many years before the main suspect was brought to book (see Chapter 35) but while the hunt for him began throughout Britain the bank offered a reward of 500 guineas, equivalent nowadays to almost £50,000. The advertisement which was first published in the *Caledonian Mercury* was repeated in other newspapers first in Scotland and then in England but despite the immense prize on offer no one came forward.

Just as rewards had their failures, they had successes too and in 1821 it was a relatively small reward that brought an end to a most remarkable story. John Gunn was an extraordinary character from Raisgill in Caithness who went on the run after stealing a horse and some cattle. While police throughout the Highlands hunted for him, twenty-five-year-old Gunn put a considerable distance between him and his hunters by managing to make his way to Peterhead on the north-east coast and joining the crew of a whaling ship sailing to Greenland.

Perhaps he was confident that the matter would fade and even disappear if he stayed away long enough. He was an eccentric character, prone to bouts of seeming madness and his appearance in Peterhead had been remembered resulting in police being tipped off that he was on board the whaler *Alpheus*. When it arrived back in Peterhead, officers were waiting to arrest him. Gunn was taken back to Inverness, where he was locked up in September 1819 to await his trial, which was delayed by his behaviour, suggesting lunacy, antics that were eventually found to be merely acting on his part.

After nineteen months Gunn decided enough was enough and having managed to cut through his cell door fled still wearing the sailor's jacket he had on when he was arrested. A newspaper notice offered a twenty guineas reward for his recapture and warned, 'It is suspected that Gunn intends to escape to America and that he will endeavour to secure a passage from some of the ports in the west coast.' The reward, however, succeeded and within days of it appearing Gunn was back in custody. After he was sentenced to transportation for fourteen years he told jailers that at least he would get 'plenty of twopenny grog on the voyage'. This time the authorities were taking no chances; within three weeks he was chained up below decks on the convict ship *Claudine*, which left him on Tasmania in December 1821.

23

REVENGE

In 1991, as she sat in her car with her children, the looks and life of a beautiful young Edinburgh woman were destroyed when a maniac threw sulphuric acid over her face and body. The attack left her blinded and horribly disfigured and had been the idea of the man who was once her husband following the break-up of their marriage. He and another man were each jailed for twenty years but could count themselves lucky because more than a century and a half earlier perpetrators of similar acts were more than likely to end their days on the scaffold. In the modern tragedy the motive was revenge and the desire for revenge lay behind some of the cruellest cases in the saga of crime and punishment.

Another case in the capital city, this time in 1827, bore many similarities. The victim was dancing teacher Archibald Campbell. He and his wife had fallen out with their neighbours Hugh and Euphemia McMillan, who lived on the same floor of the apartments in the High Street, and, as is so often the case, the dispute began over a petty incident. The Campbells had an infant child and, worried the youngster might stray and fall down a staircase, had placed a chair over the stairway, a measure that enraged the McMillans with horrific results. When Euphemia suddenly threw open their door and angrily threw in the chair the Campbells called police, resulting in twenty-six-year-old Mrs McMillan being taken to the police station, where she was held overnight, the next day appearing before magistrates and given a formal caution to behave.

According to a report in the *Morning Post*, when she arrived back home Euphemia had told Campbell 'I'll do for you', while Hugh was alleged to have told him he would, 'have his revenge though he should hang for it'. Shortly afterwards sulphuric acid was thrown over the eyes, head and face of the dancing teacher as he was about to climb the stairs to his home. He was taken to the Edinburgh Royal Infirmary, where he lingered for two weeks before dying, but at the subsequent High Court murder trial of the McMillans there was doubt as to who was responsible.

Although tests confirmed he had been deluged with acid, the immediate cause of his death was inflammation of his arm, where doctors had bled him, justifying that action on the grounds that one effect of the acid in his eyes had been to form water on his brain, causing swelling. One of the doctors reported, 'The letting of blood was a necessary step in the treatment where inflammation of the brain was anticipated; and inflammation of the brain often followed surgical operations on the eye. Letting of blood was a universal remedy to prevent, or rather to anticipate, effects on the brain.' But was it the doctors or the McMillans who killed Campbell?

The victim had given police a bedside statement saying, 'On going to his own house and where he had nearly reached the landing-place, at the head of the stair, he observed McMillan's door open, and an arm and hand holding a jug thrust out. Believing that to be intended for him, he turned about, but before he got more than half way round, the contents of the jug were thrown upon him.'

In December the McMillans were tried on an indictment alleging murder under, 'An act to prevent the malicious shooting at, and attempting to maim or disfigure any of His Majesty's subjects', which accused them of throwing acid over Archibald causing his death. The jury found the charge against Hugh not proven and while they convicted Euphemia recommended she should be shown mercy. The judge had no alternative but to sentence her to death, however, pleas on her behalf pointed out it wasn't acid but the bleeding of Archibald that cost his life and shortly before she was due to be executed she was reprieved.

The deadly combination of revenge and acid surfaced again seven years later, this time in Glasgow, when twenty-seven-year-old Hugh Kennedy was accused of a particularly nasty killing, one made all the worse by the fact that before attacking his victim, in order to make sure the sulphuric acid he planned using would be effective, he tested it out on two harmless pets with appallingly painful consequences.

Married with an infant child Kennedy had at one time run a public house in Edinburgh but when it failed he had been taken on at the Bucks Head Inn in Glasgow as under boots, a fairly lowly menial job as a general assistant for which he was paid seven shillings a week with free bed and board. Having at one time been his own master, he resented having to take orders and after a time had approached his immediate boss, head boots James Goodwin, and asked for a pay rise which was turned down with Goodwin telling him he was already getting a fair wage. Revenge would quickly follow.

Goodwin and Kennedy shared a bedroom in the Bucks Head but the early hours of an August morning in 1833 were shattered by the screams of the former, who would later say to police that he was awakened by 'feeling something thrown upon my face, which was followed by an explosion as if fire had flown from my eyes and a strong sulphurous smell'. When he pleaded for help, there was no word from Kennedy and when Goodwin tried opening the bedroom door he was unable to get out. Eventually other hotel workers came to his aid and his face was bathed with cold water, but Kennedy at first refused to go to find a doctor until he was ordered to do so. One of the waiters discovered the bedroom door handle had been removed and a rope used so that someone on the outside could prevent it being opened.

Despite hospital treatment Goodwin was blind for three weeks and although he made a partial recovery his left eye was burned out and his face and neck disfigured.

The inn owner told police that a few days before the incident something had been thrown into the eyes of a dog and about the same time he had seen a cat apparently in great distress with, 'Its head much swollen and the hair destroyed.' When police questioned him Kennedy claimed he had been asleep at the time of the attack and said other inn staff were responsible for the attack. However he was convicted of having 'wilfully and unlawfully thrown at or otherwise applied to the face' of Goodwin 'sulphuric acid or some other corrosive substance with intent, in doing so, or by means thereby, to murder or to maim, disfigure or disable' him and was convicted and condemned to death. He was executed in Glasgow in January 1834, the *Caledonian Mercury* reporting that he had 'made a full confession of his guilt, and at the same time stated that he had not stood alone in the planning and commission of the crime; but to the last he steadfastly refused to give the name of any person associated with him in the act'.

Revenge is said to be sweet but nineteenth-century courts made sure its taste was bitter for those caught enacting it. In 1855 Belfast-born William Kelso, alias Alexander Stewart, aged twenty, discovered to his cost that when society decided to take its own revenge on evil-doers the consequences were fatal. Kelso was a petty thief who pilfered from workmates at No. 1 Clayband Pit in Kelvinside, Glasgow. They were acts of meanness that cast suspicion of many innocent men and boys working at the mine.

Miner John Welch, fifty-five, was from the old school that detested thieving especially when the blame fell on those who were not involved. He had gone to his job at the pithead one November Sunday morning, but when he didn't return to his home in Walker's Land, Maryhill, three-quarters of a mile away, his wife started worrying and his children set out in darkness to look for him. One of his sons Francis thought his dad might be in a small hut where workmen often sat chatting during breaks, but when he tried opening the door he heard his father's voice inside asking who was there and calling weakly, 'Come in for you've been lang, lang a coming.'

Inside it was obvious the elderly miner was badly hurt and as he was being taken out of the hut he was asked by his family and other searchers who had attacked him. 'Collier Stewart,' he said and pointed to a bloodstained pick and shovel. He was taken home but died within a few hours. Stewart was arrested and despite pleading not guilty convicted of murder and condemned to death. The *Cheshire Observer and General Advertiser* told how on the eve of his execution he had finally confessed: 'The only reason he could assign for the rash and bloody deed was that the old man had interfered with him in the exercise of his thieving propensities about the works and threatened to inform upon him. They had no quarrel or fight when the fearful and fatal blows were given with the pick on the afternoon when the deed was perpetrated, and he admitted that the striking of Welch was simply to gratify a feeling of revenge,' a report in the newspaper said. He was executed by hangman William Calcraft before a crowd of 20,000 at Glasgow in May 1855 after a plea by the jury for mercy had been rejected.

It was little wonder Stewart did not want his thieving reported to the police. Judges in Glasgow at the time were coming down especially hard on miscreants. John Dornow was given twelve months jail, six of them with hard labour for bigamy; Robert Souters Macdonald was jailed for four years for stealing a snuff box; Francis McEwan served four years imprisonment for stealing a coat, the same penalty imposed on Mary Watson for stealing a piece of beef while Hugh Gray was jailed for four years for stealing a lump of coal.

When farmer George Dickson had to disappoint three men who asked him for work he could not have imagined his rejection would almost cost him his life. The trio were angry at being turned down and plotted revenge, taking it a week later as Dickson was riding home from Dalkeith market to his home a few miles away at Cousland. As he passed a plantation, four men leapt out, three of them grabbing the bridle of his horse then striking at him with long clubs they had cut from trees in the woods a few minutes earlier. Dickson recognised three of them as having called previously seeking work. He was viciously beaten about the head and body as one of the attackers shouted, 'Murder him, murder him,' and after being dragged to the ground and again bludgeoned and robbed he was left in a pool of blood. Once his assailants fled Dickson managed to haul himself back on his horse and ride for help. A doctor described injuries to his head and chest as serious and although for a time there were concerns for his survival he eventually recovered. He gave a detailed description of the gang, resulting in their arrest soon after, but the youngest, sixteen-year-old William Leslie, agreed to give evidence against the others, William Thomson, James Thomson and John Fram, who were charged with highway robbery when they appeared at the High Court in Edinburgh in January 1827.

Another witness said on the day Dickson was attacked, William Thomson had asked him to 'rumble a cove' at Dalkeith, a slang expression he said meant robbing a man and one he had read in the book written by David Haggart (see Chapter 15) at which point the Lord Justice Clerk intervened to say the book was, 'one of the most base and infamous works ever printed'. All three were convicted of highway robbery and sentenced to hang with the judge telling them, 'The crime of robbery has of late become so frequent that it has become necessary that those who are entrusted with the care of the safety of the public should stretch out the strong arm of the law, that examples may be made to deter others from committing like crimes; therefore I entreat you to prepare for eternity.'

The jury recommended James Thomson and Fram should be shown mercy, as they had been acting under the influence of William Thomson, and both were later reprieved and transported for life to New South Wales. William, the elder of the Thomson brothers, married with a young son, was executed at Dalkeith.

'I wished I had fallen in the field of battle,' said Captain Charles Munro of the Black Watch as he lay dying in a bed at Chapeltown, Cromarty, in 1812, the victim not of an enemy soldier but a vengeful coward who would end his own miserable life starving on bread and water before his launch into eternity from the unforgiving scaffold.

Munro was said to be a man who was sometimes hot tempered and after calling on his blacksmith George Thomson late one afternoon was followed into the smithy shortly after by Robert Ferguson. Stiff-necked Munro was a man who would not tolerate indiscipline or bad manners, traits of which Ferguson was frequently guilty and, almost inevitably, the pair began arguing, with the dispute ending when the officer grabbed the other man by the collar of his coat and pushed him into the street. Ferguson disappeared and it seemed that might be the end of a trivial affair but just minutes later he reappeared carrying a knife. Munro had only a small switch used for controlling his horse and although he tried fending off Ferguson he was viciously stabbed in his side. A broadside gave an account of the tragedy, telling that as blood poured from him and his intestines began falling out, he cried, 'I'm gone, take hold of the man', then, 'Why do you not seize the murderer?' Thomson's apprentice George Home leapt on Ferguson, who at first made no resistance but then his attitude altered with the broadside relating, 'On the way to the Justice of the Peace, in custody (of Home) and his fellow workman, he suddenly stopped and refused to go further without a warrant, threatening to use any man who should offer to seize or detain him.'

Meanwhile the blacksmith's wife helped Munro to a bed in their house, where the soldier told her, 'I did not think the man would have done this to me; God knows I would not have done it to him; we had but a few words, and I only put my hand to the back of his neck to throw him out for giving me insolent language.' A doctor who tried saving Munro said his intestines had poured out through a three-inch gash in the side of his stomach and he had to make the cut bigger to get them back in. But there was never any hope of his being saved and he died the following evening. At his trial for murder in Inverness in September Ferguson, in a written defence, 'denies the murder, but acknowledges the slaughter by a knife held up in self-defence'. He was found guilty and sentenced to hang.

The official Dead Warrant detailing the court finding held at the Highland Archive Centre shows that Ferguson was 'ordered to be held in the Inverness Tolbooth and fed on bread and water only until Friday October 20 then between two and four hanged.' He duly was, the broadside revealing how in prison he had been taught to read and had studied the scriptures and reporting his last words on the scaffold: 'He believed that his condemnation was in the hands of providence, the occasion of his conversion and he said he had full assurance of the forgiveness of sin, through the merits of Jesus Christ. After his exhortation he mounted the drop without the least intimidation, and, after delivering a most impressive prayer, he was launched into eternity without a struggle.'

24

THIRSTING FOR BLOOD

Crimes involving sex were looked on with extreme distaste and loathing in a nineteenth-century Scotland where religion played such a dominant role. Rapists and deviants expected no mercy from judges who almost without exception refused to allow reporters or spectators to hear details of sexual offences. While the names of victims of sexual crime, even youngsters, were allowed to appear in print the judiciary did its best to prevent the public hearing graphic descriptions of their ordeals and as a consequence generally added to suspicions as to what actually took place and a general abhorrence of offenders. At the same time the population's thirst for the blood of beasts and perverts frequently extended to those guilty of preying on the innocent.

Farm worker Alexander Gillan, aged nineteen, had set off on a Sunday morning walk in 1810 to visit relatives living in Lhanbryde in Morayshire and, crossing a moor, spotted Elspet Lamb, aged ten, who was looking after her father's cattle. For a reason he could never explain Gillan suddenly launched a violent sexual attack on the girl before battering her to death with a stone. His behaviour became all the more bizarre because he then went off to a nearby church, leaving some of his blood-soaked clothing at the murder scene, and joined the other worshippers. He was still there when he was arrested. At Inverness in October that year Gillan was convicted of rape and the comments of the Lord Justice Clerk, Charles Hope, in sentencing him to death reflected a nationwide fury and horror.

According to *Trewman's Exeter Flying Post* the judge told the teenager, 'Guilt such as yours has seldom appeared in evidence before any Court of Justice. Either of the crimes of which you were accused, would have been amply sufficient to have brought you into your present wretched predicament. Either would have been sufficient to have weighed down the soul of any human being to the lowest pit of perdition; but both combined exhibit a picture of depravity which human nature has seldom displayed. Under such circumstances of accumulated and aggravated guilt, I look upon any punishment which you can receive in this world as mercy. Did you flatter yourself, that if you escaped detection here, you could have lived or taken your place among the industrious in the peaceful occupations of men? If so, you have greatly deceived yourself. The mangled corpse of this innocent would have unceasingly haunted you. Her departed spirit would have drawn aside your curtain at midnight, and horror and despair would have driven you to take vengeance upon yourself to escape the stings of an agonized conscience.

'Such is the nature of your crime and such the enormity of your guilt, I have not thus dwelt upon them to insult you; far be it from me to triumph over the weakness, the misfortune, or misery of a fellow creature. I know too well the frailty to which, in common with the rest of mankind. I am incident, to offer you any insult. I only dwell on your crimes to awaken you on the threshold of eternity to the sense of the enormity of crimes not often heard of in the annals of mankind.

'The law has declared that the crimes of rape and murder shall be punished with death; and for that of murder, which is the highest that can be committed, because the injury is irretrievable and the consequences can never be undone, the law has added certain additional stigmas. It has decreed that the criminal found guilty of it shall be bereft of privileges common to all others; that he shall be deprived of burial and that his body shall not be permitted to descend to its mother earth like those of Christians.

It is therefore ordered to be delivered to surgeons to be publicly dissected and anatomized. And in any other place, that might, perhaps, have been the punishment in your case; but, as there is no school for medicine here, where you can be publicly anatomized, and as the enormity of your crimes cry for the severest punishment, I have resolved, by virtue of the powers committed to me by the laws of the realm, to make a more lasting and memorable example of the fate which awaits the commission of such crimes.

'There is another circumstance which weighs with me in determining on the nature of the punishment. The particular situation of that part of the country where this crime was committed is but too well calculated to invite the perpetration of crimes by the means it affords of concealment. Its extensive and vast woods; its uninhabited moors and the peace which reigns over it, are but too well calculated for that purpose. I am therefore anxious that the solitary woods and extensive wilds of this part of the country may be traversed by every person of both sexes, at all times, and even at night, with confidence and security, and it is my duty to make them as safe as the streets of this populous city.

'I have therefore determined, that after your execution, you shall be hung in chains, until the fowls of the air pick the flesh off your body, and your bones bleach and whiten in the winds of Heaven, thereby to afford a constant warning, to the fatal consequences, which almost inevitably attend the indulgence of the passions; and hoping that the example may operate in the prevention of crimes, and for the more permanent safety of the people.'

Gillan was fed only bread and water in the tolbooth at Elgin until Wednesday, 14 November when, guarded by soldiers from Fort George, he was taken on a cart to the spot near Fochabers where he had committed the appalling attack on little Elspet and where a gibbet had been specially built. 'An immense multitude of people from every quarter, and of every age and sex, assembled to witness the awful spectacle,' said the newspaper. Trembling and fearful, Gillan had to wait on the scaffold while hangman William Taylor argued with ministers and magistrates over who was to have the prisoner's clothes following his execution, Taylor pointing out that according to the agreement made at the time of his appointment they were rightfully his. The matter having been resolved in favour of Taylor he went ahead and after Gillan's body had hung for an hour took it down, removed his outer garments then helped a blacksmith shackle the corpse in chains and hoist it back up to the gibbet where it remained, unloved, rotting and mouldering, welcomed only by hungry birds and rats.

The same open horror and revulsion that had led the huge crowd to follow Gillan to his doom surrounded the trial in 1821 of itinerant Irishman James Gordon for the murder of a harmless wandering pedlar who had strayed into Scotland from his native Hexham in Northumberland. Just as nowadays there would be much sympathy for teenager John Elliot, described in the *Caledonian Mercury* as 'rather weak in his intellects', gained much sympathy from farmers and villages, who would give him a meal, a barn in which to sleep or the odd coin to help him along. The paper reported Elliot was of a 'slender, delicate frame, gained his livelihood by carrying a small pack, or box, containing a few trifling articles of hardware and stationary through the pastoral parishes on both sides of the Border.' In fact the box was red; it had been made for him by a relative while his sister Elizabeth and her husband John who lived near Carlisle had helped pack it.

This harmless soul met many strangers during his travels, but in November 1820 was fastened on to by Gordon, also known as James McDonald or O'Donnell, who stayed by his side for three days with his iron-bound shoes clattering on stone paths and in farm buildings. John's was a familiar face in south-west Scotland and so when a farmer's boy out tending sheep discovered his body near the village of Eskdalemuir he was soon identified. Not far away lay a pair of bloodied iron-bound shoes. The red box, so familiar to many and containing items worth a pittance was missing. The youngster's head had been smashed, almost certainly with one of the shoes but of Gordon there was no trace and his description was circulated all over Scotland,

Northumberland and Cumberland. Other pedlars and hawkers, incensed by the murder, vowed to look out for the five-foot-two Irishman with a heavily pockmarked face and blind in his left eye, and gradually it emerged that after the killing Gordon had taken the red box around farms and hamlets in south-west Scotland and the Borders, selling the pitiful pieces inside it for a few pence before throwing it away and heading north.

He was discovered 180 miles away at Nairn in the north of Scotland, where he was arrested and taken south to be tried at Dumfries for the killing. The murder had caused deep anger. Although the courtroom was packed, many were unable to get in so they waited outside to hear the outcome, which was inevitable considering the number of witnesses who had seen Gordon selling items from the red box. Despite pleading innocence he was convicted and sentenced to hang. The *Caledonian Mercury* proclaimed, 'Judging from what was brought out in evidence, the whole property possessed by Elliot could not have exceeded the value of a few shillings, and nothing can more strongly evince the utter disregard which many of the low Irish display for human life than the barbarous and painful circumstances under which this murder was committed.' The paper said that, 'On receiving sentence the prisoner behaved in the most hardened and outrageous manner, declaring that he had not received justice; and when the judge earnestly called on him to prepare for eternity and to throw himself on the mercy of the Redeemer, he muttered between his teeth, "I renounce it, I renounce it." He was taken from the bar imprecating curses on the whole Court. The trial occupied about ten hours and from the intense interest it excited, the court was crowded almost to suffocation. Indeed hundreds of persons found it impossible to gain admittance.' Watched by a big, resentful crowd, Gordon was hanged at Dumfries in June 1821.

Equally vile in the eyes of the public was the terrifying burglary in 1817 by three Irishmen on the Greenock home of farmer Robert Morris. The first part of the indictment against the trio was bad enough; it was alleged that they did 'wickedly and feloniously break and enter the house of Robert Morris by forcing open one of the windows, and did then and there wickedly and feloniously attack and assault the said Robert Morris, and did drag him out of his bed, and having blindfolded him did forcibly hold him down upon the ground and then take and carry away a banknote of one pound, or one pound one shilling sterling, twenty shillings or thereby in silver and copper money, together with a vast variety of wearing apparel'.

It was the second part of the accusation that caused such fury and disgust because it charged them with 'a rape or an assault with intent to commit a rape on Janet Crawford, sister-in-law of Robert Morris and Mary Black, his servant'.

As was usually the practice in sex hearings, only court officials were allowed to hear the evidence, newspapers and the public being left to speculate on the details. This frequently led to grossly exaggerated accounts of what was said to have happened and this case was no different. But at the end of the trial in Edinburgh the trio of brothers Bernard and Hugh McIlvogue and Patrick McCristal, who had denied guilt, were convicted and hanged at Greenock. In a final letter to his mother McCristal had written, 'My present situation must be very distressing to you all – but I send you this with a joyful heart, in hopes that I will get a favourable sentence from my blessed Redeemer.' No one would ever know whether he did, but there was little sympathy for the three at their hanging and extra constables were sworn in to guard the scaffold during their brief appearance.

Judges rarely went into detail as to why evidence in sexual trials should be heard behind closed doors. But an exception was made in July 1830 when carters John Thomson, aged twenty-two, and twenty-six-year-old David Dobie were accused of raping, murdering and robbing Margaret Patterson, a young woman they had met outside a public house near the village of Gilmerton on the outskirts of Edinburgh. The thirty-three-year-old victim was the daughter of a retired gardener to the Duke of Buccleuch. She had become addicted to drink and on the night of her fatal meeting had been in an inn and was unsteady on her feet when the pair offered to help her along the road. What happened next was, according to the *London*

Standard, an example of 'fiendish brutality'. And while the indictment was required to give precise details of the attack newspapers such as the *Hampshire Advertiser* and the *Bury and Norwich Post* published part of it in Latin, knowing that while a tiny percentage of their readers would understand, the vast majority would remain in ignorance. What was known was that after the assault Margaret managed to get to her parents' home, but because she gave the appearance of being drunk they refused to let her in and instead she ended up in the poorhouse, where she died as a result of a beating from Thomson and Dobie but also through internal injuries committed during the sadistic assault.

The case caused outrage. Lord Meadowbank said to his fellow judges after the jury returned a verdict of not proven on the rape charge but convicted the pair of murder, intent to ravish and robbery, causing Thomson and Dobie to be sentenced to die, 'I am perfectly certain that were the details of this case unfortunately made public, as, thank God, the power of law has enabled you to prevent, those details would have excited such feelings in this Christian community as never were before excited. It is hardly possible to imagine that persons would have been found living in this Christian land who would have brought their minds to the commission of such atrocious crimes. Melancholy it is to think, that had this unprotected female been wandering the world among the most barbarous people, she would have been in a state of comparative safety to what she was within three miles of the metropolis of this most civilized country.' His fellow judge Lord Moncreiff commented that the case 'beggared all power of language to describe, and all terms of condemnation to characterise'.

In a leading article the *Sheffield Independent* stated, 'From the very decent practice of the Courts, and the respect which the Scotch newspapers are compelled by the character of their readers to pay to public morals, no particulars of the trial have been published.' Told that after the executions at Edinburgh his body and that of Thomson was to be handed over to surgeons after their hanging, married Dobie shouted, 'My Lord, it is a grand thing that you canna dissect the soul. I'm as innocent as the child that's unborn.'

The *Caledonian Mercury* reported that on the 'appearance of the criminals on the scaffold there called forth something like a smothered shout from the assembled multitude, but it was immediately checked'. And after they were dead the newspaper told that, 'The nature of the crime for which they have so justly forfeited their lives was such as almost to preclude all feelings of pity towards them; and accordingly we do not recollect any persons, in their situation, whose fate excited less commiseration or about whom less was said between the period of their condemnation and execution.'

Few cases of mass murder have attracted the same degree of attention as that involving William Burke and William Hare, two Irishmen who established a thriving trade in the supply of bodies for dissection in Edinburgh. They sold their first corpse for £7 10 shillings in 1827 to well-known city anatomist Dr Robert Knox. It was that of an elderly pensioner who died of natural causes in lodgings run by Hare, and realising surgeons were constantly on the lookout for corpses the pair set about satisfying the demand simply through murder. Usually they chose victims who were unlikely to be missed and preferred suffocating them so the bodies would be sold unmarked. Targets were lured to Hare's lodging house and included a grandmother put to permanent sleep with a huge dose of painkillers, her blind grandson and prostitutes. However, greed and suspicion by Burke that Hare was trying to organise separate deals with Knox resulted in the killers falling out and when other lodgers became convinced something evil was taking place in their midst and went to the police, the racket was exposed and both were arrested.

Burke's days were numbered when Hare agreed to give evidence against him in exchange for his freedom. He was accused of three murders, but it was widely believed at least sixteen people had been killed. His trial was a sensation. News that vulnerable people had been dragged to their deaths in exchange for a few pounds caused fury in the capital, with as much anger directed at Hare for escaping justice as his one-time accomplice. The finding of guilt over the slayings was a formality but even after he was condemned the authorities had to lay on extra protection for Burke in the Edinburgh prison, with furious crowds baying outside for his blood. Workmen who erected the scaffold were cheered by a huge waiting mob as they completed their task in the Lawnmarket in January 1829. Many in the crowd waited for twenty-four hours, often in pouring rain, to be near the gibbet and owners of buildings surrounding the site did a roaring trade in hiring places in their windows to onlookers with prices of up to twenty shillings (£100) being paid. Such was the demand for viewing spaces that even the great Sir Walter Scott had to share his window with his friend, the artist Charles Kirkpatrick Sharpe.

Tiredness and frustration combined with drink worsened the fury of the spectators and by the time Burke was led to the scaffold screams of 'Strangle him', 'Burke him', 'Choke him' and 'Hang him' echoed around the Lawnmarket and it was almost with a sense of relief that he went to his doom.

The feeling of intense disgust and hatred for what Burke had done penetrated to the pages of the *Caledonian Mercury*. 'Essentially and in his real character an ignoble, base, mean spirited wretch, this wholesale assassin, by the mere extinction or obliteration of every moral principle and feeling of his nature and by a consequent abandonment of the faculties bestowed upon him to the commission of crime has succeeded in obtaining a bad pre-eminence even among those who had prostituted and degraded far higher endowments to the ways of iniquity; and a name which ought never to have been heard of beyond the precincts of the lowest and meanest compartments of society, is now damned to immortal infamy.'

Had the crowd been able to get their hands on William Burke it is probable he would have been torn apart. Six years before his one-time co-director in death turned King's evidence to condemn him, another Irishman could count himself fortunate to have survived to reach the gallows. Janet Anderson, aged eight, and her younger brother had, in all innocence, accompanied twenty-year-old Irishman James Burtnay to a field at Prestwick in Ayrshire to help pick potatoes. Once there Burtnay sent the boy home and as soon as he was out of sight launched a vicious and vile sexual attack on the girl, who eventually managed to struggle from him and, bloodstained and out of her mind with terror, get home to tell her parents what had happened. As soon as the alarm was raised a huge number of furious local residents joined in a hue and cry, the hunters including a procurator fiscal, the wealthy owner of a coal works and Sir Alexander Boswell of Auchinleck, the well-known Scottish poet and writer, along with scores of neighbours of the victim's family. They found Burtnay four hours later and he was arrested and carted off to jail. In November 1822 he went on trial at Edinburgh for raping and assaulting Janet, who gave evidence against him, as a result of which he was found guilty and sentenced to hang at Ayr.

The vileness of the assault on the child which left her severely mentally distressed had incensed parents in the area and, following rumours that an attempt might be made to attack Burtnay at his hanging, extraordinary measures were taken to protect the scaffold. A wooden fence was built around it. Thirty Freemen of Ayr were issued with arms and were joined by a force of the Ayrshire Militia and a party of special constables while town officials were given fearsome halberds. In fact a tiny group was waiting to seize the rapist's body; his few friends wanted to see whether they could revive his corpse but had to wait forty minutes before they were allowed to rush off with his coffin to jeers from elements of the crowd that had remained. It was a hopeless exercise, however, and the principal drama involved the arrest of a pickpocket among the spectators.

Just as with Burtnay even the most evil offenders, while surrounded by the hate of ordinary folk, occasionally discovered a semblance of pity. James McWheelan, aged thirty-two, was condemned at Ayr in October 1848 for the brutal and bloody murder with a chisel of a young peasant, James Young, on a remote road outside Kilmarnock. Before his trial he tried to kill himself and from that moment until his hanging was permanently watched in case he made another attempt to cheat the law and his executioner. Despite that, McWheelan almost managed to evade justice because a search of his cell uncovered a small pair of scissors. That search had not been sufficiently painstaking because a few days later another examination revealed he had hidden a sharpened nail. In the condemned cell at Ayr, security was tightened up and when he was visited several times by a young woman friend from Ardrossan the couple were never allowed to be alone together. The authorities had encouraged McWheelan, who denied being a killer, to make a full confession and it was hoped that if the woman continued to see him she might persuade him to come clean. However, by the time he decided to admit his guilt she had vanished.

Of all those cases in which executions brought out the hatred of ordinary folk none did so with more devastating consequences than that in 1736 surrounding Captain John Porteous, commander of the Edinburgh City Guard. A remarkable letter held at the National Library of Scotland written by eyewitness Allan Ramsay, the poet and publisher, graphically describes the beginning of this ghastly tragedy that had its roots in the English capital.

Scottish resentment at having to conform to laws laid down in London was increased by the imposition of a tax on malt that pushed up the price of beer and caused widespread protests. A particular target for demonstrators was excise officials whose job included collecting the tax and catching smugglers trying to evade duty.

When smugglers Andrew Wilson, William Hall and George Robertson were arrested at Pittenweem in Fife for trying to rob exciseman James Stark, they were tried at Edinburgh and sentenced to hang, although Hall was reprieved after giving evidence against his co-accused. There was considerable sympathy for Wilson and Robertson as they waited in the Edinburgh Tolbooth to be executed and friends plotted to free them. One escape attempt in which a smuggled saw was used to cut through bars on their cell window saw Robertson wriggle through but failed when Wilson became stuck in the gap. Undeterred they tried again during a kirk visit days before they were due to hang when Wilson literally threw his companion over pews then held guards, allowing Robertson to get away to friends waiting with 'money and a swift horse and fairly got off nae mair to be heard of or seen again', according to Ramsay. In fact Robertson managed to reach the Netherlands and spent the rest of his life running an inn in Rotterdam.

By sacrificing himself to let his friend go free Wilson's stock rose even higher in the eyes of many Scots and the strength of support for him led to suspicions an attempt would be made to snatch him from the scaffold. City officials ordered Porteous and his 150-strong City Guard to be on hand at the execution which, said Ramsay, went off quietly 'with all decency and quietness'. As often happened when the body was cut down youngsters threw a handful of stones at the hangman. It was the spark that ignited an inferno of bloodshed and hatred and, 'On which the brutal Porteous (who it seems had ordered his party to load their guns with ball) let drive first himself amongst the innocent mob and commanded his men to follow his example which quickly cleansed the street but left three men, a boy and a woman dead upon the spot, besides several others wounded.'

Not content, Porteous ordered another volley which killed, 'a taylor in a window three storeys high, a young gentleman and a son of Mr Matheson the minister's and several more were dangerously wounded and all this from no more provocation than what I told you before, the throwing of a stone or two that hurt nobody. Believe this to be true, for I was ane eye witness and within a yard or two of being shot as I sat with some gentlemen in a stabler's window opposite to the Gallows. After this the crazy brute march'd with his ragamuffins to the Guard, as if he had done nothing worth noticing but was not long there till the hue and cry rose from them that had lost friends and servants, demanding justice.'

Porteous was eventually, largely as a result of demands from thousands of Edinburgh citizens, tried for murder and condemned to be hanged, but on the eve of his execution word reached the capital that Prime Minister Robert Walpole wanted a delay to give him time to get Porteous a reprieve. The result was a march on the tolbooth by a furious 4,000-strong mob that overpowered guards, dragged Porteous to the Grassmarket and lynched him. Following a parliamentary inquiry into what became known as the Porteous Riots, the city was fined £2,000 (£420,000).

Sir Walter Scott used descriptions of the riots in the opening chapters of his novel *The Heart of Midlothian*, while paving stones arranged to resemble a heart mark the site of the much loathed tolbooth in the High Street near St Giles' Cathedral.

25

DEADLY DINNERS

'What is food to one man is bitter poison to another,' wrote the Roman poet and philosopher Lucretius more than half a century before the birth of Christ. Almost 2,000 years later he might have been a journalist reporting on a horrific case in which a grasping landlady killed two of her lodgers. What made this devilry all the more hideous was that before murdering the main target of her spite she experimented with the effectiveness of her ghastly killing concoction on the other.

Elizabeth Jeffrey and her husband ran a boarding house in the then mining village of Carluke in Lanarkshire where most of her lodgers were mine workers or weavers. The couple also had a nearby but and ben which was home to others, including elderly widow Ann Carl, who helped pay for her board by assisting Mrs Jeffrey with cleaning, cooking and going for the occasional message to the village shops.

Ann's was a familiar face about the community, but then in early October 1837 she became ill, complaining of sickness and stomach pains. She was a harmless old woman and other lodgers including Janet Meikle were sympathetic and worried, asking as she lay bedridden whether she had eaten or drunk anything out of the ordinary, but they were told she had taken only her normal dinner of porridge prepared for her by Mrs Jeffrey. The landlady had handed the sick woman a glass of whisky and water, insisting she drink it and waving aside her protests that she did not want it. Next morning the old woman was dead and although Mrs Jeffrey refused to help wash the body she almost immediately arranged for a coffin, helped sew a shroud and watched the burial that afternoon. Neighbours thought there was nothing unusual in the death of an elderly woman.

Another of the boarders was miner Hugh Munro, a canny Highlander from Skye who had saved a few pounds in case he found himself out of work. He had loaned money to his landlady but after getting some of it back to send to relatives told her he would need the rest because his job had come to an end. On the day he broke the news she made him porridge and within an hour he was unwell, complaining of the same symptoms as those suffered by Ann Carl just over three weeks earlier. Mrs Jeffrey refused pleas by other boarders to send for a doctor, angrily telling them, 'Highland people are narrow minded; he'd groan about the expense,' and instead fed him rhubarb mixed with a powder she falsely claimed had been bought from a doctor and was a remedy for stomach troubles. But as his condition worsened she would not go near him and he died after days in agony. Once again she organised an immediate burial.

After two similar sudden deaths in such a short time neighbours were gossiping: some of the other miners quit the lodgings, remembering how Hugh had suddenly fallen ill after saying he would be asking for the repayment of his money; a druggist recalled twice selling arsenic to Mrs Jeffrey, each time just before the deaths, allegedly for killing rats; and another lodger told how she had been buying new dresses for her daughter's wedding not long before Munro died.

Rumour that all was not well reached the police and, after the bodies were exhumed, tests revealed arsenic in both. Mrs Jeffrey was charged with double murder and following an eighteen-hour trial at Glasgow in May 1838 during which she fainted several times and which ended with guilty verdicts in the early hours of the morning, she was sentenced to death. During the trial the prosecution said the accused woman had 'tried her hand' on Ann Carl to find out how much arsenic would be needed to kill a man. The jury recommended she was shown mercy and hundreds signed a petition asking for her to be spared. At first the condemned woman was confident of a reprieve but after the government rejected the appeals she became bedridden in jail, where she showed little interest in the goings-on around here even when her heartbroken husband visited her. She was still protesting her innocence on her way to the scaffold in May.

The *Morning Post* commented that Jeffrey 'seems to have been noted by her neighbours for her revengeful spirit' but if that was the case then that certainly applied in an even greater degree to evil Margaret Wishart, who fatally fed porridge laced with arsenic to her blind sister Jean in October 1826. Wishart's was the classic mixture of passion and poison, once again the story of a landlady with lethal intentions although here jealousy and not money was the inspiration for wickedness.

Margaret ran a lodging house in Orchard Street, Arbroath, and among her boarders was Andrew Roy, a good-looking and devout churchgoer with his own business as a millwright. Jean, blind from birth, stayed in the house doing what she could to help out, but unknown to either sister was the fact that each was in love with Roy. However, in Jean's case her passion led her into Roy's bed when Margaret was not at home and as a result she fell pregnant in 1824, giving birth to a child who died after nine months but refusing to reveal the name of the father even though Margaret suspected Roy might be responsible. She was hurt but kept her pride and pain to herself, believing his protestations during secretive trysts with him. The pair did their best to carry on an affair in darkness or behind closed doors or curtains. However, in September 1826 Roy suddenly announced he was selling his business to finance a long-held dream of settling in America. Within days he had gone and the following month the real reason for his decision emerged when Jean admitted to her sister she was once again pregnant, yet again refusing to tell Margaret who had bedded her but admitting to a fellow lodger that Roy was responsible.

As she went about the business of running the lodgings and

taking care of a blind, pregnant sister, jealousy began eating away at Margaret Wishart, delving into sisterly love and slowly polluting her sense until it bordered on insanity. She hid her thirst for revenge on a sister who she determined had betrayed her until just before the birth of the second baby in October 1826 when she gave her a deadly dinner of porridge into which she had stirred arsenic she claimed was bought for use as a rat poison. Despite falling severely ill Jean gave birth to a healthy baby boy but within three days both were dead and buried in the same coffin in St Vigeans churchyard on the outskirts of Arbroath.

Margaret went on running her lodging house while tearfully accepting the condolences of neighbours. She was well known in the area, but not everyone was so sympathetic because whispers about the sudden and surprising demise of mother and baby began spreading until the authorities ordered their coffin to be exhumed and tests showed the presence of arsenic in Jean although none in the body of the tiny baby.

Margaret was arrested and went on trial at Perth for double murder. Among the spectators who packed into the courtroom was a gloomy figure who kept his scarf around his face as if he did not want to be recognised but who some likened to Andrew Roy. At two o'clock in the morning the jury decided Jean had been poisoned, however, on the charge of killing the baby decided the prosecution case was not proven. By then many who knew Margaret were convinced the ordeal had driven her insane and her execution was delayed for a fortnight so experts could decide whether she ought to end her days in an asylum. The respite gave extra time for local magistrates, councillors and leading citizens to press their appeals for a reprieve, but in the end she was ruled sane and deserving of death.

Edinburgh hangman Thomas Williams was paid ten guineas (£900) to hang the forty-year-old at Forfar. 'Don't tie me too tight,' she pleaded with him as he began to pinion her arms as she set off on the miserable walk to the gallows. She told officials who accompanied her, 'I am not guilty and God will plead my cause.' The *Caledonian Mercury* described how there was more drama on the scaffold as Williams patiently waited for her to throw away a handkerchief, the signal for him to launch her into eternity. 'She was placed on the drop and remained in that situation for twenty-five minutes, fervently engaged in prayer. In this last appeal, though she confessed herself a great sinner and worthy of death she again asserted her innocence of the crime for which she was to suffer. She repeatedly shifted the handkerchief from one hand to the other as she concluded her prayer, nature struggled hard, reluctant to give the fatal signal. At length it was necessary to inform her that the time fixed for the sentence was fast expiring; she faintly answered, "Two minutes yet", and after a solemn pause, lifting up her face to Heaven, she gave the signal.'

But there is even more to this astonishing and terrible story. Weeks after the execution some youngsters out fishing near Arbroath discovered the body of a man floating in a river; it had been there for some time but the features were those of Andrew Roy and local people wondered whether he had finally been unable to live with the conscience of knowing his lust had taken three lives.

And still the saga continued. A broadside account of the life of Margaret revealed, 'In the house formerly occupied by her in Arbroath there is occasionally heard (particularly in the night time) a fearful noise, as if of tongues, doors rattling, fire irons clattering so the present occupants lose many an hour and night's sleep. Mr William Prophet, stone-ware merchant, and family, occupy the whole house. Several people who have had occasion to be in the house, have heard the noises and concur with the family in speaking of them. Whatever the cause of them may be, the truth of this statement is beyond all controversy. Ghost or no ghost, the family are fearfully annoyed.'

Just as lust ripped apart the Wisharts, so it slithered like a cancer into the lives of Thomas Leith, his wife Ann and their six children with dire results. Leith had come from the humblest of beginnings; as a toddler his penniless mother carried him about on her back as she begged from door to door for penny or a piece of bread. When he was older he worked as a tailor then a seaman, saving hard until he was able to marry and then open a furniture and clothing shop, initially a small unit but later moving to an impressive establishment in the Westport area of Dundee. The business boomed and he was able to buy up properties that he rented out. The future for the Leiths seemed rosy; he and Ann had twelve children of whom six survived to youth and beyond, a fair percentage of life over death in Georgian days. But then pretty teenager Isabella Kenney turned up at his store begging for a job and her looks turned his head.

Soon squabbles and distrust clouded the air in the Leith household in Hawkhill, Dundee. Deeply religious Ann confided to her minister that she and Thomas were becoming estranged, that he was threatening to hit her but she still loved him and wanted them to remain together. She was followed to the manse soon after by Thomas, who complained he and Ann could no longer stay together and pleaded for advice on how to go about formally separating. At home Ann accused him of being a womaniser, of casting his eye too frequently in the direction of Isabella, an allegation that infuriated him all the more because it was true. He and the girl were lovers but when she fell pregnant, alarmed by the humiliation that would be heaped upon him if it became known he was fathering an illegitimate child, he ordered her to leave, setting the youngster up in a home where he could visit her regularly.

Leith was smitten by her gentle looks and firm body and despite her pregnancy wanted to be with her. The problem was that his wife stood in the way. One day in April 1847 he sent a message to Ann asking her to deliver a pot of tea to him at the shop; after drinking it he was ill but recovered. Three weeks later when Ann went to mix porridge for herself and four of the children who were then living at home she discovered there were not sufficient oats and mixed in barley meal from a sack in the kitchen. Very quickly all five became sick, with a doctor fearing for their lives. In the case of Ann his concerns were justified because she was dying, but on her deathbed when the minister with whom she and her husband had previously discussed separation asked what she thought might be the source of her illness she told him how the barley meal had 'tasted of sand'. Hours

203

later she died after suffering agonising stomach pains, although her children survived. Following her death the minister visited the Leith home to console the family and Thomas told him about the tea, revealing he was convinced his wife had poisoned it and later the porridge to divert suspicion from herself and make it appear he was the culprit.

But the churchman remembered how Leith had wanted rid of his wife. When he questioned why the businessman had not gone to the police over his wife's actions he was told he did not want the authorities involved to avoid embarrassment to his family. It was when Leith demanded the bag of barley meal, saying he wanted to destroy it, that the minister refused to hand it over and contacted the police.

Tests showed Ann had died from arsenic poisoning and Leith was charged with her murder, tried at the High Court in Edinburgh and convicted, a verdict that produced a bizarre statement from the jury. It recommended mercy be shown to Leith and when as was customary the judge asked on what grounds this appeal was made, the chancellor (foreman) replied that they disapproved of capital punishment. It brought no support from the bench because the poisoner was sentenced to die on the gallows at Dundee, an outcome that gave anti-hanging campaigners the opportunity to demonstrate their revulsion and anger.

Posters appeared placed by the growing anti-hanging movement urging, 'WORKMEN OF DUNDEE, DO NOT GO TO THE EXECUTION OF THOMAS LEITH. Tomorrow the disgusting spectacle of a public execution will be exhibited in Dundee. It is time that scenes so degrading to the dignity of human nature should cease, and that a decisive testimony should be borne by the community, that capital punishment, for whatever crime, should be abolished, and something more efficient for the good of the public, as well as of the offender, substituted in their room. As a means of bearing this testimony, do you, working men of Dundee, by universally absenting yourselves, on the present occasion, show that public opinion in this town is against capital punishments?' In fact the hanging was temporarily postponed to allow police time to investigate an allegation by Leith that a female prosecution witness was in fact the poisoner. His claims were found to be groundless and he was put to death, protesting as he went to the gallows, 'I have no doubt that my unhappiness with my wife is the cause of my being here.'

In 1857 Scotland and much of the rest of Britain was shocked when a twenty-two-year-old woman from a highly respectable Glasgow family went on trial accused of murdering her lover. Madeleine Smith had been the mistress of Pierre Emile L'Angelier, an apprentice nurseryman, but when she ended the affair and demanded the return of love letters he blackmailed her, threatening to reveal intimate details of the scandalous relationship if she did not marry him. He died soon after from arsenic poisoning but after a sensational trial she walked free on a not proven verdict.

Reports of the hearing filled newspapers and among those taking an unusually keen interest was tailor John Thomson, aged twenty-six, who had returned from a transportation sentence for theft, and was working and living at Eaglesham, West Renfrewshire. On the floor above in the same house stayed twenty-seven-year-old mill worker Agnes Montgomery and although other curious residents believed there was a romantic attachment between the two, Thomson would always deny this.

During the Madeleine Smith trial in July it emerged she had originally tried buying prussic acid but when druggists refused to sell this she instead bought arsenic, a commonly used poison for exterminating vermin. Thomas listened as accounts of the trial were read aloud and asked workmates what prussic acid might be used for and where it could be bought. He handed a short shopping list to a colleague, knowing the man could not read and telling him to show it to a druggist. On the list was prussic acid. In mid-September Agnes Montgomery died suddenly after drinking from a glass of Tennent's beer and a couple of weeks later Thomson left the house after it was discovered that first bread then money had gone missing. He went to lodge with Archibald Mason and his wife Agnes at their home in John Street, Paisley, and almost immediately they were stricken after drinking whisky given to them by Thomson. Despite being very ill they recovered, but gossip about Thomson and Agnes led to the exhumation of her body and the discovery she had died through drinking prussic acid.

Thomson was arrested, accused of murdering Agnes Montgomery and trying to kill the Masons, and ultimately hanged; but nobody could work out what his motives were and throughout he insisted he was innocent.

There was never any doubt about the motive of John Stewart and his wife Catherine Wright when they poisoned merchant Robert Lamont on the Toward Castle steamboat during a voyage from Inveraray in 1829. Lamont from the Isle of Ulva in the Inner Hebrides had left his farm to do business in Glasgow and other passengers were not slow to notice his bulging wallet containing the current equivalent of £2,000. Among them were Stewart and Wright, who had married at Gretna six years earlier and were now broke and hoping to find work in Glasgow. They quickly realised that in the friendly Highlander was the opportunity to solve their money worries and not long after joining the boat had invited him into their company, plying him with drink and greedily eyeing the lump in his coat behind which was their target.

Lamont felt he had drunk enough but twenty-two-year-old Wright pushed another beer bottle before him, insisting he swallowed the contents and within minutes of doing so he was, in the words of a fellow passenger, 'insensible'. The skipper of the vessel suspected foul play because when Stewart and Wright had boarded his ship they told him they had no money and yet now appeared to have plenty. After Lamont's empty wallet was found under the table where they had been seated the master ordered Stewart and Wright to be detained. By the time the boat docked at Glasgow Broomielaw it was obvious Lamont was seriously ill and although doctors were called he died, tests showing he had been given a lethal dose of laudanum. Stewart and Wright were arrested and while he was in prison awaiting their trial for murder the former told other inmates that his wife carried a phial of laudanum that they had used to knock out and then rob other victims. They intended using it on a woman smuggler who had been on board but after seeing Lamont realised he was an easier target. The couple were convicted and condemned, the judge telling them, 'This was a crime of a most novel, most dangerous, most subtle and daring nature.'

A broadside giving an account of their trial equally pulled no punches, describing it as a 'horrid affair' and going on: 'Although not equal in extent to the murders which Burke committed, yet it is equal in enormity. Burke murdered that he might get money for their bodies; they murdered that they might get money from their victim's pockets.'

Following their execution together at Edinburgh, the *London Standard* proclaimed, 'After a short career of iniquity, and in the bloom of youth, two wretches have been cut off, by the outraged laws – who will long hold a conspicuous part in the book of record of human depravity. Their crimes were of the most dangerous description, particularly in a commercial country. They watched the actions, the motives of their intended victims, surrounded their footsteps, and, with the coolest deliberation and fiendish hypocrisy, changed the social into a mortal cup, and converted excursions of business or pleasure into "journeys to the dark region and valley of death". It is to be hoped that the example just made will be an effective preventive of such enormous crimes.'

It was not to be. Just two years later a near identical crime resulted in the execution of an Irish couple, James Byers and his twenty-five-year-old wife Mary, for murdering elderly John Martin, who they met up with on a voyage from Belfast to Glasgow. On their arrival the Byers persuaded the old man, who had brought with him £200 (£20,000) because he intended settling in Scotland, to accompany them into a series of public houses in the city centre. They started with Walter Lea's in Stockwell Street and finished in a bar in the High Street where Mary Byers briefly left the company, having earlier asked where she could find a druggist. She had crept out to buy laudanum and on her return slipped the drug into a glass of porter. Soon after drinking it Martin fell ill, dying the next day despite efforts by a doctor to save him.

James Byers fled back to Belfast, where he was arrested, and while in jail awaiting the arrival of police to take him back to Scotland for his trial attempted to escape but was discovered and in another desperate effort to save himself offered to turn King's Evidence against his wife, who had remained in Glasgow, where she was detained. He told a jailer in Belfast that although his wife had put laudanum into a drink they only meant to rob the victim not kill him. They were convicted of murder and robbery and sentenced to death, and from that moment Byers said he never wanted to see Mary again. However, he did when they stood together but acted as strangers on the scaffold at Glasgow in October 1831 and both were said to have struggled agonisingly and severely once the hangman launched them into eternity.

While there was no sympathy for the callous pair, it could be argued that kindness killed fifty-three-year-old Elizabeth McNeil and her second husband Peter in 1835. The couple had not been married long when she determined that whatever love had brought them together had gone. Her first marriage had been happy, she had given birth to a dozen children, but then she was widowed and after depression set in was rescued from despair by Banks. But it was as if she nursed a death wish, a longing to be reunited with her first love with whom she had spent almost a quarter of a century. With so many youngsters still to feed she and collier Peter struggled to make ends meet and day after day she wandered from house to house in the Borders trying to sell pottery. When she trudged up the long drive to the door of beautiful Chesters Hall near Jedburgh, the housekeeper there, Ann McGregor, felt so sorry for her that she gave her a shilling.

It was an act of charity meant to do good, but it gave birth to evil because McNeil used the money to buy arsenic with which she poisoned her husband. After her arrest she claimed she had originally meant to kill herself but changed her mind at the last minute, telling neighbours at Dewarton in Midlothian worried by Peter's gaunt look that he was suffering from cholera and there was no point in calling a doctor. However, after his death doctors decided to examine his corpse and discovered the presence of the poison. In prison she tried several times to starve herself to death but was always persuaded to eat.

As housekeeper Ann McGregor had demonstrated pity, so did the jury at Edinburgh because after convicting Elizabeth of murder they recommended mercy for her. However, when they were asked on what grounds, the foreman stated that this was merely because some jurors felt sorry for her. She was executed in Edinburgh in August.

Pity had been absent too in the tragic case of married Margaret Cunningham in 1807. When she discovered she was pregnant by her butcher lover John Skinner the pair plotted to murder her husband John Mason by slipping poison into his tea. It was third time unlucky for him because after the first two attempts failed she increased the dosage and he died in agony at their home in Pathhead, Midlothian. The affair of she and the butcher had been the subject of considerable gossip and the sudden and unexplained death of flax dresser Mason caused eyebrows to be raised, then lifted further when it became firstly obvious that a baby was due and then by the disappearance of the butcher. Once tests confirmed Mason had been poisoned, Margaret was charged with his murder and a warrant was issued alleging Skinner was involved in the killing.

At Perth in May 1806 Margaret was found guilty but because she was obviously heavily pregnant sentence was postponed until after the birth. The baby was born in the Edinburgh Tolbooth on 12 October and the young mother hoped the existence of a new-born child would win sufficient sympathy to save her life. But when she appeared before judges at Edinburgh the following month holding the gurgling infant in her arms she heard the awful sentence of death pronounced on her and she was hanged at the tolbooth in front of a huge crowd in January 1807, the baby being brought up in the workhouse.

By the middle of the century an increasing percentage of the adult population was becoming sickened by the sight of a woman dangling from a gibbet. In England rallies were held to raise support for demands for a reprieve for pregnant Charlotte Harris convicted at Somersetshire Assizes in 1849 of murdering her husband by putting arsenic in his tea. She was told that once she gave birth she would be hanged, a ruling that sparked a massive campaign against what a series of petitions to Queen Victoria, who would shortly announce that she was herself once again pregnant, this time with her seventh child, described as 'an outrage to humanity'. Public pressure would lead to Charlotte's sentence being commuted to two years' jail followed by transportation for life and now similar support was being raised in Scotland for another pregnant woman facing death. In this case the circumstances were remarkable.

Margaret Hamilton, aged twenty-five, lived at Strathaven in South Lanarkshire. Her niece, Jean Hamilton, had been working as maid for a church minister, the Reverend George Campbell in Edinburgh, and the pair began a passionate and sexual affair as a result of which the girl became pregnant. Discovery would mean his being sacked and it was agreed she should return to live with her aunt in Strathaven, where she gave birth in June 1848. Jean wrote to tell the minister he was a father and he sent her a note for £20 (£2,400), which she could take to a bank where she would sign it and be handed the cash or as much of it as she wished. Margaret was desperate for money and when she discovered the existence of the note stole it and paid the daughter of a neighbour a penny to cash it and bring her the proceeds. However, the bank refused the youngster saying the holder had to be there in person to sign it. Shortly afterwards Margaret forged Jean's signature, took the note to the bank saying the girl was unable to be there in person through illness, and pocketed the money. She now needed to get rid of Jean who she knew would, with a growing infant to feed, be looking for her note.

Much to the distress of her family and friends the young mother became ill. She appeared to recover but then worsened and died after taking a powder given to her by Margaret, who said it was from her doctor. The powder was in fact arsenic and the killer might have literally got away with murder had the little girl to whom she had offered a penny not told her mother about the gift and as a result police were informed and Margaret arrested. She was convicted of murder and sentenced to death, with the jury recommending she be shown mercy. Immediately a campaign was launched to save her. A crowded public meeting in Glasgow unanimously agreed to petition Queen Victoria to show Margaret mercy and there were demands for the trial jury to make a statement saying on what grounds it had sought mercy for her. In fact it was all in vain and in January 1850 Margaret was helped on to the scaffold in Glasgow, as was her eighty-two-year-old executioner John Murdoch.

The full horror of what happened next was described by the *Glasgow Herald*. 'As she thus stood on the drop her body was observed to sway backwards and forwards, and finally she fell back altogether, having evidently gone off in a swoon. She thus swung into a recumbent position, supported by the rope, while her feet partially rested on the drop. A momentary thrill of horror ensued; The Chaplain hastily descended with the prayer unfinished; but the executioner, in the next moment, pulled the bolt, and the drop fell. The unhappy woman died almost instantly having evidently been hanged while in a state of insensibility.'

26

WHOOPS!

The degree of suffering a hanging victim was forced to undergo in Georgian and early Victorian times was very largely a matter of pot luck. Executioners were often criminals who saved themselves from the gallows by agreeing to hang others; some took on the job because there was no other work. Their only training was by watching how other hangmen carried out executions. As a result, nooses were frequently clumsily tied and placed, resulting in victims dangling in extreme agony for minutes, slowly strangling themselves instead of being instantly killed through the bodyweight helping break their neck.

It was not until 1872, when William Marwood advocated the long drop, that hanging became a more humane method of execution. Until the gradual introduction of stricter guidelines and the ending in 1868 of public executions, hangings were often an excuse for executioners to boost their fees by selling the clothes of victims or other of the regalia used, such as the noose, a section of rope or the hood placed over the head of a victim immediately before the drop. In June 1856 the rope used to hang infamous poisoner Dr William Palmer at Stafford, England, was on sale in Lochmaben, Dumfriesshire, at five shillings (25p) an inch, the seller a friend of hangman George Smith.

While Palmer died quickly many others were not so fortunate.

Robert Tennant, aged twenty-four, was forced to suffer a terrible ordeal as he was about to hang at Stirling in October 1833 for the brutal murder of seventy-year-old road foreman William Peddie, whose boss had ordered him to sack the killer for being regularly drunk and unreliable. The *Glasgow Chronicle* reported, 'While the executioner was being told that he had not removed the prisoner's neckcloth, the signal was dropped, after a few seconds spent in imploring mercy. At this moment the unhappy man was considerably agitated by the executioner again going up to him to remove the neckcloth (which he had intentionally left around the neck, as tending to shorten the period of suffering). The rope being readjusted the unhappy criminal stood trembling for a few seconds with his hands uplifted and engaged in uttering such ejaculatory expressions as "O God, O God have mercy" and having given the signal the drop fell.'

Tennant's suffering was far from over, according to the *Caledonian Mercury*, which said, 'The convulsive struggles that shortly succeeded were violent,' and the bungled manner of his execution infuriated friends in the crowd. The *Morning Post* told how, 'As the executioner was proceeding through the Castlehill, on his return to Edinburgh, a crowd followed him till he reached some gardens near the bridge, in one of which he took shelter to escape the vengeance of the mob, who had become outrageous. They pursued him into the garden where they got hold of him, and struck and abused him. Seeing his life in imminent peril he made a desperate effort to escape, and ran towards the river followed by the crowd, who showered stones after him, several of which struck him. On reaching the river he plunged in and swam towards the opposite side, where he was in great danger till the High Constable arrived and drove at the crowd and conveyed him to the gaol for safety.'

Even more distressing for the condemned man and those close to him was the ordeal of Irish-born Moses McDonald at Greenock on Friday, 5 June 1812. He and an accomplice, John Gray, had been condemned for shop-breaking but while Gray was reprieved there was no such luck for father-of-six McDonald, who would suffer a horrendous experience on – and off – the scaffold; one described by the eminent writer Sir Walter Scott for the *Edinburgh Annual Register*. 'At ten minutes past three o'clock he took farewell of the magistrates and clergy and ascended the scaffold with a firm step, by a stage erected out from the church railing; the executioner then put the rope round his neck, drew a white cap over his face, withdrew, and at a quarter past three, he gave the signal by dropping a handkerchief; the drop fell, when, dreadful to relate, the rope broke, and he fell to the ground; his sister, who was near, instantly assisted him in rising (his arms being tied), when he got up, and walked steadily without the least attempt to escape, to the church door; he was then taken into the church, and became faint; the back of his head being bruised by the fall – another rope was procured, the drop was supported underneath by a plank, he again mounted the scaffold with a firm and quick pace, the executioner put the rope round his neck, tied the other end on a hook above, and drew the cap over his face. He then went below, and, on the signal being given, knocked the prop away, when the drop fell and he was launched into eternity at twenty minutes before four o'clock. He made three or four feeble convulsive throes, and was apparently dead in three minutes.' McDonald's nightmare had lasted more than half an hour.

Ten years later at Aberdeen the luck of the drop left farm worker Robert McIntosh suspended in agony while at his side William Gordon, aged forty-five, died apparently quickly and painlessly. The former, aged twenty-two, had cut the throat of his mistress, Elizabeth Anderson, who was in her early forties and twice his age, when she told him she was three months' pregnant with his child. Elizabeth had been reading the Bible at her home in Crathie, Aberdeenshire, when McIntosh asked to see her and attacked her with a razor before rifling a chest to take away a letter in which he had promised to marry her.

Fishing tackle maker Gordon's wife bled to death after he stabbed her in the thigh with a pair of scissors.

The two men shared the condemned cell while strenuous efforts were made to save both, with the *Aberdeen Journal* reporting that many had been 'impressed with the conviction that the lamentable catastrophe had taken place from no previous malice; but had been perpetrated by the unhappy man while under the influence of that most baneful of human vices, and, of course, a prey to all the evil passions which it naturally engenders. These considerations, combined with the once respectable character of Gordon induced many gentlemen (including several of the jury who tried him) to join in Petitions to the Throne for a commutation of his sentence; while the unhappy man himself, in a well written letter, presented the same prayer to His Majesty.'

McIntosh's elderly, sick father travelled to London to plead with government officials to spare his boy but in each case their efforts failed and it was then that the doomed pair made their own efforts to save themselves by escaping.

Unfortunately a letter written by both and signed by McIntosh and intending to be sent to an accomplice on the outside of the prison at Aberdeen was found by a clergyman, who handed it to the jailers. 'It showed that the minds of both the unhappy criminals had not been wholly employed as become men on the brink of eternity,' said the *Caledonian Mercury*.

On the scaffold, where both refused to wear the customary shrouds, instead choosing to die in black suits, it was as though they sensed something was about to go wrong because each did his best to delay their end; Gordon praying long and fervently while McIntosh, waiting patiently by his side, became faint and matters had to be delayed so a glass of water could be fetched for him. Finally, the trapdoor on which they stood opened and both dropped with a crash, the *Aberdeen Journal* reporting, 'The sufferings of Gordon seemed to terminate very quickly, but owing to the rope having been improperly placed McIntosh struggled considerably and was convulsed for some minutes. This painful sight occasioned some commotion and shouts of disapprobation among the spectators who surrounded the scaffold.'

It is not unusual for a man or woman about to die an excruciatingly agonising death to feel faint on the verge of reaching eternity. At Ayr in October 1817 Margaret Crossan, aged thirty, was joined on the scaffold by twenty-seven-year-old William Robertson and Irishman Joseph Cairns, twenty-four, the men having been convicted of robbery and stouthrief, Cairns committing the offences after deserting from the army.

Crossan was to die for setting fire to a barn, stable, byre and stack yard at a farm at Carsegowan in Galloway. She started the blaze in revenge for having been turned out of her house by the farmer. It took the lives of a dozen cows, a bull and three calves and afterwards she confided to a neighbour that she was sorry it was the livestock who were burned and not the farmer. She even warned that if the buildings were rebuilt she would return and give them another 'whiz'. As death neared it was Robertson who was the most terror stricken of the three, having to be supported after he came close to fainting, while once the rope was around his neck he appeared to lose consciousness and was held up only by the noose. A huge crowd was present and after fears of trouble troops surrounded the scaffold from where they were addressed by Cairns, who pleaded with them never to desert, saying that absconding from his regiment led him into crime. Once the hangman pulled the bolt, dropping them through the trapdoor, the men appeared to die quickly, but Crossan struggled and gasped for some minutes resulting in the angry crowd surging forward and having to be held back by soldiers.

Her distress was almost certainly the result of the hangman not allowing her a sufficiently long fall. It was another bungle by an executioner that led to the agony of George Warden being extended on the gallows at Edinburgh in 1819. A clerk in the Aberdeen post office, he had been caught opening letters and taking out money. Warden was a mild, inoffensive twenty-one-year-old who used the small amount of money he stole to help support his parents and two sisters, aged fifteen and five. That he had committed a crime of any sort shocked all who knew him and there was considerable support for efforts to save him, but these came to nothing. The judge who sentenced him had said, 'Would to God you had continued in your original path of life, where you might have risen to eminence and rank, instead of being the shameful spectacle you this day present.'

The unassuming figure dropped to his death watched by an immense crowd surrounding the gallows in Libberton's Wynd on an April afternoon. Newspapers were agreed that the spectators had considerable sympathy for the doomed man and were angered when the death ceremony went wrong. The *Caledonian Mercury* reported: 'Just before the drop fell a circumstance occurred which excited considerable alarm among a portion of the crowd but fortunately no serious result followed. When the executioner and his assistants descended from the drop, the unhappy sufferer fainted and swung upon the rope, while the handkerchief, unperceived for an instant, fell from his hand. A loud cry of "Let down the bolt" issued from those close by, while others at a greater distance, alarmed by the shout, ran with violence in different directions from the scene. In a moment, however, the drop fell and in less than two minutes Warden's sufferings were at an end.'

There was an appalling mishap, too, seven years later when it came to the execution of twenty-year-old James McManus at Dumfries for assaulting and robbing a man near Lockerbie. What happened before, during and after the hanging was graphically described in the London-based *Morning Chronicle*, which said a huge crowd had gathered to watch the demise of McManus. 'Pity for the fate of a fellow creature appeared to pervade every mind, though we were sorry to see so many decently dressed females present, and could not help regretting that curiosity should have triumphed over their better feeling. McManus was ready to leave his cell before the devotions had been concluded on the scaffold, and that on finding his exit opposed by the temporary absence of the gaoler, he knocked violently against the under door. His feelings at this time appear to have been wound up to the highest pitch; he was anxious, if we may so express it, to die and ran rather than walked across the courtyard. The prisoner's face was a little flushed, and his frame, at times, slightly convulsed; but his step was firm.

'At this time he truly stood on the brink of eternity; the messenger of death was armed and ready; an awful gulf lay before him and it was consoling to observe, that instead of wasting a single thought on the crowd, or the dreadful apparatus before his eyes, he gave his whole heart and soul, to the important duties in which he was engaged. Everything being finally ready, the cap and rope were finally adjusted, the signal given, the prop which supports the drop withdrawn, and the prisoner launched into eternity. To all appearances McManus's sufferings were long and severe. Being of a slender make, no dislocation of the neck took place; the noose shifted as the drop fell, and rested, we understand, on the lower part of his head; the rope in this way was imperfectly lightened, and before strangulation had done its work, his frame was very violently convulsed for six or seven minutes.'

Even after McManus was pronounced dead and his body put into a waiting coffin, the niceties of death were not yet over, as the *Morning Chronicle* described. 'The parties who attended the waking ceremony were cautioned against making any unnecessary noise, and, from all we can learn, it was conducted with every regard to decency. The coffin with the body was placed on chairs in the corner of the jury room, and those who wished it were indulged with a view of the face of the corpse. The practice of howling, though common in some parts of Ireland, was altogether dispensed with here; and McManus's mother, at the command of the priest, restrained her feelings in a wonderful degree.'

That same decorum could hardly be said to describe the execution at Edinburgh in 1835 of Irishman James Bell, a dragoon guard who had shot dead his overbearing and unpopular sergeant major for refusing to allow him a short leave. His execution for murder was described at length in the *Caledonian Mercury*, which had little liking for the behaviour of the hangman. It emerged that while prayers were being said for him Bell was having his arms pinioned, 'And here it was that the executioner gave a sample of that inefficiency that was afterwards like to have been attended with such disagreeable consequences on the scaffold. He cried like a child and made one or two abortive attempts before he could accomplish the task. Whether this irresolution and incapacity, on the part of this functionary, proceeded from a want of nerve, or from some other cause, we cannot say. The culprit, during the course of this painful ceremony, shed tears.'

There was worse to come when the official party, including the hangman, arrived on the scaffold.

'As soon as this official was recognised, he was greeted with horrible yells and groans by the crowd, which the unfortunate culprit seemed to think were directed against himself, and this feeling for a moment quite unmanned him. He again burst into tears and, turning round, beckoned beseechingly with his hands, to the multitude. The executioner then made one or two awkward attempts to adjust the rope, but not hitting the length; he tried to rectify his mistake, and was equally unsuccessful.' At this point one of the officials, afraid of the farce turning into a riot, had to intervene, pushing the executioner aside and adjusting the rope himself. And still things worsened. 'This lamentable course of bungling however, had not terminated, for when the culprit gave the fatal signal, with which the drop should have simultaneously given way, a few moments of dreadful suspense occurred during which the miserable victim shook with a sort of convulsive tremor, at the same time stretching out his hands in the attitude of prayer, as if to snatch the last moment of intercession.'

A policeman fainted as Bell dangled and it was hardly surprising that after the execution the hangman was pelted as he ran off along Libberton's Wynd. Other newspapers were more forthright about their view of the execution, with the *Morning Post* suggesting his incompetence was down to an 'over quantity of stimulants'. In other words they believed he had been drunk.

If that was tragic, however, an even worse calamity due to bungling by the hangman had occurred on the Edinburgh scaffold a year earlier at the execution of Robert Johnston. He along with George Galloway and James Lees had been convicted of assault and robbery, but while Johnston was sentenced to death Galloway and Lees were transported to Australia.

Johnston made the mistake of giving his haul from the robbery, the very considerable sum of £314 (equivalent now to almost £25,000) to an acquaintance, who told the police, with the result that he was arrested and convicted. Johnston was twenty-four and well known in the then Edinburgh underworld, so it was no surprise that a large number of his cronies turned up to watch his hanging in the city Lawnmarket.

Even before the fatal ceremony started some in the crowd doubted enough room had been left under the trap to allow Johnston to drop fully. The horror they saw after the doomed man dropped the handkerchief, the signal for the hangman to act, would go down in history. It was related in the *Newgate Calendar*. 'Nearly a minute elapsed, however, before the drop could be forced down, and then it was found that the toes of the wretched culprit were still touching the surface, so that he remained half suspended, and struggling in the most frightful manner. It is impossible to find words to express the horror that pervaded the crowd, while one or two persons were at work with axes beneath the scaffold, in the vain attempt to hew down a part of it beneath the feet of the criminal. The cries of horror from the populace continued to increase with indescribable vehemence; and it is hard to say how long this horrible scene might have lasted had not a person near the scaffold, who was struck by a policeman while pressing onward, cried out: "Murder!" Those who were not aware of the real cause of the cry imagined that it came from the convict, and a shower of stones, gathered from the loose pavement of the street, compelled the magistrates and police immediately to retire. A cry of "Cut him down – he is alive!" then instantly burst from the crowd, and a person of genteel exterior jumped upon the scaffold and cut the rope, and the culprit fell down in a reclining position, after having hung during about five minutes only. A number of the mob now gained the scaffold, and taking the ropes from the neck and arms of the prisoner removed the cap from his head, and loosening his clothes carried him, still alive, towards High Street.'

Half naked and almost dead, Johnston and his kidnappers were chased by the police, who eventually caught up, grabbed him, dragged him along the ground, the remainder of his clothes being torn off, and hauled him into a police station where, astonishingly, two doctors bled him then declared he was well enough to be hanged again. He was carried back to the scaffold and laid on a table while the noose was once again put around his neck.

'At last the table was removed from beneath him, when, to the indescribable horror of every spectator, he was seen suspended, with his face uncovered, and one of his hands broken loose from the cords with which it should have been tied, and with his fingers convulsively twisting in the noose. Dreadful cries were now heard from every quarter. A chair was brought, and the executioner, having mounted upon it, disengaged by force the hand of the dying man from the rope. He then descended, leaving the man's face still uncovered, and exhibiting a dreadful spectacle. At length a napkin was thrown over his face, amidst shouts of "Murder!" and "Shame, shame!" from the crowd. The unhappy wretch was observed to struggle very much, but his sufferings were at an end in a few minutes.'

The appalling demonstration resulted in the sacking of the executioner and demands by judges for an inquiry, although many blamed the city magistrates for not making sure the trapdoor through which Johnston should have dropped was working properly.

27

BIRTH OF FORENSICS

Much modern crime is solved thanks to remarkable increases in the science of forensics; at the same time just as was the case 200 years earlier it is the police officer's eyesight that often puts he or she on the trail of wrongdoers. Police in the Georgian era had an added advantage because travel by horseback or carriage was restricted to the relatively wealthy while the only means of escape for the average criminal was on foot, and that frequently meant being noticed by other travellers.

Sophisticated security systems now protect banks to bothys but in 1809 it was that oldest of safeguards, a dog, that was responsible for bringing a prolific thief to the scaffold.

Andrew Hosack thought he had quietly crept into a cottage at Rubislaw in Aberdeen and stolen away with a pile of clothing, valuable articles at that time. He worked at the nearby granite quarry and was used to clambering about cliffs and heights, and having 'sized up' the building sneaked on to the roof and down the chimney one night. Hosack ought to have left by the way he came but instead he decided to use the door and the creak set a neighbour's watchdog barking, arousing other residents, who chased the thief and cornered him in a cornfield while he was still carrying his booty. A search of his home uncovered an Aladdin's cave of property taken during a spate of other thefts and the fifty-six-year-old quarryman was sentenced to death.

After his arrest it was noticed that he bore a resemblance to a man wanted in connection with a brutal double murder near Keith in 1797, when a robber had broken into the cottage of George Milne and his daughter, slaughtered them with an axe, ransacked their home and then burned it and their blood-soaked bodies. Despite a 100 guinea (£10,800) reward for information nobody was ever caught and when he realised he was being blamed for the horrific slaughter Hosack waited until he stood on the Aberdeen scaffold and told the crowd of spectators, 'I was not directly or indirectly concerned in the said horrid murder,' adding, 'I know nothing whatever of the perpetrators involved.'

Not everybody was convinced. The slaughter of the Milnes had been appalling and after hangman Johnny Milne had hanged Hosack it had been intended to put the body in a cart and take it to a nearby cemetery where it would be put in a shallow grave until surgeons were ready to dissect it. But nobody was prepared to lend the Aberdeen magistrates a cart and attempts to borrow one at the quayside where coalmen were loading up ended in a punch-up, with seamen joining to chase the officials off. Eventually someone remembered that Milne had a horse and cart and the search moved to the hangman's home, where his daughter was pushed and jostled before the horse was led off, dragging the cart behind.

The sharp eyes of a constable sent evil Robert Edmond to his doom at Edinburgh in March 1830 to be watched by an even bigger crowd than that which turned out for the execution of William Burke the previous year. The reason for the huge turnout was the horror and anger that his crime caused. Cheerful, good-natured Marion Franks had been widowed in July 1829 and was still grieving in October when Edmond, her brother-in-law, broke into the home at Haddington, East Lothian, she shared with her daughter Madeleine, aged fifteen. In a terrible onslaught he butchered both women, leaving the body of Marion in a pigsty. Neighbours found the women, and police who examined the bedroom where Madeleine's body lay hidden under a carpet spotted marks of dried blood on the floor made by a shoe. Closer scrutiny revealed the heel of the shoe had double iron rims with small round tacks between the outer and inner rims. The inner rim was said to be especially distinct. Locals remembered a recent argument between Marion and Edmond and Constable Charles Ramage arrested him at his home in North Berwick, where the policeman found bloodstained clothing and shoes that had recently been washed and brushed. They had iron-rimmed heels and on one there was blood between the heels and soles.

When Edmond went on trial for double murder, long before the proceedings began the court was packed with hundreds of people unable to get in. The *Aberdeen Journal* did its best to make Edmond out to be a loathsome creature, describing him as 'a mean, puny looking fellow with a thin, pallid countenance – the profile rather bold, misshapen head and sandy coloured whiskers'. The evidence of the bloodstained shoe proved to be the final nail in his coffin and he was convicted and sentenced to death. He had wanted to be hanged wearing his wedding suit but was told it could not be found. 'These shoes are the only remains of my wearables which I shall die in,' he told jailers. 'In remembrance of that unfortunate day which has brought on all my sorrows and led to this my untimely fate.' On the scaffold watched by an unsympathetic crowd, he complained the noose was too tight and then realised Williams the executioner had once lodged with his wife. 'Tell her I die in peace with all mankind,' he whispered and seconds later was launched into eternity, struggling violently for some minutes before dying.

Andrew Hosack had climbed down a chimney and in 1849 that was the means by which twenty-five-year-old James Robb entered the lonely home at Auchterless near Turriff, Aberdeenshire, of Mary Smith, aged sixty-three. Robb had been drinking and after climbing in through the lum, a wooden canopy over the hearth of the fireplace, discovered the elderly woman in her bed and was instantly aroused. A violent struggle followed in which Mary was raped and then battered and finally suffocated. Robb was arrested shortly afterwards and it was forensic evidence that convicted him, even the lum being brought into court as an exhibit. When his clothing was examined, soot on his corduroy trousers matched that in the chimney of Mary's cottage and a button missing from his coat matched one found in her bed. When Robb was sentenced to hang, the judge, Lord Cockburn, told him, 'I would be the worst friend that you have upon earth if I did not most solemnly advise you not to be deluded by the hope of a commutation of your sentence.'

As he was about to walk to the scaffold at Aberdeen for his fatal meeting with hangman William Calcraft, brought specially from London, Robb asked for a statement to be read in which he admitted, 'I hereby confess that I entered the house of Mary Smith, when I was under the influence of drink, with the intention of ravishing her; that, while struggling with her, in order to accomplish my purpose, she coughed twice or thrice and then ceased to breathe; and I hereby declare that the crime of rape was not committed. Lust, drink and Sabbath breaking have brought me to a shameful and untimely death. God grant that others may take warning by my sad example.'

The *Aberdeen Journal* noted that, 'The concourse of spectators was very numerous, chiefly of the working class; and, as is always to be remarked, comprised a vast number of females, hardly on the verge of womanhood. It is much to be wondered at, that such distressing scenes can afford satisfaction to anyone; and the fact of their attracting so many in whose minds they might be expected to excite only pain and horror, is an evidence of a state of feeling among a portion of the rising generation, which is far from creditable to them.'

By 1857 the benefits of photography to police work were being well recognised, and photographic evidence to confirm identity was used at the trial in Glasgow of Madeleine Smith. In current times, photographs would certainly have been taken at the scene of the December 1866 murder in Blairingone, Perth and Kinross, of thirty-six-year-old carter Alexander McQueen, who drove around remote villages selling bread and cakes and collecting money. McQueen was shot at close range as he went on his round, the blast blowing away part of his face. When his body was discovered, witnesses noticed a set of footprints at the scene. They were measured with a ruler and found to be twelve and a half inches long. Police discovered poacher Joseph Bell, aged twenty-eight, had boasted to an acquaintance that he knew a man who collected money and said he would kill him. Even though he later claimed he had only been joking it was enough to have him arrested and when his boots were examined and measured they were found to fit the prints examined at the murder scene. Bell was sentenced to death and such was the interest in the murder that special trains were laid on to carry crowds from Dundee to the hanging at Perth in May 1866. Some local employers threatened to sack workers who took time off to attend the execution, which was carried out by William Calcraft, who was greeted with booing and groaning when he appeared on the scaffold to check the gibbet.

Calcraft was an old hand at hanging; regarded as the prime expert. He had sent hundreds of men and women to their deaths but despite his long experience many felt he was becoming increasingly slipshod, a belief confirmed by what happened as he sent Bell on his way. Newspapers reported that after he drew the bolt Bell did not fall immediately as should have been the case. Instead he slipped before dropping suddenly, with the body swinging to one side, at which Calcraft put his hands on the shoulders of the doomed man to steady him. But it meant Bell suffering minutes of agony before breathing his last.

The bungling enraged the already angry crowd whose fury increased even more when, as the body was being lowered to the ground, the rope snapped and it fell with a crash. There were screams of 'Hang the murderer' aimed at Calcraft and some of the mob tried clambering over a barricade around the scaffold to reach the grey-haired and bearded executioner, but they were held back by a police cordon.

Two years later Robert Smith was another to be caught by the eagle eyes of a policeman. In the plantation where the body of his little victim (see Prologue) was discovered, a footprint, seemingly that of a common labourer's boot, was found and after Smith's arrest matched his own exactly. Had there been any doubt as to his guilt, now there was none.

Scotland – or at least one of her sons – can legitimately claim to have played a major role in giving police massive advantages in the fight against crime. Henry Faulds, born in Beith, North Ayrshire, in 1843 became a missionary in Japan for the United Presbyterian Church of Scotland and set up a hospital for the blind there. After a break-in, police blamed a local man who worked there but Faulds was convinced of his innocence and showed police officers that his fingerprints were different to those left by the culprit. Although Faulds passionately believed in the use of fingerprints to solve crime, his work was only given the recognition it deserved after his death in 1922.

28

MISCARRIAGE

In April 1840 James Wemyss, a thirty-five-year-old umbrella maker, was hanged at Edinburgh for the murder of his wife Sarah. It was alleged that the two had been out drinking in the city and soon after they returned home a neighbour heard the sound of fighting during which Wemyss hit his wife over the head at least twice with a stool. The indictment went on to accuse that he, 'otherwise abused and maltreated her, by all which she was bruised, wounded and mortally injured and soon after died'. Wemyss was described at his trial at the High Court as a 'quiet' man, while his wife was 'always drunk and quarrelling' and he pleaded not guilty, admitting that although they had been fighting, Sarah had often fallen and fainted after drinking. He said that after the quarrel he had kissed his wife, who was still alive, and he had then gone to bed. He was unanimously found guilty and condemned to death. But was an innocent man hanged?

Almost immediately the judge put on the black cap and sentenced Wemyss, a campaign began to save him. He was known to have hit his wife in the past, but never viciously and only when she became abusive after drinking. A petition was sent to Queen Victoria pleading for the sentence to be mitigated. It was signed by more than 300 prominent people, including most of the jury, seven Edinburgh University professors, the Lord Provost and all the city magistrates. It read, 'We confess that, upon reading the evidence on the trial, we were grieved and surprised at the verdict of the jury. To confound a case of death caused in a quarrel between two persons, both in a state of intoxication, and in which the deceased had given great provocation, with a deliberate murder, did appear to us to be an error against which the general intelligence of Scottish juries was a sufficient safeguard. We are opposed to capital punishment in all cases, believing it is to be founded in a mistaken view of the real preventives of crime; but surely there is a broad distinction between a cool, premeditated murder, in which the criminal calmly selects his victim with a view to the amount of booty, and a case of drunkenness in which there was no forethought, and in which the party killed was, at the outset at least, as much in fault as he whose act became the immediate cause of death.' It concluded, 'If, unhappily, the error which has been committed in this instance should prove beyond remedy, and the fearful sentence which has been passed should be carried into effect, we trust that future juries will take warning, and, in all cases like that of James Wemyss, exercise their own judgement and undoubted right by returning a verdict of culpable homicide.'

This was an appeal for clemency and the execution was delayed for two weeks while the government considered whether there were enough grounds for a reprieve. While this was being investigated there came an astonishing revelation that followed investigations into Sarah's medical past in which the *Caledonian Mercury* claimed she had, 'By long habits of intemperance, debilitated her constitution and induced a diseased condition of the brain, so as to make her liable to fatal injury from a comparatively slight cause.' This resulted in another letter to London requesting a further respite. However by the time it was sent off the government had rejected the first plea and the news that Sarah may have died from natural causes appeared to have been ignored.

If Wemyss was unlucky, his misfortune continued to the end. As he stood on the scaffold with the noose around his neck, the executioner pulled the wrong bolt and the trapdoor through which he should have dropped to his death remained closed. The *Standard* reported that the hangman, 'Then attempted to beat it down with his feet but without effect. A gentleman rushed from the street, withdrew the bolt, the drop fell and Wemyss was dead in a few seconds. The executioner, dreading violence from the crowd, from which a terrific howl and cries of "shame" burst forth, instantly left the scene and sought shelter in the Sheriff's office.'

Wemyss was not the first to die with a question mark over his guilt. Nor would he be the last. In 1819 in a case with many similarities to that of Wemyss, soldier hero John Buchanan had been hanged despite doubts about what had actually caused the death of the prostitute he was alleged to have murdered. Buchanan had served with the 2nd Battalion of 21st Foot, the Royal Scots Fusiliers, fighting at the bitterly contested siege of Bergen op Zoom in the Netherlands in which a strong French force inflicted heavy casualties on British attackers. Among the casualties was Buchanan, who was wounded and returned home, eventually making his way back to his native Glasgow where, having left the army, he returned to his old job as a flesher. He was well known and liked, but angered when in June 1817 one of his friends, William Pringle, was convicted of housebreaking and of being a habitual thief and sentenced to death. One of those who gave statements against Pringle was a young prostitute, Jean McKenzie, and although Pringle was reprieved and transported to Australia for life, Buchanan's anger against the girl remained.

On a night out he and a group of pals found themselves in the house where she and other prostitutes lived. Within minutes she had agreed to sleep with him but no sooner had the door of the bedroom closed than she was heard calling out 'Murder' and there was the sound in the room of a beating being dished out. Buchanan and his companions left almost immediately and the next day when McKenzie complained of pains in her heart and stomach a doctor was called and quickly became convinced she had a fatal stomach disease which might have been the result of 'cold ardent spirits or unhealthy indigestible food'. Despite his treatment she died eight days later of 'mortification of the bowels'.

Buchanan was arrested and charged with murder. He pleaded not guilty and in court the doctor admitted the disease might have been brought on by blows to her stomach, but said that at the time he examined her there were no traces of violence. In his speech to the jury Buchanan's counsel said, 'To deny the brutal assault on this woman would be both futile and foolish, but to lay the crime of murder is equally absurd. The disease of which she died was an inflammation of the bowels, Jean McKenzie was a girl, young and vigorous and just one of those patients on whom this complaint made the most rapid stride; and when we consider the diet, and the probability of her having got spirits, and the place where this poor girl was confined, our wonder will not be how she lived so short but how she survived her complicated troubles so long.'

Buchanan was found guilty by a majority verdict and as he sentenced him to die Lord Pitmilly told him, 'The motive which induced you to commit this deed, renders your crime still more diabolical. You have confessed that it was because the unfortunate girl gave evidence against some of your companions; if witnesses were frightened and assaulted by people who conceive themselves aggrieved and thereby deterred from appearing in a court of justice there would be an end to all justice.'

Despite the doubts over what caused the girl's death, Buchanan was executed at Glasgow in November; but before his last march to the scaffold friends had to bring him the news that his wife had died of typhus, falling ill almost immediately after he had been arrested. And like that of Wemyss his execution was not without drama. As his body dangled a woman in the huge crowd was discovered stealing the watch belonging to one of the spectators. The *Morning Post* reported, 'The noises occasioned by this, as well as the appearance of the crowd, transcends all description. Hundreds of heads were seen for a second darting above their fellows, the grumbling noise, the prancing of the horses, the anxiety visible in the faces of many women and children running, tumbling and screaming in all directions, formed a scene indescribable. The woman, the cause of the tumult, received a terrible panelling and was afterwards lodged in the police office.'

Mary McKinnon ran a public house on Edinburgh's South Bridge. She had been out one night in February 1823 visiting friends and on her return discovered a group of drunken young men fighting with her female staff; furniture was being smashed, ornaments broken and some of the women being badly hurt. McKinnon intervened, ordering the drunks out, but according to statements made later to the police by both parties, she was attacked, pushed to the floor of her kitchen and beaten. By the time the fracas was sorted out one of the visitors, William Howat, was found to be bleeding from a stab wound to his chest. He was taken to hospital, where he died twelve days later. Howat had been drunk at the time but soon after arriving at hospital made a statement in which he said his attacker was thirty-two-year-old McKinnon, who was brought to his bedside so he could identify her. She denied stabbing him and named another woman as the killer.

Other witnesses painted a picture of a drunken, confused battle in the public house in which McKinnon was the victim of a brutal attack by Howat's friends, who tried throwing one woman into the fire, while no one apart from the victim claimed to have seen her stabbing him. Nevertheless, she was convicted of murder by a majority verdict.

Curiously, the chancellor, Robert Cockburn, having told the judge, Lord Pitmilly, that a majority of them requested McKinnon should be shown mercy, was given short shrift by his Lordship, who said he couldn't see any grounds for their plea but would forward it to the authorities. As the government would automatically ask Pitmilly for his view it was clear he would not advocate sympathy; he had made up his mind she was guilty and should hang. Was the fact that the dead man had been a solicitor's clerk a factor in his decision?

Along with many in Edinburgh Mary McKinnon hoped for a reprieve and twice applications for her to be spared were turned down. On the scaffold she asked to keep on her bonnet and veil but was ordered to remove them so the crowd could see her face and to the very end insisted she was innocent.

Who fired the shots that killed three men during a horrific riot at Greenock in 1820 during which soldiers fought a bloody pitched battle against sailors and town's tradesmen? The riot would claim a fourth victim when John Dempsey, a private in the Somerset Light Infantry, was executed having been found guilty of murdering the three, Robert Simpson, Henry Pearson and Archibald Morrison. But from the outset Dempsey denied firing the fatal shots and even on the scaffold protested his innocence.

The battle kicked off after a disagreement over a woman in which a sailor punched one of the soldiers who was with infantrymen garrisoned in the town. It quickly escalated, not least after a sailor said Private Robert Surrage, a friend of Dempsey, was a 'Lobster backed bugger'. At one stage a sailor tried pacifying the soldiers by offering them a drink but when he was dragged up a close and given a beating other seamen were joined by trades people, who chased the blood-covered soldiers into a house and besieged it, smashing doors and windows. Suddenly someone shouted, 'Fire' and a series of shots rang out.

By the time the town guard arrived to disarm the soldiers Simpson and Pearson, both watchmen who had tried to stop the fighting, and Morrison, a sailor, lay dead. Dempsey and Surrage were convicted of murder, while four of their comrades were cleared. Surrage was later reprieved and transported after the jury pleaded for him to be shown mercy. The judge who sentenced them said he hoped their executions would, 'Have its due weight upon the country at large and teach the army that the arms they are called to use for the protection of the country were not to be made instruments of oppression upon their fellow subjects.'

While Dempsey admitting firing his musket in self defence, he had denied shooting anybody and in the confusion of the fighting witnesses agreed the soldiers had been badly assaulted and had come under a terrifying attack from the mob. Did he receive a fair trial? Before the evidence began at the High Court in Edinburgh, leaflets lambasting the soldiers had been circulating in central

Scotland, a fact pointed out by the accused men's counsel; nevertheless the proceedings went ahead. Dempsey's last words as he stood on the scaffold with the noose about his neck were, 'I am innocent of the charge against me.'

Dempsey was a stranger to Greenock, where the often raucous behaviour of the soldiers made them few friends and there was little local support for him. That was not the case with fifty-nine-year-old Arthur Woods when he and his thirty-year-old wife Henrietta went on trial for their lives in the High Court at Edinburgh in 1839 for the murder of his son John at their Dundee home. Pedlar John had regularly scrounged money from his father and step-mother, telling them he wanted to start up his own business. Finally the couple who were expecting their third child decided they had had enough and when John turned up one day in late July refused to hand over any more with the result that father and son ended up fighting. A neighbour claimed to have overheard Woods say he would put an end to his son's existence. In the early hours of the morning a week later a policeman heard the sounds of fighting as he passed the Woods' home and about twenty minutes later saw the body of a man lying outside at the bottom of a set of stairs.

Woods told the police he did not know where his son was, while Henrietta admitted John had called but they had refused to let him in. Marks seemingly made by a rope were found around the dead man's neck and a search of Woods' home uncovered pieces that a doctor said fitted the marks. However, Dundee was one of the world's most prominent importers of jute used in rope making and most of the town's population was engaged in its manufacture and had lengths hung up in their homes. John had earlier been seen coming out of a public house and the couple said they believed that after being turned away from their door he had fallen down the stairs and died as a result. However, they were charged with his murder, the trial having to be put back as Henrietta was pregnant, but it went ahead after she gave birth. By majority verdicts the jury decided the case against her was not proven but her husband was guilty and condemned to hang.

Efforts immediately began to win Woods a reprieve; petitions on his behalf were sent to the Home Secretary Lord John Russell and hopes these would succeed rose when experts said the injuries to the dead man were consistent with him having fallen. The *Aberdeen Journal* said, 'Woods still insists that he is innocent and it is thought his sentence will be commuted.' But the outrage caused by the verdict and sentence rose to anger once Russell had rejected the idea of Woods being saved. The *Manchester Times and Gazette* reported, 'There is much in the case of this unfortunate individual calculated to excite a deep interest in his fate and the determination of the Home Secretary has created a very unpleasant feeling generally among the people of Dundee.'

The *Chartist* went even further after Woods was put to death. Under the headline, 'AN INNOCENT MAN HANGED!' it declared, 'If we are not mistaken the execution of this unfortunate man will cause great dissatisfaction throughout the country. We know that everything was done that could be done by Dr Carruthers, the Roman Catholic Bishop of Edinburgh, and eighteen other gentlemen of the greatest eminence and respectability in Scotland, to obtain further time to investigate facts which had come to light since the trial and which convinced them of the innocence of this man not only in Dundee.'

Courts were used to hearing accused people insist on their innocence. Usually clear evidence could be produced of their guilt from eye witnesses or the discovery of items linking them to a victim. However, in 1808 even the trial judge admitted James Gilchrist had been convicted on purely circumstantial evidence, although the absence of corroboration didn't stop him from sentencing Gilchrist to death for the murder of his wife Margaret in a drunken row. The circumstances were simple; stocking maker Gilchrist, aged forty-seven, and his wife frequently rowed after drinking sessions and one January night neighbours in the Slatefield area of Glasgow smelled burning and, going into the Gilchrists' home, found Margaret dead in a chair with her clothes burning. Had Gilchrist beaten her senseless then set her alight to cover his tracks, or had she been drunk and set herself on fire?

He was convicted on the evidence of what neighbours claimed they heard but nobody had witnessed him attacking his wife.

Still, the jury convicted him of murdering Margaret and although the judge told him, 'The evidence against you is circumstantial,' he sentenced him to death. After the verdict was announced Gilchrist told the court, 'There certainly must be some misunderstanding in this case; but I declare before God and this audience, and as I have to answer to God at the day of judgement, I am as innocent of this crime as the child unborn.' And on his way to the scaffold at Glasgow in July Gilchrist was said by the Annual Register for 1810 to have told the Lord Provost, 'My Lord, you are parting with an innocent man.'

29

MAD HATTERS

They were the hours of hope, the last of the old year and first of the new, a time for fun, good wishes and friendliness. But in Edinburgh the celebrations would herald evil and murder because for weeks adolescent firebrands had been plotting to wage a campaign of mayhem against law and order. And now it had kicked off and was out of control. Blockmaker's apprentice John Thomson would later tell a packed High Court, guarded by 100 soldiers from the 1st Regiment of Royal Edinburgh Volunteers, that during the dying moments of 31 December 1811 he was in the city centre when he watched a mob armed with bludgeons pursue a man into Assembly Close, where he was knocked down. He saw police watchman Dugaid Campbell – nicknamed the Royal Arch – chased by a howling pack near the Stamp Office Close, where he was tripped and fell and then was kicked and set on with some of the crowd screaming 'Take his life' and when he went to the officer's aid Thomson too was beaten. Suddenly a roar was heard from the direction of the Tron Church, sending most of the attackers off in that direction, allowing Thomson to help Campbell, badly bleeding from a gash to the head, stagger to the nearest police office where he collapsed and was taken to hospital only to die three days later.

Harmless students who had gone into the city to enjoy the

festivities said they were confronted by gangs, threatened and robbed. And it emerged that at the height of the trouble brave Campbell had ignored warnings from other officers not to tackle the rioters but had waded in, telling them, 'Damn the fear.' Other witnesses told how weeks before the new year a gang known as 'Kellies' had been overheard scheming to 'give the police a licking', some promising to 'have a good hat'. The plan had been for a full-scale attack on the police with Campbell, who had a reputation for coming down hard on young miscreants, being singled out for revenge. Now he was dead and a murder investigation was launched. It led to a number of arrests, but so many crimes had been committed that trials were delayed as prosecutors interviewed scores of witnesses.

First to appear in court in March was gunmaker's apprentice John Skelton, who denied three charges of robbery, including one of stealing an empty purse from penniless divinity student William Jolly. Witnesses spoke of being beaten unconscious by mobs of up to fifty 'lads', their pockets rifled while they were helpless and of seeing young men climb trees to snap off branches and break them into clubs with which to batter bystanders. One of Skelton's friends said the plan had been to 'steal gentlemen's hats' and wear them as souvenirs.

Skelton was found guilty and the jury asked for him to be shown mercy. However, in a warning of what was to come for the others who were yet to appear in court, he was sentenced to be hanged at Edinburgh on 15 April.

Just over two weeks later it was the turn of five more rioters to face the music. Hugh McIntosh, Neil Sutherland, Hugh McDonald, George Napier and John Grotto faced eleven charges, the first being the murder of Dugaid Campbell, the second of knocking down and robbing solicitor's clerk Roger Hog Lawrie. Other charges on the indictment alleged that they knocked down and robbed ensign Humphrey Cochrane of the Renfrew Militia; knocked down and robbed Gustavus Richard Alexander of property including his hat; knocked down and robbed Francis James Hughes near the Tron Church of his watch, gold seals and hat; assaulted and robbed Nigel Allan, manager of the

Hercules Insurance Company of a watch, gold chain and seals and money; knocked down and robbed Duncan Ferguson near Barclay's Tavern in Adam's Square; assaulted and robbed David Scott Kinloch of his hat and other property; knocked down and robbed John Buchan Brodie of gold seals, money and his hat; assaulted and robbed medical student Duncan McLauchlan of his handkerchief, gloves and hat; and knocked down and robbed another medical student, Peter Bruce, of his money and hat.

Significantly, the indictment added, 'And all the said acts of robbery, or one or other of them, were committed by all and each or by one or other of you in furtherance of previous agreement or plan; to which plan or agreement, you were, all and each, or one or other of you, parties.'

They all denied murdering Campbell and committing the robberies except Napier, who admitted the offence involving Bruce and Grotto and who pleaded guilty to attacking and robbing Brodie. One after another witnesses trooped into the courtroom to describe being beaten, kicked, punched, threatened and robbed during the rampage of terror.

It was a well-organised plot in which the rioters were divided into three gangs – Niddry Street, Canongate and Grassmarket – each carrying a distinctive whistle that was to be blown as a signal to the others as to where to move next. They carried weapons, mostly wooden clubs, and even a saw. The plan had been for a full-scale assault on the police, the mob meeting at nine o'clock on 31 December and whatever was taken was to be given to sixteen-year-old McIntosh, who would divide it up the next day. However, it ended up with most of the loot packed into two trunks and sent to Glasgow, the new arrangement being for it to be sold to fences there dealing in stolen property and the proceeds returned to Edinburgh and shared out. However, here the conspiracy foundered. McIntosh had arranged for it to be handled by John Lyall in Glasgow. Lyall and his brother Adam had been indicted at Edinburgh in 1811 accused of highway robbery (see Chapter 19) but John had managed to convince doctors he was insane and so escaped the death sentence passed on Adam, who was hanged in Edinburgh in March 1811. John had adopted the false surname of Duncanson but after being set free had again been arrested in Glasgow and was in jail in the city facing another robbery allegation.

John had asked a woman friend, Janet Gemmell, who lived in Glasgow and who visited him while he was in prison, to go to a coaching stop, collect a trunk, open it and bring him the contents. She told the murder trial she had taken the trunk to her mother's home and on opening it had been 'astonished' to discover an array of watches, gold, bank notes, silver and other items. She gave some of the contents to John but claimed she refused to have anything to do with most of it. She gave one of the watches to a soldier who discovered it had been stolen in Edinburgh and, fearing repercussions, took it to magistrates in Glasgow and gave details of how he came to have it. That led police to Gemmell and Lyall who, it was discovered, had been shouting from his cell window to associates in the street outside to come and visit him and when they did were given watches and gold to sell and return the money to him. Following the riot, McIntosh and McDonald had moved to Glasgow, where their links with Lyall led to their arrests.

McIntosh and nineteen-year-olds McDonald and Sutherland were convicted of robbery and McIntosh of murdering Campbell. They already knew what their fate would be but before their death sentences were formally pronounced had to listen to the angry words of the judges who had conducted the trial. Lord Armadale told them, 'Ever since I have had the honour of sitting on the bench, I have never seen any case more alarming, more distressing or more criminal. The atrocities you committed were the consequences of a deep laid plan.'

Lord Meadowbank said it was the fact that some of the accused had been given a good education that had enabled them to organise the plot. 'I am at a loss for terms to express my indignation at the conduct of parents who allow their children without restraint to follow, as by their own declarations these boys have done, lewd women and idle associations.' He also blamed employers for not keeping a closer eye on what their apprentices got up to out of hours. And he said the spot where they were executed should be at the scene of their crimes. 'The blood which has stained our streets and which cries for vengeance should be expiated on the spot where it was shed.'

Lord Gillies told the trio, 'You have been found guilty of crimes the mention of which ought to make the blood curdle in the veins of boys like you. It is astonishing that, armed as you were, more murders were not committed.'

Skelton was reprieved on 6 April and he along with Bruce and Grotto and two others, Robert Gunn and Alexander MacDonald, would all be transported for life to Australia. However, unlike Skelton, who had the advantage of the jury's mercy plea, McIntosh, Sutherland and McDonald were never in any doubt that salvation was a distant dream. On the day of their execution the route from the Edinburgh Tolbooth to the spot opposite Stamp Office Close was lined by hundreds of troops – men from the Perth and Renfrewshire Militia, Royal Edinburgh Volunteers, the 1st Regiment of Edinburgh Local Militia and members of the 6th Dragoon Guards were stationed in Nicolson Street while police officers mingled among the enormous crowds. The three had refused the offer of being carried to the gallows in a coach, instead deciding to walk, McIntosh and Sutherland in blue coats and pantaloons with white vests, McDonald in a blue coat with white trousers. All wore white gloves. A church bell tolled as they reached the scaffold where, after shaking hands, they were simultaneously launched into eternity

Later that year, a book about the trial published by William Reid of Leith commented, 'These young men by their own confession had lived very thoughtlessly for some time past. They frequently and painfully acknowledged even before their trial, that they were very guilty before the great Searcher of their hearts; that the first cause of their ruin was listening to the solicitations of an artful and dangerous class of females who lay in wait for them, to invite them to their rooms and to drink with them.'

Meanwhile the remarkable saga of John Lyall continued. Convicted of robbery he was transported to New South Wales in 1813 from where he eventually escaped and managed to make his way back to Britain where, to avoid another brush with the gallows, he enlisted as a soldier.

Too often celebrations ended in tragedy and even an apparently innocent day out could lead to the scaffold. Alexander Cain had gone to watch a hanging but found himself at the end of a rope being executed just two months before McIntosh, Sutherland and McDonald. Cain was an itinerant who had been hanging around central Scotland for some time, his scruffy appearance arousing suspicion. He had been seen at Falkirk Tryst, a major cattle market in the town to which drovers, many from the Highlands, took livestock every year for sale to dealers looking for supplies to send on to the great cities of Scotland and northern England. One of those dealers was Archibald Stewart, and he had had a particularly successful time. His pockets bulged with more than £1,000 in cash (£72,000) along with other bills made out to him and he was intent on enjoying himself. Crafty Cain had spotted the dealer counting as payments were being made and when Stewart headed for Stirling to watch the double execution of Robert Anderson and James Menzies for housebreaking and theft Cain followed.

After the two had been put to death in October 1811 Stewart met up with a prostitute and would later claim the two only had a drink together. He had called in at public houses for a dram or two but insisted he was not drunk when some hours after the hanging he was suddenly set upon in a back street after going out to check his horse, stunned by a blow to the head. He then felt his pockets being searched. By the time he came to, his money was gone. Police found it relatively easy to follow Stewart, who had most of the stolen cash; he headed south-west towards Dumfries often stopping along the way at public houses or tolls to change some of the notes, and was finally arrested and thrown into Dumfries jail. His stupidity was hard to believe. In prison he first told a police sergeant guarding him that, 'He wished he had given him 100 guineas the day he took him to let him make his escape.' The sergeant pointed out others were also on guard duty and so Cain tried again, telling him, 'I think I could trust you with a secret, if you would keep it, it would make you up for life, and save me.' If the sergeant would keep his secret, Cain promised him £400 but when asked if this was part of the money taken from the cattle dealer at Stirling, blurted, 'Don't, don't ask that question; you shall have an equal share.' It was as good as putting the rope around his own neck, and Cain was later convicted of robbery and hanged on the same scaffold where he had watched Anderson and Menzies die.

Markets and fairs were a feature of Georgian and Victorian life, the chance to meet up with friends, enjoy games and compete in dancing and sports contests. Mostly they went off peacefully although from time to time drink caused the merriment to develop into violence. Such was the case at St Boswell's Fair in the Borders in 1849 when a huge mob of Irishmen, mostly railway workers and at least 300 strong, rioted and attacked a contingent of twenty-two police officers who had arrested one of their number. After breaking up a fight two policemen arrested one of the belligerents and were taking him to a barn, their temporary headquarters for the day, when a crowd gathered and immediately matters became ugly. At the later trial in Jedburgh the *Caledonian Mercury* reported that witnesses spoke of the mob screaming, 'Killing, killing,' rushing forward to rescue the prisoner and battering the arresting officers. Other police rushed for safety into the barn and were attacked by rioters wielding sticks, clubs and stones. The terrifying barrage only calmed down when a senior officer decided to free the prisoner.

Local blacksmith John Lauder had been enjoying himself at the fair when the trouble erupted. Lauder was not involved in the fracas but witnesses alleged some of the rioters, including Irishman John Wilson, aged twenty, had turned on him and he was fatally smashed over the head with a club, blood soaking his clothing. In court when his father was shown his son's bloodied coat and asked to identify it he broke down in tears. Wilson and fellow railway labourer John Brady were accused of murdering Lauder. They denied the charge but were convicted and sentenced to death at which Brady burst into tears. He would later be reprieved and transported for life to Australia. Wilson insisted he was innocent but his claims and a recommendation from the jury that he be shown mercy were ignored. He went to his death at Jedburgh in October 1849 and seconds before the noose was put around his neck said, 'I am going to be launched into eternity to face my God, and I am not going with a lie in my mouth. I neither lifted stick nor stone on the fair day. I am about to suffer for another man.' Guards surrounding the gallows were said to have fainted as the body swung gently, but Irish workers stayed away from the grim scene, a handful arriving after it was over.

Not far from St Bowell's and at the foot of the Lammermuir Hills lies the ancient town of Lauder. In 1826 cow-feeder James Hunter had enjoyed a day at the annual fair and was walking home to Edinburgh when he was attacked by three men. Hunter's pockets had been filled with most of his savings; he was intent on having a good time but had spent very little and now after a ten-mile walk suddenly found himself beaten to the ground, his pockets rifled and the robbers disappearing into nearby fields with all his money and even his umbrella. Bloodied and shocked he was helped by other travellers to nearby houses, where locals went off to fetch police. Two days later Andrew Fullarton and James Renton were arrested but police still sought the leader of the gang, James Reid.

After a trial at Edinburgh Renton walked free, the jury deciding the prosecution case was not proven, but Fullarton was found guilty and burst into tears when he was sentenced to hang. A plea for him to be reprieved mainly on the grounds of his youth – he was aged twenty-two – was made to the government, but his refusal to implicate Reid or tell the police where Reid had gone went against him. With just days to go before his death Reid was caught but hopes by Fullarton that he would earn him a reprieve by confessing to being the principal fell on stony ground. If there was honour among thieves, it vanished when the noose went about Fullarton's neck and he was sent off to eternity.

30

THE DREAMER

From time to time police forces, baffled in their search to find a dead body, have called in the services of a clairvoyant. There have even been occasional claims that this odd strategy has worked. In March 1831 the body of pedlar Murdo Grant was discovered floating near the banks of Loch-tor-na-egin in Sutherland. It was soon clear he had been badly beaten about the head and dragged through heather, then dumped into the water. There were no other clues as to who the killer might have been but Murdo's pack was missing and police reasoned that if they could find it then it might well lead them to his murderer. As April dawned the trail seemed to have gone cold but then Kenneth Fraser, a local man well known for visions that appeared in his dreams and which sometimes gave predictions as to the futures of people in the district, came forward with a remarkable story.

Fraser was known as 'The Dreamer' and said he knew where the dead man's pack was to be found because he had seen the hiding place in a dream. What was so astonishing was that he'd had his dream in February – the pedlar had been killed after this, in March, a fact that was later confirmed by the man responsible for his death and who had been caught as a direct consequence of Fraser's vision. Former schoolmaster Hugh Macleod, aged twenty-two, at first denied being the culprit but eventually made a full confession.

At the accused's murder trial in Inverness the *Caledonian Mercury* reported Fraser's amazing evidence. 'I was at home when I had the dream in the month of February. It was said to me in my sleep by a voice like a man's that the pack was lying in such a place. I got a sight of the place just as if I had been awake; I never saw the place before. The voice said, in Gaelic, "The pack of the merchant is lying in a cairn of stones in a hole near their house." The voice did not name the Macleods, but I got a sight of the ground, fronting the south, with the sun shining on it and a burn running beneath Macleod's house. I took the officer to the place I had got a sight of. It was on the south-west side of Loch-tor-na-egin. We found nothing there. We went to search on the south side of the burn. I had not seen this place in my dream. It was not far from the place in my dream that the things were found, there were five silk handkerchiefs lying in a hole.'

Macleod's home was close to the spot where the handkerchiefs were discovered and police decided to search the property, uncovering hidden blood-stained clothing. Macleod was convicted of murder and sentenced to hang, protesting he was innocent, but finally he admitted being responsible, saying he had been short of money and had tricked his victim into meeting him by the side of the loch on the pretext of buying the entire contents of his pack, then smashing him over the head with a hammer hidden in his coat. And just as The Dreamer had seen, he hid the pack in a cairn of stones near his home. He added, 'No person in court was more astonished at Fraser's evidence than I was.'

Judges had ordered Macleod's body to be handed over for dissection and a broadside published after his execution at Edinburgh in October revealed his ignominious ending. 'His body, after hanging three quarters of an hour, was cut down, placed in a coffin, and taken to the jail. It was then crammed into a square box, and a couple of pecks of salt thrown over it and sent in a cart to Edinburgh as neither carrier, coach nor ship could be got to take it.'

Five days previously, another killer whose case prominently featured a dream had been put to death, this time 200 miles away at Jedburgh. Thomas Rogers, a Coldstream carter, had been with a group of local men when they became involved in a violent argument with a party of Irishmen who had travelled to the Borders hoping for farm work during the harvest season. Stones were thrown at the Scots, who retaliated by chasing after the Irishmen. They caught Neil McKernon, who was severely battered unconscious with a stick by Rogers. As he lay helpless the injured man was again attacked by Rogers and later died.

The *York Herald and General Advertiser*, reporting on Rogers' trial when he was convicted of murder, stated, 'During the time of his confinement in jail, Rogers has repeatedly declared that the whole transactions connected with the murder of McKernon were to him like a dream; and that when he awakened from sleep the morning after the crime was committed, upon putting on his clothes and finding them wet, he asserted he had no knowledge of being in the water in pursuit of the Irishman, and was quite unconscious of having stained his hands in the blood of a fellow creature.'

There were two other odd features of the tragedy. Rogers had a bizarre fixation with executions and in 1822 after watching the hanging of William Robertson in Jedburgh for housebreaking had been desperate to get his hands on the rope which was used, even bargaining with the jailer who eventually agreed to sell it. And aware of considerable local interest in his own execution had sat in prison for his portrait to be painted two days before he was put to death.

There were times when canny Scots took one look at their compatriots and instantly felt uneasy. That was so in 1814 when Andrew Black and his friend Samuel Payne had passed two men on a road to the south-east of Edinburgh and the former had commented to Payne, 'Those are gallows looking fellows.' His prediction was appallingly correct. The previous day Irishmen Thomas Kelly and Henry O'Neil had committed two violent and terrifying robberies. Their first victim was schoolmaster William Welch, viciously attacked as he walked to his home, one of the assailants putting a pistol to his head and threatening to kill him if he resisted. Welch was robbed of his watch, money, coat, shoes, gaiters, hat and even his wig, although the assailants came back and returned it. Soon afterwards they pounced on two farmworkers near Haddington, taking their money and badly beating them before running off with gaiters, an umbrella and a pair of shoes.

Next day they were looking for more victims as they passed Black and Payne, whose description was about to once again prove chillingly true. The Irishmen were hardly out of sight before Black and Payne heard screams and ran towards them, Kelly and O'Neil passing them heading in the opposite direction. Lying in a ditch covered in blood was carter David Loch, who had been dragged from his horse and bludgeoned with a club then robbed.

When they appeared in the High Court at Edinburgh convicted of highway robbery, the pair pleaded for mercy but were shown none, the judge ordering the erection of a gallows half a mile south of Morningside, where Loch had been almost killed. On a cold afternoon in January 1815 the 'gallows looking fellows', both in their fifties, were slowly hauled in a cart accompanied by an immense crowd along snow-covered roads to their doom at three o'clock.

The vast majority of criminals did their best to evade arrest. Seaman David Balfour actually ran to prison to hand himself in after murdering his wife Margaret at the home of his in-laws in Dundee in 1826. While he was at sea Balfour had moodily told shipmates he suspected the wife he loved was having affairs with others during his absences. His skipper had told him, 'David, man, you a sailor and break your heart for a woman! Cannot you engage yourself on board some foreign vessel, and leave her to her own doings?' Balfour had told the captain, 'That would be no use, even at the furthest extremity of the globe she would be as much in my thoughts as if she was in the room beside me. I have no happiness away from her.' Lovesick, he returned to Dundee and begged his wife to give up seeing other men, but she had refused.

He had called in a family friend, Margaret Ireland, telling her, 'I'll be in jail tomorrow.' Then he went to see his wife, pleading with her to sleep with him, saying, 'Oh my dear, can I not gain your heart?' only to be coldly told, 'Not tonight.'

Next morning he went to a butcher's shop and asked for a knife, saying it was needed to 'kill a beast' and soon after this at the home of her father Margaret screamed out she had been murdered by her husband. Twenty minutes later breathless Balfour banged on the door of Dundee jail and told turnkey Charles Watson, 'Let me in, I've murdered my wife.' By then a doctor had confirmed Margaret was dead, a terrible stab wound penetrating through her ribs and lungs and into her heart.

Balfour, who killed because of love, was executed in Dundee in June 1826, the *Caledonian Mercury* reporting, 'He seems, from the beginning, to have made up his mind to the fate which awaited him; and yet, in the full possession of his faculties, he resolved to pay the forfeit, in order that he might avenge himself for what his feelings had suffered from the unfaithfulness of one whom he loved. He has all along declared that he was, even to the last moment of her life, prepared to forgive his wife, had she shown any wish to give up with her other associates, and to live with him; but her indifference and contempt were what he could not bear.'

Like that of Balfour, marriages that went wrong all too often had tragic endings. James and Catherine Humphrey had a relationship that would nowadays be described as 'open' in that sometimes she slept with her husband, a former soldier, and at others with one of his employees, James Petrie, at the public house they ran in Aberdeen. The Humphreys drank a lot and often argued, she at one time threatening to cut his throat and on another telling Petrie, 'Lord God if any person would give him poison and keep her hand clear of it.' She had once said to a customer that, 'Arsenic is the best thing for that scoundrel,' while he had retorted that she would 'hang with her face down in Marischal Street' – the usual place for executions.

One night in April 1830 Petrie had been waiting for Catherine to join him in bed when she asked him to look at her husband, who seemed to be ill. According to the *Morning Post* Petrie said at Catherine's later trial for murder that she was smiling as she showed him James 'writhing from side to side and foaming at the mouth'. A doctor was called but quickly realised sulphuric acid had been poured down Humphrey's throat while he slept and although he was taken to hospital he died two days later. Just as her husband had predicted, Catherine, fifty-one, was hanged in Marischal Street.

A year later, Thomas Gow, whose marriage to his wife Georgina had badly deteriorated due to his heavy drinking, went berserk and killed her at their home in Edinburgh High Street and in doing so fulfilled a prediction to Georgina that he would, 'Hang at the head of Libberton's Wynd for her.' A neighbour, Alexander Polson, had heard her screams for help and rushed to try to save her as a consequence of which he was himself badly stabbed, with doctors at one point fearing for his life. There was never any doubt over Gow's guilt, the only question being whether he might be declared insane, but once he was confirmed as having been aware of what he was doing he was condemned. Telling him he was to be hanged, the judge reminded Gow, 'You rashly and precipitously and regardless of the attempts made by the unfortunate man to rescue your wife, imbrued your hands in the blood of her, who, by every tie of nature and humanity you were bound to have defended even at the risk of your own life.' As he was being led off to the condemned cell Gow told a jailer, 'The game is up, all is over, my wife has put an iron ring on my leg but I put a gold ring on her finger.'

Thomas Miller was working at his weaver's loom in Girvan, Ayrshire, one evening in December 1853, chatting to his fellow worker Janet Cunningham as she told him about her marriage woes. She said she had left her husband Alexander on a number of occasions because he had often been violent to her. Janet said she'd always gone back to him but had now told her husband she was finally leaving him for good. She said to Thomas the announcement had angered Alexander, who had muttered threats against her. It was dark outside and the weavers worked by candlelight when suddenly Miller heard a bang, a shot and to his horror turned to see blood pouring from Janet's chest. 'Tom, Tom!' she cried and he grasped her but within seconds she was dead.

Unknown to her Alexander had earlier predicted her and his own fates, saying to a friend he wanted to shoot his wife and was told, 'Do not let such thoughts enter your head or else they will hang you.'

Even more chilling were the words of the dead woman's sister, Agnes, at the trial in Ayr the following year of Cunningham for murder. 'Two months before she was murdered I heard him threaten her and say he would be hanged for her,' said Agnes. 'She said she was afraid he would shoot her through the window when she was sitting at her loom.' Inquiries showed that Cunningham, aged thirty-six, had borrowed a gun, sneaked into a garden next to where the weavers were working, thrown gravel at the window to attract Janet's attention and fired. He was hanged at Ayr in May 1854.

While all of these predictions had come true another would not and it was perhaps the strangest of all. In April 1837, Alexander Miller, known by the nickname of 'Scatters', was hanged at Edinburgh for the brutal murder near Denny of elderly William Jarvie. The two had quarrelled after Jarvie complained he was being bullied and later that night noted troublemaker Miller turned up at the home of a friend whose daughter, Susan Brown, immediately realised something was wrong. Miller had been drinking and she asked him what he had done. Susan told his murder trial in the High Court in Edinburgh about their conversation. 'He said, "Wish to God that your soul may be damned in Hell to all eternity if you tell and I'll tell you." I refused to be sworn to silence. He told me, "Say as sure as death you will not tell." I said I would keep his secret and he said, "I've killed Willie Jarvie. I broke into his house and he came and catched me and I took a paling slab and drove in his skull."'

After the discovery of Jarvie's body a police officer went to arrest Miller, who fled out of a back door dressed in women's clothing. Up to forty local people joined in the chase after him but it was four hours and fifteen miles later before he was caught hiding in a ditch wearing a woman's gown and hat. He was found guilty by a majority verdict and Lord Medwyn told him, 'I think you went only to commit a minor offence but on being detected by the old man, in order to remove a dangerous witness hesitated not to commit murder. It is somehow ordained in the providence that directs the affairs of this world that a murderer seldom escapes, that the blood which is shed seems to cry from the ground for vengeance.' And the sentencing judge, Lord Meadowbank, said, 'You stand there a most extraordinary and miserable example, an example the like of which I have never witnessed before.'

But something extraordinary was yet to occur as the *Caledonian Mercury* described at his execution before a huge crowd at Stirling. 'On his coming to the platform, contrary to the usual practice, the executioner placed the rope round his neck and the cap over his face. This was said to be a precaution ordered by the magistrates, in case he should attempt to bolt as he was known to be of running propensities. Mr Leitch (one of the ministers) offered up a most suitable and appropriate prayer, which seemed to be more responded to by the audience than by the unhappy man in whose behalf it was uttered. At its commencement he, by rubbing the one foot against the other, was enabled to put off his shoes, which he kicked from him to a considerable distance. This was done, it is said, to falsify a prediction made by an old woman on whom he had been playing off some cruel sport that "he would die with his shoes on yet", meaning he would be hanged.'

31

KILLED BY KINDNESS

Can kindness kill? Scattered among the hundreds who have climbed the grim steps to Scotland's gibbets are those who have died either because of their own kindness or through that of others to them. For example William Baird and Walter Blair might almost have been looked on as nineteenth-century Robin Hoods, but instead of their generosity winning the hand of a beautiful Maid Marion it cost them their lives.

In 1817 the *Glasgow Herald* reported on an extraordinary incident at Haghill. As John Somerville, who worked for a wealthy estate owner, was on his way to guard sheep, part of a flock that had recently been rustled, he was confronted by two well-dressed men who held a pistol to his heart and demanded his money. 'He told them he had none and that they had more need to give him money than to take anything from him,' the newspaper reported. 'After searching him and finding that he had told the truth one of them gave him sixpence and told him to be off.' And off the astonished man went, but not to match the generosity of his would-be robbers. Instead, he ran for help, collected three of his fellow workers, a firelock and a dog and went back to the spot where he had been held up.

'After searching about two hours his party met the villains. Somerville went up to them and said, "You are not robbers now," on which the one who had presented the pistol to his breast instantly fled but he called to him to stop or he would blow his brains out. The fellow, however, still continuing to run, ordered the dog to catch him, which he very soon did and drove him headlong into a ditch by which his arm was dislocated.'

As the two villains were being arrested by Somerville and his colleagues, quarry worker Richard Ferrie appeared complaining he had been robbed of two pounds of gunpowder and instantly recognised the pair; a search of their pockets produced the missing gunpowder. The newspaper named Baird and Blair as the kind-hearted scoundrels and it turned out that by the time of their trial for robbery other victims had come forward. There were so many witnesses that there was little point in their denying the charges and so both pleaded guilty, knowing this would bring certain death sentences but it gave them hope that they might later be reprieved.

It was a distant prospect, however, despite the jury recommending mercy, and when it was clear that salvation had passed them by they made a dramatic last-minute attempt to escape from prison at Glasgow. The *Caledonian Mercury* described it as 'foolish' but it was also daring. The day before they were to be hanged, 'A boy was introduced into their cell, accompanied by a turnkey and two soldiers with drawn bayonets, for the purpose of shaving them; and they were about to leave the cell when one of the prisoners asked change for a shilling. The turnkey was turning over some copper in his hand, looking for two sixpences, when Blair presented a pistol at his breast and ordered him to give up the keys.' But the attention of the prisoners was distracted when the pistol was handed to Baird and the turnkey took advantage of the situation to grapple with Blair. The *Caledonian Mercury* continued, 'The soldiers ran to the end of the passage and with their bayonets barricaded the back of the door; and the boy crying out in terror, the alarm was given to the people on the outside. When assistance came the keys were thrown out at a window by the turnkey. On searching the cell a pair of common pistols were found. They were loaded with powder, and pieces of pewter, which the prisoners said they procured by breaking down their spoons.'

Baird and Blair, both in their early twenties, at first refused to tell how they were able to get the guns, but with all hope of freedom gone said friends had waited outside the prison at midnight, thrown a length of string in through their cell window and once the two had this they had attached the guns so they could be pulled up. Asked who the friends were, the doomed men claimed they were sympathetic soldiers. Although the authorities doubted the story, they were taking no chances; extra Dragoons and police being drafted in to guard the scaffold. Baird in particular was well educated, from a respectable family and with many clever and resourceful associates, but the execution in front of the jail went off without trouble.

Five years later Francis Cain, aged seventeen, discovered there was no reward for kindness. The young cotton spinner had been one of a gang of seven teenagers who set upon businessman James Maxwell near Shawfield, Glasgow, one night in June 1823 as he walked home after dining at the home of a friend. Maxwell would later tell a court he was repeatedly knocked down, robbed of his gold watch and chain, hat and money, and as a result of injuries to his head and shoulders inflicted with a club bedridden for nearly a fortnight. The gang split up after sharing out the loot, each getting one pound, but most of them were caught and two gave evidence against the others to save themselves. Both admitted some in the gang had not wanted Maxwell attacked.

Cain was sentenced to death after being convicted of assault and in the condemned cell at Glasgow, with time running out, and nothing to gain, made a remarkable confession in which he said, 'I freely acknowledge that I got a fair trial and I forgive my enemies and all those who have borne evidence against me. I regret exceedingly that Mr Maxwell was so much hurt but I declare in the face of that awful tribunal before which I am about to appear, that I never struck nor abused Mr Maxwell. I took nothing from his person – on the contrary I advised my companions not to rob him.' His solicitor said Cain wanted it known that just before the attack he had offered to share out to the others a few shillings he had in his pocket if they left Maxwell alone.

Cain was executed at Glasgow alongside twenty-year-old

George Laidlaw, who had been sentenced for housebreaking, and there was considerable ill feeling in the city over the decision to execute them. On the scaffold near Glasgow Green the two were deep in prayer when they were told it was time for them to die. A large number of women were said to be moaning and crying, and when their prayers were disturbed many in the crowd muttered angrily and shouted 'shame' while others cried.

Just as kindness cost culprits their lives, more often than not it led to the deaths of the kind. In 1843 James Bryce demonstrated particular callousness to his sixty-year-old brother-in-law John Geddes, who had helped him out in the past by lending him money, a loan that had not been repaid. What seemed to make the crime he would commit all the worse was that it was carried out at Christmas. Bryce, aged forty-four, was an unpleasant character. After the death of his first wife, who gave him four children, he set up home with Geddes' half sister and together they had three more children. He later admitted, 'She has often warned me about my wicked life, and advised me to leave it off and go to church. She is not to blame in any way for my present condition, for had I taken her advice I would never have done anything wrong.' By his condition he meant lying in a condemned cell awaiting the hangman's noose.

Broke and out of work, Bryce relied on handouts from relatives to keep the family going, admitting the husband of his sister had been 'kind and often supported us with meat' and that, 'I had, too, sometimes got assistance from John Geddes, and at one time I got one pound from him and left him my watch as a pledge. After that I sent my daughter to him and got another pound.' Geddes might not have been the most generous of souls, but he had also paid school fees for the Bryce children and his help was about to cost him his life.

Bryce had gone back to visit him at remote Blaw Weary, West Calder, West Lothian, and, after a series of requests for more money, had been turned down, concocted a vile lie, saying one of his children had died and he needed a pound to bury her. His host had given him bed and board but was adamant that until the first loan was repaid nothing more would be forthcoming.

He was suspicious of the story that Bryce wanted to buy a coffin for the dead child, especially when the cost began dropping until it reached five shillings. Raging at being knocked back, when Geddes' back was turned as he made up the fire, Bryce admitted in a statement to police, 'It came into my heart to murder him,' and so he picked up a set of fire tongs, brutally and repeatedly smashed his victim over the head, then seeing signs of life took a cord and strangled him.

After taking what money he could find as well as the dead man's shoes Bryce went walkabout through central and southern Scotland while, following the discovery of the murdered man's body, police searched for him. He was finally tracked down and arrested in Dumfries. High Court jurors at Edinburgh who convicted him of murder were said by reporters to be upset, with some in tears when they returned their unanimous verdict before a packed court. The judge told the doomed man whose hanging was later watched by 30,000 people at Libberton's Wynd, 'You are to pass in the period specified in your sentence into the presence of Almighty God, in presence of that great being who can destroy not only the body but the spirit and by whose unerring wisdom the punishment due to the guilty is brought to pass. What do you suppose when this awful sentence is executed and when the first sight of eternity bursts on your bewildered soul?'

Landlady Janet Anderson was another whose generosity proved her undoing when she was brutally murdered by a man to whom she had shown nothing but kindness. The elderly woman took in occasional lodgers at her home in Buttergask near Blackford in Perth and Kinross, and was not averse to giving a bite to eat to men and women down on their luck who called at her door as they tramped Scotland in search of work. One of her lodgers had been Irishman John Kellocher, aged twenty-six, who had stayed with her with fellow workers helping to build the Scottish Central Railway. One day he announced to friends he wanted to go fishing in Ireland, where a good catch would be more profitable than railway wages. The venture was a disaster and Kellocher returned to Scotland in late 1848 almost penniless.

However, he had a plan to resolve his cash problem and it

was revealed at his murder trial in Perth in May the following year when his fishing companion Patrick McKean recollected some of the conversation as they wandered along a road outside Perth. 'He said he would murder the woman to get money. He meant Janet Anderson. I thought he was joking. I left him in consequence of what he said. I ran before him as I was afraid he would kill somebody on the road.'

But in a confession to police following his arrest, Kellocher confirmed he had not been joking, saying he had gone to Janet's with the intention of killing the old woman and robbing her, but she had invited him in and been so kind to him, giving him bread and milk and saying how sorry she felt for him and hoped his bad luck would soon change for the better that he couldn't bring himself to harm her and when he left she even gave him her blessing. But he had only gone a few yards when his feelings of warmth towards her changed to evil and he turned, went back and murdered her. He had thought nobody would see him because her neighbours were in church that morning but on a hill overlooking Janet's house William Eadie, aged eleven, was herding cattle and saw him enter and leave. The boy's evidence and that of others who saw the killer later in the day set police on his trail and he was arrested in a boarding house in Glasgow and hanged at Perth.

The horrific manner of Janet's death shocked her community, but even greater was the outrage that followed the murders in October 1852 at Kittybrewster, Aberdeen, of elderly widow Barbara Ross and her six-year-old grandson John. The killer was 51-year-old George Christie, who had served in India in the Bengal Artillery for twenty-seven years, at one time briefly reaching the rank of sergeant before being demoted for misconduct. When he left the service he received a pension of a shilling a day but found himself destitute when he lost the right to the money after being jailed for theft. Freed from prison he returned to his native Aberdeenshire, where he found occasional work at one stage near Kittybrewster and taking his meals at Barbara's home. He watched one evening as she counted her cash, a fatal mistake on her part because desperate for money he went to her home, slaughtered her with an axe and then set about the help-less boy, knowing the youngster could recognise him. Christie was still in the house when a farmer friend of the widow looked through her window and saw him wandering about inside holding a candle at which point he ran for help. By the time it arrived Christie had gone but he was arrested the next morning, his clothes bloodstained and in his pockets a ring belonging to the dead woman and her money.

While he waited in jail to be hanged Christie tried for a time to starve himself to death, telling warders he was a fiend who could not bear thinking about what he had done to the boy. The *Aberdeen Journal*, reporting his execution at Aberdeen in January 1853 said, 'The crowd numbered probably some 8,000 composed largely of working people and the class who usually frequent such scenes. When the wretched man sunk below the platform, it was remarked that scarcely a single expression of sympathy was uttered for the murderer – an indication of the universal abhor-rence of his dreadful and fearfully aggravated crimes.'

William Noble was another whose conscience beat down upon him as he languished in prison waiting to be launched into eternity. In 1834 the twenty-year-old soldier had deserted from the Sutherland Highlanders at Fort George and was in need of help and money. He knew he was in for a savage whipping if he was caught because he had deserted previously and been branded with a 'D'.

In the past kindly William Ritchie had helped him when he had been on the run after absconding from his regiment, helping him evade army searchers by warning him soldiers were in the area looking for him. Now Noble was again on the run and, desperately needing money to get away, hung about Elgin one night resolving to rob the first person he met.

He told police he spotted a man and in the moonlight thought he might be a soldier, so he battered him to death with a club. It was only later that he found his victim had been penniless Ritchie walking home from work to his waiting family. 'I'm very sorry, he was a real fine man,' he said in a statement after being caught when he went to Fort George pretending to be somebody else. To show his contrition was genuine he wrote a letter of apology to his victim's widow and begged her forgiveness. He also asked to meet Jessie Smith, a teenage girl whose evidence that she had spotted him near the murder scene about the time of the killing was vitally important in his conviction. Jessie was taken to Inverness prison where Noble was said to have assured her he knew she had spoken the truth and before they parted shaken her hand.

On the scaffold he had another message, telling a vast crowd that included many young people, 'I hope you will all take warning by my fate. Avoid drunkenness and bad companions and breaking the Sabbath. It was drunkenness that was the cause of my ruin and that brought me to this.'

It was not the first time that the authorities had allowed a face-to-face meeting between victim and culprit. In 1829 glazier John Craig, aged thirty-four, and forty-year-old labourer James Brown had broken into the home at Paisley of bleacher William Robertson and badly battered him on the head with a club. When his sister Elizabeth went to his aid she too was smashed over the head and hit in the face, the attackers making off with a number of valuable items including a set of silver spoons. Newspaper reports about the attack described the pair and an accomplice, and as a result they were recognised by fellow passengers when they sailed on a steamer heading to Belfast, where they sold their haul to a jeweller. But the other passengers had tipped off police, who arrested them in Belfast as they left the jeweller's. They were condemned for stouthrief but asked Robertson to meet them at Glasgow jail where, still in irons and heavily guarded, they tearfully begged his forgiveness and their victim assured them he gave them his pardon. But two other meetings brought even greater distress as Craig said goodbye to his wife and three children and Brown to his wife and their seven youngsters.

Kindness and love killed mother-of-eight Nancy Laffy. The love was for her imprisoned husband Thomas, who was facing his day in court at Airdrie, North Lanarkshire, for a breach of the peace. His lawyer had said there was a chance that if he offered to pay a fine he could walk free. The trouble was the couple had no money. Then kind Nancy came up with a solution; if she pawned his coat the proceeds might pay a fine and bring her husband home to her and their family. Nancy received ten shillings for the coat, but had to set off home alone to the hamlet of Legbrannock near Holytown, North Lanarkshire, after Thomas was jailed for twenty days. It was 7 December 1863 and on the way she stopped for a drink with a woman friend. It was to be her last. Hours later her body was discovered at the side of the road she had been walking along, her head smashed in apparently with a stone and other horrific injuries covering her body.

Suspicion fell on Irish railway worker John O'Neill after bloodstained clothing belonging to him was found dumped in a plantation. He had vanished but advertisements appealing for information about his whereabouts appeared in the *Police Gazette* and led to him being spotted in the Borders towns of Biggar, Peebles, Galashiels, Hawick and Jedburgh, all the time heading south.

Seven weeks later Northumberland Police Superintendent John Gillespie read the *Gazette* and realised he had seen a man answering the description working on a railway line in the Redesdale area in the west of the county and sent Constable John Hurles to arrest him. Hurles' evidence at Reilly's trial for murder proved crucial. The officer said on the way to prison the man, claiming his name was O'Brien, had said, 'I killed a woman.' Hurles told the court, 'I said, "Who said so?" He said, "Didn't you say so?" I said, "No; you are charged with murder, but there was no person mentioned." I did not know it was a woman who had been murdered. In the *Police Gazette* there was no person mentioned.'

Shortly after one o'clock in the morning, by a majority of nine to six, the jury found O'Neill guilty of murdering Nancy and he was watched by a crowd estimated at 20,000 when he was hanged at Glasgow in May.

32

LADY LUCK

In July 1820 as the country reeled from the violent reaction of the government to efforts by workers to improve the lot of the working classes, a young man named John Sharp appeared before the High Court in Edinburgh on a capital charge that would have a remarkable outcome. Many thousands before Sharp who had stood in docks all over Scotland and many thousands who were to come after him had wondered on their day of judgement whether Lady Luck might play a part in their fate. Sharp, though, would have been warned by his defence counsel that he needed a miracle to survive.

He was charged with 'firing a loaded pistol upon the constables of the county patrol of the county of Lanark, about four o'clock in the morning of the 19th January last, upon the main street of the Bridgeton of Glasgow, they being in search of him, on suspicion of having the same night broken into the cellar or warehouse of the Bridgeton Old Victualling Society and stolen therefrom, same night, various articles, in consequence of which Alexander Livingstone, one of the patrol, was severely wounded in the right groin, to the imminent danger of his life.'

In a forlorn hope of saving himself, Sharp pleaded not guilty, but the evidence was overwhelmingly against him and after retiring for just a few minutes the jury found him guilty.

Sharp was then arraigned on a second charge of stealing items that included a ten-gallon jar of whisky and to this he jokingly pleaded, 'Guilty of standing beside the jar', a plea that was taken to be a denial and once again he was convicted.

Shooting at and almost killing a policeman was a serious matter and after being sentenced to be executed at Glasgow on 16 August Sharp was packed off to jail in Glasgow to await the appearance of the hangman. But the mythical Lady Luck now put in an appearance. By chance, one of the jurymen was again called up for duty in another case and this time a keen-eyed clerk noticed he was just nineteen, when the minimum age for a juror was twenty-one, making his earlier service invalid. As it would in the case of Hugh Hosey and Alexander Mackay (Chapter 15) the law stated that a jury had to consist of fifteen men.

As he sat in irons in the condemned cell at Glasgow prison jailors told Sharp his hanging was to be delayed while lawyers and judges argued over what to do. The matter dragged on until December, with Sharp wondering whether every knock on his cell door was to bring good or bad news. During lengthy legal debates there had been suggestions that the absence of a full jury meant he had not received a fair trial and the entire matter should be thrown out. In the end, though, it was decided Sharp should be retried.

His shoulders must have slumped at the prospect of facing a repeat of the first trial with the same inevitable outcome of death, so Sharp simply decided to plead guilty and shorten the proceedings. But once again luck came to his rescue. Instead of ordering his execution Lord Pitmilly said that because of his 'long confinement and anxiety of mind suffered since his late trial' he would be spared and he was ordered to be transported. Sharp, the man who might have died twice, spent the rest of his life in Tasmania.

What appeared to be curious inconsistencies must have led to the condemned wondering why they had to die while others who were guilty of near identical cases survived. In August 1816 the convict ship *Lord Melville* left England bound for New South Wales, a voyage that would take six months. On board were 101 female convicts, among them Helen Reid and Susan Tinny. Despite the misery of being sent to a world 12,000 miles from their own they were astonishingly fortunate to be still alive. Reid, the mother of five who was frequently drunk, had viciously knifed her husband in the back at their home in Keith, Morayshire, killing him. At her trial for his murder she had received the inevitable death sentence from Lord Pitmilly, who told her, 'You were going down the hill together and ought to have continued the journey of life, assisting and supporting each other in its trials and difficulties. You deprived your children of one of their parents, you are to leave a legacy of shame to them from the other.'

Tinny's was a more complex case. Using a lighted candle in April 1815 she had set fire to the home, barn, cart shed and stack yard of farmer Andrew McDowall in Wigtonshire, causing immense damage. She was accused of wilful fire raising and theft and had no defence to the allegations other than that she was an imbecile. A doctor who rejected the claims told her trial at the High Court in Edinburgh, 'Religion was the only subject that remained on her mind for any time. She said she was under the immediate influence of God Almighty, and could only do what God allowed; she said she had no ill will at the people, as she did not know them, and that God Almighty had left her to herself and the Devil tempted her to burn the barn.' She too was sentenced to death.

Yet fortune intervened on behalf of Tinny and Reid because they were reprieved and transported for life, an outcome especially surprising in Tinny's case because just two years later pleas on behalf of Margaret Crossan, who had committed a similar crime, were rejected. Did Margaret die because cattle were killed when she burned a farm, whereas none perished when Tinny and the Devil went about their work?

Luck smiled too on Andrew Ewart in 1828. A married man with a big family and his wife expecting another child, Ewart had taken his gun along to Libberton churchyard in Edinburgh to hopefully provide a meal by shooting a swan or two. He met up with a group of friends, including Henry Pennycook, who went off to wander about in search of the birds while Ewart and the others were chatting to a patrolman in his watch house.

The conversation concerned grave-robbing. A few nights earlier John McQuilton had been caught in the process of creeping into the churchyard to dig up a body and sell it to medical students. Now it was dusk and as darkness fell the watchman was reminding Ewart and the others to keep a particular lookout for anyone trying to steal the dead. A broadside revealed that as he spoke, one of Ewart's friends spotted 'a dusky figure' at which he 'gave an alarm that another resurrection man was in the yard'. Tragedy followed. 'Firmly impressed with this idea, [Ewart] snatched up a loaded gun, ran to the door and instantly levelled it at the supposed intruder who pacifically said, "Surely you'll not shoot me?" But the words had scarcely escaped his lips ere he received the contents in his arm. It was then too late discovered that the unfortunate man was Pennycook and that a friend's life had been sacrificed instead of that of a sacrilegious depredator.'

Despite frantic efforts to save him, Pennycook died a few days later and Ewart went on trial for his life, charged with murder, of which he was found guilty. He was sentenced to death even though the evidence pointed to it having been an accident. At the same court McQuilton, whose actions were indirectly the cause of the fatal shooting, was jailed for six months for 'violating the sepulchres of the dead'. Judges showed no mercy to men who used guns to kill and harm, pointing out that a strong recommendation by the jury was no guarantee of Ewart's life being spared. As he lay in heavy chains in the condemned cell frantic efforts were made on his behalf, at the forefront of which was a petition to King George IV signed by the Libberton church minister and 650 influential parishioners. Days before he was due to hang, Ewart was reprieved and eventually his sentence for shooting dead his friend was commuted to just twelve months in prison.

Did his good luck bring a smile to the face of Ewart? It produced a remarkable reaction from clerk David Bartie at the end of his trial at Edinburgh in 1830 for allegedly raping a fourteen-year-old girl, an offence that carried the death penalty – hanging for rape was not abolished until 1841. The girl worked as a servant at twenty-eight-year-old Bartie's lodgings in East Cumberland Street, Edinburgh, and claimed that after she rejected his advances while the landlady was out shopping, he had made a series of offers of money to her to sleep with him, starting off with a pound (£100) and going up to three pounds before he realised she wasn't interested in him. After this he chased her through the house and when he caught her dragged her into his bedroom, where he committed the offence.

Bartie was forced to sweat in the dock as the youngster gave her version and a broadside revealed that when the jury retired to consider their verdict he 'remained in a state of the utmost agitation and anxiety. He repeatedly gazed round him with an indescribably haggard expression on his countenance, over which hung a cloud of the blackest gloom and most dismal melancholy. At times he laid his head down on his hands and arms; and for a few moments seemed asleep; and then he would raise his head again with the same unaltered expression. It struck almost every person in Court that his appearance now was like that of a maniac or rather of a drunk man arousing from sleep and trying to collect his dissipated ideas.'

Bartie's nightmare lasted twenty minutes before the jury reappeared and announced a not proven verdict, at which, according to the broadside, 'On hearing these joyful words the prisoner sprung to his feet, clapped his hands, uttered an exclamation of gratitude to the jury and (all in an instant) appeared as if he wished to seize his hat, bound at once out of the Court.' It added that a solicitor who shook Bartie's hand said it, 'Felt like the clammy hand of a person newly dead or dying.'

And so Bartie, through the unique Scottish verdict that has saved by a thread so many from death or years in prison, had joined the ranks of the lucky while fate had mocked at so many others.

In 1819 four men went on trial in the High Court charged with housebreaking, theft and reset of theft. It was alleged that Alexander Robertson, Alexander Archibald, James Dickson and James McMillan had entered sale rooms in Candleriggs Street,

Glasgow, known as the City Auction Mart, and stolen what was described as a huge quantity of watches, gold seals, gold keys, pencil cases, jewellery, spectacles and two hats worth altogether about £230 (£18,000 in present day values).

Immediately the robbery was discovered police informers had passed on the names of the culprits who fled, Robertson, Dickson and McMillan heading first to Grangemouth, where they caught a steamer to Leith and from there to Edinburgh, where they began reselling much of the loot. However, police, tipped off by an informant, were waiting when they went to a pawn shop in Cowgate, Edinburgh, and they were arrested. Archibald was detained in Glasgow. Although they had planned to equally share the proceeds it was Robertson who was to carry the lion's share of the punishment. He was convicted of shop-breaking and sentenced to be executed while the others were found guilty of theft and reset and ordered to be transported.

Robertson, aged twenty-four, had an especially hard luck story to tell. As a young man he had run his own business successfully and even travelled to America to set up there as a trader. But after returning to Scotland, his pockets filled with money, he became an easy although willing target for loose women and his savings soon ran out. Finally broke he turned to crime in the hope of reviving his fortunes, only to end his days on the scaffold while his accomplices spent the remainders of theirs in Australia.

His decision to deal in crime turned out to be a loser. That same year Irishman John O'Neil and his brother Joseph gambled with their lives by praying that a guilty plea to charges that they broke into a series of houses in Ayrshire and stole anything from money to teaspoons would win them favour with judges at Ayr. While it was a strategy that had paid off for others, the gods were not with them that April day because both were sentenced to death.

Luck had not deserted them totally, even if she made a late appearance. On the morning they were due to dangle, news arrived from the government in London that Joseph, the younger of the brothers, had been reprieved, while John was told he had to die. It was an odd decision because both had been equally guilty and the jury, required to listen to evidence and formally return a verdict in a case involving a capital offence, even where there was a guilty plea, had recommended both brothers should be shown mercy.

Four years later two more sets of brothers were forced to suffer a similar ordeal at Aberdeen. Following a series of thefts and robberies in Aberdeenshire at Cuminestown, Belhelvie, Ellon, Tillydrone and Rathen, a number of men were arrested, including brothers Thomas and Alexander Donaldson, William and Neil McLeod and William Buchanan.

While they waited for their trials some of the group escaped from the Aberdeen prison. Police in the north of Scotland were urged to be on the lookout for Donaldson, the McLeods and two cronies, William Dunn and Alexander Martin. They were eventually caught but not before they had broken into the home of Margaret Murray in the north of the shire.

When the brothers and Buchanan appeared before their judges in April 1823, they denied all the charges, the worst of which was a cowardly attack by Thomas Donaldson and Buchanan on seventy-year-old John Cooper, who farmed at Monquhitter near Turriff. Cooper had heard a gang was travelling through the area breaking into homes and, determined not to join the growing list of victims, decided to sit up all night to defend his house. He had a gun but no powder or shot and at two in the morning heard the sound of footsteps and warned he would fire if they didn't go away. However, the evil pair sneaked into Cooper's home and savagely beat and stabbed him, leaving the old man covered in blood with broken ribs and a deep slash on his arm. Robbing the brave veteran was a fatal move because he remembered that years earlier Donaldson had worked for him and this led to his arrest and then those of the others.

Cooper was determined to see the gang given their due deserts on the scaffold. Despite his injuries not yet having healed he walked nearly thirty-five miles to the courthouse to give his evidence; however, after completing the return journey he became ill. He had listened as William Buchanan, twenty-six, Donaldson, twenty-five and twenty-seven-year-old William

McLeod were sentenced to death. Fortune, though, was on the side of Neil McLeod and Alexander Donaldson, who were ordered to be transported for life. At least they would live, unlike the others or poor Cooper, who died in his bed shortly before they were hanged together. In the condemned cell, knowing there was no hope of a reprieve, McLeod and Donaldson's final partings had been from their brothers whose youth may have been a factor in the decision not to condemn them.

Youth often turned out to be the saviour and so Thomas Black, aged seventeen and fifteen-year-old John Reid were confident their adolescence would save them from death sentences passed on them at Edinburgh in 1823 after their conviction for house-breaking. They had been caught red-handed climbing through a second-storey window. However, the jury unanimously suggested both should be shown mercy. Reprieves were widely expected but Black's luck had run out because it was not he but Reid who was told he was to be put on a transport ship to Australia instead of into a coffin.

Sometimes it was impossible to understand why one culprit was spared while another was not. In 1793 sisters Margaret and Agnes Adams had gone into the Argyle Street, Glasgow, home of Janet McIntyre, then bolted the door before murdering her and plundering the house. They were seen by a chance caller who, having knocked and not been answered, looked through a window and saw the sisters at which she shouted for help and neighbours smashed down the door, found Janet dead with one of her eyes gouged out and the sisters hiding under a bed. They were charged with murder but while Agnes was reprieved Margaret went to the gallows.

There were times when it seemed impossible to predict the mood of judges. In 1818 John Forster was merely sentenced to be banished from Scotland for life for 'illegally and clandestinely solemnizing marriages' at Lamberton toll-bar, just over the Border with England. Couples had flocked to Scotland since 1753 when marriages by simple declaration before two witnesses conducted by unauthorised 'priests' were made unlawful in England. As if to show what he thought of the verdict Foster simply walked to the River Tweed, bought a boat and moored it exactly on the Border and continued marrying. Yet earlier that year Edinburgh minister Joseph Richardson and spirit dealer William Pearson had been jailed and banished for life for running a similar racket and in their cases Richardson had been properly ordained. Their crime was to commit a technical breach of the procedure by forging the signature of a clerk on an official document giving formal permission for a wedding to take place.

33

THE RADICALS

Since the fall of the Bastille in Paris in 1789 the British establishment had been terrified that the subsequent revolution would spread across the Channel. Four years later the execution of King Louis XVI followed by that of his wife Marie Antoinette confirmed the power that working classes could wield when they were organised and led. News of the revolution encouraged those in Britain who were intent on reforms giving workers a better deal and the population in general a fairer say in the running of the state.

In Scotland, running parallel with the call for change was the demand for independence. However, the establishment treated reasonable requests for a fairer society as threats to start a revolution and their reaction led to appalling violence and bloodshed, and the judiciary would not be slow to demonstrate its power and influence. Often the authorities when scared by the events that had led to such turmoil in France had been quick to call in troops, leading to a general mistrust of the military by workers.

In 1797 the introduction of the Militia Act authorising the government to conscript young men into the military caused general anger and acted as fuel north of the border to organisations such as United Scotsmen, a secretive group with more than 2,000 members striving for reform. It felt the establishment already had too much power and that year in Scotland encouraged the holding of a protest demonstration in late August at Tranent in East Lothian. The response of the authorities was merciless. Heavily armed troops fired wildly into a contingent of miners, killing and wounding, while members of the Cinque Ports Light Dragoons chased innocent men, women and children trying to escape the melee, slashing with sabres and stabbing with lances. By the time it was over at least a dozen townspeople were dead, including a woman and a boy of thirteen, while the soldiers escaped retribution. This decision created even greater anger when it was compared with the prosecution of weaver George Mealmaker from Dundee and a group of others who had come under government surveillance for writing pamphlets and booklets advocating reform and who were transported as a result.

Five years after the soldiers escaped judicial punishment for their murderous rampage at Tranent more civilians were shot down in apparent cold blood at Aberdeen. Towns and villages traditionally celebrated the birthday of the King and in the Granite City in June 1802 what began as a party deteriorated into horror as the *Caledonian Mercury* described. 'It now becomes our painful duty to relate the melancholy events of the evening which led to consequences that we can never sufficiently deplore. An unfortunate affray took place between the boys in the street and some of the officers and privates of the Ross and Cromarty Rangers then on guard in Castle Street, who being joined by the rest of the corps from the barracks ran upon the people in the street with their arms in their hands, and began firing upon them with ball, indiscriminately and in every direction, and some were even seen taking deliberate aim at individuals. Many of the bullets went through windows and doors in the west end of Castle Street and in the head of the Shiprow and Narrow Wynd and others were found at a greater distance through the town.

'As far as we can learn the following were the fatal consequences that ensued; one man, a native of this place, and a private of the Rifle corps recruiting here who was standing at the corner of the Plainstones, was shot through the head and instantly died on the spot. Thomas Milne, a mason; John Moir, a young boy and only son of a widow, and William Gibb, apprentice to a barber, were all mortally wounded and died next day; and ten more persons, as near as we can learn, were variously wounded. Upon being informed of the unhappy affair the Provost and Magistrates, with becoming spirit, instantly interfered and the whole corps were ordered into the barracks. A sufficient guard of armed citizens was immediately mounted, to prevent all communication with the regiment which in the irritated state of the public mind might have led to further fatal consequences.'

What didn't help the situation was that the Crown was reluctant to prosecute even though four people had been murdered and it was left to individuals in Aberdeen to open a fund to raise enough cash to pay for a prosecution. Money poured in and in January the following year Lieutenant Colonel George Mackenzie, Captain J. B. Macdonach and Sergeants Andrew Mackay and Alexander Sutherland appeared before the High Court in Edinburgh accused of murder, while a fifth man ensign George Lanigan failed to appear and was outlawed. A succession of witnesses told how some officers and men from the Ross and Cromarty Rangers had been drunk, fighting among themselves and at one stage soldiers fixed bayonets and threatened onlookers. The trial ended with Mackenzie and Macdonach being found not guilty and the jury deciding the allegations against the sergeants had not been proven.

During the next twelve years the Napoleonic Wars occupied the military but the gradual introduction of machinery was leading to diminishing workforces, especially in the weaving industry on which so many Scots depended for their livelihoods. The lucky who still had work found their wages getting smaller and there was an increasingly strong feeling that the government in London did not care about the plight of starving families in cities such as Glasgow, with the result that these became a breeding ground for unrest. In Glasgow a huge reward of £300 (£23,700) was being offered by the Crown for anyone giving information leading to the arrest of the writer of handbills secretly printed in London claiming friends of German-born Queen Charlotte, wife of George III, were behind a plot to stir up trouble, while placards were being distributed in central Scotland urging workers to strike and take up weapons until electoral reforms were introduced.

In February 1817 a party of men, including a schoolmaster and solicitor's clerk, were arrested as they met in the back room of a public house in the Old Wynd, Glasgow, and charged with 'having met for treasonable purposes'. They argued that their meeting was simply to discuss how to best find out how much relief the poor were entitled to from parochial relief. Three days later a man and his son were arrested at their home in Anderston, again being accused of having treasonable intentions. However, before they could be taken away an angry crowd surrounded the house. Soldiers were called and had to fire shots after they were stoned, slightly injuring a young boy.

Arrests of this nature aroused public anger and the following year a demonstration starting in Bridgeton and the Calton in the east end of Glasgow and made up of around 3,000 men and boys set off to march and link up with a similar demonstration at Paisley. However, it had hardly moved away when it became obvious that many were there simply to get rid of anger and frustration. Hundreds of street lamps were smashed, windows broken, doors kicked in and shops ransacked as the march turned into a full-scale riot. At Bridge Street the mob invaded a Methodist service, terrifying worshippers. Hussars were called out and pointed two field guns at the marchers, whose response was to stone them at which point the cavalry was ordered to charge, sending the rioters fleeing for cover. There were so many arrests that Glasgow prison overflowed and offenders had to be taken to Greenock. At their subsequent trials, culprits were mainly given a few months in jail or bound over to keep the peace for terms of up to five years.

There was worse to come. At the start of April 1820 placards published by a group calling itself 'A Committee of Organisation for Forming a Provisional Government' and demanding reforms, appeared in Glasgow calling for a national strike. It was widely suspected that government agents trying to lure leading agitators out into the open where they could be recognised and picked off were behind the placards, which had the effect of stopping work at a number of mills and plants in central Scotland. A small group led by James Wilson from Strathaven headed for ironworks near Falkirk intent on seizing weapons but at Bonnymuir was met and detained by well-armed Hussars; another group from Strathaven avoided an ambush by soldiers and dispersed while yet more protesters with their numbers increased by locals attacked militia escorting prisoners to Greenock freeing the convicts. It was claimed that protesters had been discovered making pikes while other raids by soldiers uncovered gunpowder and an array of crude weapons.

The London government had had enough and determined on revenge. It appointed a special Commission to try eighty-eight men on treason charges. Some were found not guilty but for the others there was to be no mercy. John Anderson, John Barr, shoemaker William Clackson, smith James Clelland, William Crawford, Andrew Dawson, weaver Robert Gray, cabinet maker Alexander Hart, weaver Alexander Latimer, stocking weaver Thomas McCulloch, weaver Thomas McFarlane, John McMillan, blacksmith Allan Murchie, labourer Benjamin Moir, muslin singer Thomas Pike, weaver William Smith, weaver David Thomson, bookbinder Andrew White, tailor James Wright and fifteen-year-old Thomas Pike were one by one sentenced to be transported to Australia, the majority of them remaining in irons on the convict vessel *Speke* until it reached Tenerife after leaving in December 1820. At least they escaped with their lives; others were not so fortunate.

The course of savagery on which the government had set itself by dishing out the harshest possible punishment to those challenging its authority was about to become clear. Stocking maker James 'Purley' Wilson, aged fifty-nine, married with a daughter and three grandchildren, who had headed the march to the ironworks, was accused of four offences of high treason, convicted of one, that of, 'Compassing to levy war against the King to compel him to change his measures', but cleared of the other three. The sentence silenced a packed courtroom as Wilson was told he would be, 'Taken to the place from whence you came and that you be drawn on a hurdle to the place of execution on the thirtieth day of August and after being hung by the neck till you be dead, that your head be severed from your body, and your body cut in quarters, to be at the disposal of the King; and the Lord have mercy on your soul.'

When it came to 30 August 1820, the day he was to die at Glasgow, as though to rub salt into the wound Wilson, described as 'indifferent to religion', was forced to listen to a variety of prayers, psalms and passages from scriptures before being led to the hurdle – 'a sort of black box, about three feet deep with a seat in each end', according to the *Caledonian Mercury*. The newspaper continued, 'The prisoner was seated with his back towards the horse and the other seat was filled by a person dressed in a grey great coat, a fur cap on his head, and a black crepe over his face, holding up an axe nearly opposite the face of the prisoner. The hurdle grated heavily along the pavement. The prisoner ascended the scaffold and viewed the scene before him with a vacant stare. The people sat up with a vehement cheer, mingled with a partial cry of "murder, murder" but no signal or motion of the unhappy man showed that he attended in the least to their exclamations.'

On the scaffold Wilson was met by Tam Young, the Glasgow executioner whose grim task it was to hang him. 'Did you ever see such a crowd, Thomas?' the doomed man asked as Young adjusted the noose around his neck then completed the job for which he had been engaged. After hanging for half an hour Wilson's body was taken down and placed across three boards laid over his coffin. 'When the face was turned downwards, the neck bared. And all properly adjusted, the man in the mask came forward lifted the axe and cautiously felt the neck with his left hand, and severed the head from the body at a single stroke. He then threw down his weapon, lifted the head from the box, streaming with blood, and held the ghastly and distorted purple visage towards the crowd, exclaiming, "This is the head of a traitor." Cries of "He's died for his country" and "He's murdered" were quite general.

'Just at the moment the unfortunate man was thrown off, a false report got up in the centre of the crowd that "the dragoons, the dragoons are coming", the right and left wing caught the alarm and the flight became universal. Here a scene of confusion ensued that baffles all description; some were bending their course one way, some another; all passage was completely blocked up, and men, women and children by commingling together in heaps, like swathes of hay; the tumbling and trampling one over another, the beseeching of the women and screams of the children were truly appalling. Many were seriously bruised and a child, we are sorry to say, had its brow dreadfully lacerated from the trampling.'

After his horrific execution posters appeared all over Glasgow proclaiming, 'May the ghost of butchered Wilson haunt the pillows of his relentless jurors – Murder! Murder! Murder!'

A week later it was the turn of weavers John Baird and Andrew Hardie, who, like Wilson, had been singled out as ringleaders of the trouble, to be put to death in the same barbaric fashion, this time at Stirling. On the scaffold Hardie pleaded with another enormous crowd at least 20,000 strong not to go to public houses to drink to the memory of he and Baird, but to, 'Go home and think of God,' adding, 'I die a martyr to the cause of truth and justice.' Once again after they were hanged the axeman stepped forward and completed the sentence, although he needed three strokes to sever the head of Hardie. Reporters said he had 'lost his former firmness and dexterity' probably because the crowd was more raucous and clearly angry.

The character in the grey coat and fur hat who had accompanied Wilson, bungled the beheading of Hardie and decapitated Baird, was penniless Irish-born medical student Thomas Moore, aged twenty. The authorities had searched central Scotland for an axeman after Young agreed to carry out the hangings ritual but baulked at the idea of cutting off heads. They concentrated on medical students aware they might not be too squeamish to carry out the grisly tasks, particularly when money was on offer. Moore badly needed cash to complete his studies and had been willing to chop the corpses into quarters but was relieved of this task when it was decided this might stir up too much trouble at the executions. However, fellow students had gone along to watch the butchering of Wilson and afterwards Moore was warned that friends of the dead man and those of Hardie and Baird – numbered in their hundreds – would be made aware of his identity. Immediately following the Stirling ceremony he disappeared to Ireland with his money never to be seen or heard of again in Scotland.

The executions of the three men and transportation of others did nothing to stifle widespread anger and desire for change. When continued calls for strikes failed to gather enough support, some workplaces and workers were targeted in an attempt to force employers out of business. In 1825 cotton spinner John Graham had left his workplace in Glasgow and was walking home with friends when he was waylaid by a crowd of jobless men in Barrowfield Road, booed, hissed and then shot in the back. Police had been warned of trouble in the area and were on hand to arrest another cotton spinner, John Kean, who was tried and convicted of the shooting. Desperate to save his own life Kean made a series of astonishing confessions in which he revealed the identities of the men who he claimed had provided him with the weapon, the names of manufacturers he had been instructed to kill for £100 payment and details of secret societies of cotton spinners in Scotland. In exchange for telling tales he was spared but ordered to be whipped at the front of Glasgow prison then transported for life. A few days after his trial, a huge crowd gathered to watch as he was brought out of the jail, stripped to the waist and his hands and feet tied to a frame specially erected for the punishment.

The *Caledonian Mercury* described how, 'When all was ready for punishment the executioner threw off his coat, brandished a formidable cat-o-nine tails and inflicted twenty lashes on the back of the prisoner. A short pause ensued, Kean got a draught of water, and the punishment was resumed, eighty lashes were given in all and the flogging was over in about a quarter of an hour. He appeared from the contortions of his countenance to feel the pain of the first ten lashes acutely. During the infliction of the last twenty he cried twice or thrice and continued groaning heavily till he was loosed. There has not been so large a crowd assembled in Glasgow since the decapitation of the unfortunate Wilson. While the flogging was going on there were occasional cheers, and some hisses, but on the whole there was little sympathy manifested for the delinquent except by some females.'

The brutality shown to Kean did nothing to lessen the clamouring by workers for better, fairer conditions and sporadic outbreaks of trouble continued. However, the passing of the 1832 Reform Act, making significant changes to the electoral system, came too late to prevent a major riot at a potato flour manufacturing plant near Ayr during which the machinery that had replaced a large number of workers was destroyed. The culprits were jailed, but their sentences of a few months were lighter than had been expected. Was there, at last, the appearance of the first shoots of sympathy for the poor and jobless?

Three years later King William IV, who had ascended to the throne in 1830 and who would, during his seven-year reign abolish slavery, prevent the use of very young children in workplaces and make amendments to the Poor Law to encourage the destitute to seek refuge in workhouses, reviewed the cases of the Radicals. It was too late to help Wilson, Hardie and Baird but the men who had been transported to Australia were formally pardoned, allowing them to return to Scotland. However, by then they had spent fifteen years on the other side of the world and most decided to stay.

34

LAZARUS

Ever since Jesus revived Lazarus of Bethany from the dead 2,000 years ago doctors and scientists have striven to repeat the miracle. Lazarus had died four days before his reawakening; in Scotland and elsewhere those attempting resuscitation waited only minutes and at most hours to begin experimenting on hanging victims. Some were encouraged to attempt raising the dead by total belief in the description in the Gospel of St John of the feat performed by Christ; others simply reasoned that by restarting the breathing process an apparently dead body would return to life.

In 1733 these latter were encouraged by the outcome of an experiment with convicted highwayman William Gordon who, along with three others, had been condemned to hang in London. The medical world was fascinated by a description in the *Newgate Calendar* of his hanging. A report circulated that he had cut his throat just before he was carried out to execution and that a surgeon sewed it up. The cause of this report was as follows: 'Mr Chovot, a surgeon having, by frequent experiments on dogs, discovered, that opening the windpipe would prevent the fatal consequences of being hanged by the neck, communicated it to Gordon who consented to the experiment being made on him. Accordingly, pretending to take his last leave of him the surgeon secretly made an incision in his windpipe; and the effect this produced on the malefactor was that when he stopt his mouth, nostrils and ears, air sufficient to prolong life issued from the cavity. When he was hanged, he was observed to retain life, after the others executed with him were dead. His body, after hanging three quarters of an hour was cut down and carried to a house in Edgeware Road where Chovot was in attendance, who immediately opened a vein which bled freely and soon after the culprit opened his mouth and groaned. He, however, died; but it was the opinion of those present at the experiment that had he been cut down only five minutes sooner, life would have returned.' The result did not discourage the determination of the medical profession to continue experimenting.

Forty years later a young sailor named Black had his own theories, as the *Scots Magazine* revealed. Black had contracted fever at Greenock and knew he was dying. 'He requested on his deathbed that the coffin should not be nailed closed until his friends at Dunoon might see his corpse. His body was carried to Dunoon and while one of his sisters was kissing the corpse and taking her last farewell, to her surprise as well as that of several spectators he revived, called for a drink of water which was immediately given him and he continues to life and health ever since.'

William 'Deacon' Brodie was a well-known and much respected Edinburgh councillor and cabinet maker, a profession in which he was frequently called on to mend and fit locks and security systems at the homes of the city's richest citizens. That gave him the chance to copy keys and carry out a string of thefts to fund a gambling habit and maintain an active love life that produced at least five illegitimate children. An accomplice informed on him to the authorities and Brodie fled to Holland but was arrested in Amsterdam, hauled back to Edinburgh in chains and sentenced to death. Brodie, aged forty-seven, was not giving up easily on life. Moments before he stepped on to the scaffold at the Old Tolbooth in the High Street in October 1788 he was suspected of secretly fitting about his neck a steel collar around which he had paid the executioner to fit the noose. He had also arranged for friends to whisk his body off and blow air down his throat through a silver tube, but the ruse failed and he was buried in an unmarked grave.

He had been convinced the answer to how to be revived lay just in getting air into the lungs. Doctors believed it was more complicated than that; they were sure the body had to literally be shocked back to life and began making what were known as galvanic experiments in which corpses were stimulated with electric currents.

One of the first of these efforts to bring an apparently dead man back to life was made at Glasgow on thirty-five-year-old married weaver Matthew Clydesdale, who had been convicted in October 1818 of attacking and murdering an eighty-year-old man with a coal pick. He admitted that after the killing he had gone home and thrown his cat on the fire, an action said to have 'excited an expression of horror and disgust' among spectators in the crowded courtroom. He was sentenced to death, ordered to be given only bread and water, and after the hanging for his body to be handed over to Dr James Jeffray, Professor of Anatomy at the University of Glasgow. Jeffray and a colleague, Doctor Andrew Ure, had been researching the potential of galvanism and were acknowledged as experts on the subject.

They were eagerly awaiting the execution of the murderer by city hangman Tam Young on 4 November, but to complicate matters somewhat, Clydesdale was not alone on the scaffold that afternoon; at his side was housebreaker Simon Ross, who would die with him, and inevitably with two to drop the procedure would take slightly longer than usual. As it turned out both bodies were left to hang for almost an hour while the doctors waited impatiently to get their hands on the corpse of Clydesdale. The *Caledonian Mercury* reported that once they were cut down, 'Clydesdale's was put into a coffin and by means of a cart was conveyed, for the purpose of dissection, to the Professor of Anatomy. The cart was followed by a large portion of the crowd, who huzzard when the body arrived in front of the college. In the dissecting room Dr Jeffray was waiting.'

Ure too had been nervously pacing the dissecting room, having charged up his powerful galvanic battery consisting of 270 pairs of four-inch plates with a mixture of nitric and sulphuric acids. As soon as the naked body of the murderer arrived the two experts got to work watched by a huge audience of medical students and those from the crowd who had managed to squeeze in and find a vantage point. What then took place was said to be appalling. The initial experiment involved moving a highly charged rod from hip to heel, resulting in Clydesdale's leg suddenly shooting out with such a force that one of the assistants was almost knocked down. The rod was then put to the phrenic nerve in the neck of the corpse with astonishing results because it appeared that the dead man began breathing, the chest and stomach heaving and falling. Many of the spectators were convinced that had blood not been drained from the body after the hanging to confirm death the heart might have begun beating.

In another experiment the supraorbital nerve leading to the face and forehead was touched by the rod with even more startling effects as every nerve in the face was 'thrown into fearful action', according to the *Lancaster Gazette*. It went on: 'The scene was hideous. Several of the spectators left the room and one gentleman actually fainted, from terror or from sickness. In the fourth experiment the transmitting of the electrical power from the spinal marrow to the ulnar nerve at the elbow; the fingers were instantly put into motion and the agitation of the arm was so great that the corpse seemed to point to the different spectators, some of whom thought it had come to life. Doctor Ure appears to be of the opinion that had not incisions been made in the blood vessels of the neck and the spinal marrow been lacerated the criminal might have been restored to life.'

The results of the tests on Clydesdale encouraged those who, despite his not having wakened from the dead, remained convinced life could be restored to an apparently dead body. They put their thoughts to the test on sixty-one-year-old George Thom at Aberdeen after his execution in the city in November 1821; but there were many who hoped this evil poisoner would not be brought back to life. Cattle dealer Thom had married into the Mitchell family who ran a farm at Burnside near Alford. His wife Jane had brothers, James and William, and sisters, Helen and Mary, who did not think much of her choice as a husband. The Mitchells were well off, their assets increased two years earlier when another brother had died sharing his considerable fortune among Jane and the others. Thom saw Jane as a prize catch; he knew that whenever any other of her siblings passed away, their money would be shared among the survivors. A greedy man, he plotted to do away with the others and finally his wife because even while he courted Jane he had eyes on another younger local girl.

One night Thom paid a surprise visit to the Mitchells. When he had stayed with the family before his marriage he had shared a room with one of the brothers. However, telling them he needed to be up and away early next morning he announced, to the surprise of the others, he would sleep in the kitchen. However, he was persuaded to lay his head in the same room as William. Before going to bed he joined them for a supper of porridge but next morning James heard footsteps in the kitchen. At the time he thought nothing of that or of having noticed that when Thom had emptied his pockets a white dust had fallen out.

So the Mitchells mixed their regular breakfast of porridge flavoured with salt taken from a sack in the kitchen. They would as usual be attending church and had begun downing the steaming food when James having taken a brief taste complained it had a strange 'sweetish, sickening' taste and wanted no more. The others had their porridge but almost immediately James became ill, vomiting and even losing his sight. He was still determined to be at church because missing the service might attract gossip in a highly religious community such as theirs and eventually managed to stagger off but had to leave halfway through and found brother William being violently sick in the churchyard.

Thom in the meantime, after leaving the Mitchells, had bumped into a friend and told him he had been ill, setting the stage for an alibi by saying it must have been caused by something he had eaten the previous night. He went home to his wife convinced he had finished off the Mitchells. At their farm the sickness had spread to the sisters and the family discussed what might have brought on their illness. They wondered whether a spell had been cast over them and William employed a man to go to the Highlands to ask the opinion of a sage who was an expert in spells and witchcraft. His view was that someone had poisoned them, one that was quickly shared by the sisters. William's condition worsened and he finally died despite efforts by the family doctor to save him. Thom and Jane were arrested although she was quickly cleared of any wrongdoing, but her husband was tried for murder, convicted and sentenced to hang although he protested he was innocent. However when it emerged he had been trying to buy arsenic his fate was sealed and on the eve of his execution he admitted adding the poison to the Mitchells' salt.

After being bled to make sure it was dead Thom's body was carried in a cart to Marischal College in Aberdeen, where doctors waited to experiment with electric currents in an attempt to revive him. They applied a positive wire to the spine and a negative to the sciatic nerve then switched on the power. Their battery was not as powerful as that used on Clydesdale but watchers reported, 'A general convulsive starting of the body was produced,' while 'considerable contractions' were seen in the arm and forearm when the spine and ulnar nerve were linked by the same system. Other tests resulted in movement in the facial muscles with even the tongue being seen to move. However, after an hour and a quarter with the temperature of the corpse dropping, the doctors gave up trying to make the dead man walk.

Where the professionals failed, amateurs were set on proving it was possible to bring the deceased back to join the living. In January 1823 friends of twenty-year-old Irish-born mineworker James Burtnay (see Chapter 23) waited anxiously around the scaffold at Ayr while he was hanged. They were desperate to get hold of his corpse as soon as possible so they could try to revive him and after waiting forty minutes to be told the body having been bled could now be removed, rushed off with it in a coffin. But as the *Morning Post* revealed, 'As might have been expected all their exertions to restore animation failed in producing the desired effect.'

In Glasgow James Jeffray had not abandoned his quest to revive a Lazarus of his own. Doctors throughout Britain had consulted him about his theories but despite efforts elsewhere corpses stubbornly refused to be aroused. In July 1824 he was ready to try again, this time on William Devan, who had been sentenced to death for cutting the throat of his wife Mary at their home in the Glasgow Gorbals. A *Caledonian Mercury* reporter had a seat in the packed anatomical theatre where Jeffray was to work and described what happened once the body of the killer was taken there on 21 July 1824.

'The naked body was carried shoulder high and in the most adroit manner laid on a board. The face was considerably swelled and had a deep purple appearance; but in the course of the experiments it assumed a more natural colour. The various apparatus and instruments being all ready, Dr Jeffray and his assistants immediately commenced operations. One of the assistants held the culprit's head in a proper position while another blew a pair of bellows into his nostrils. This experiment was made to endeavour to inflate the lungs and heart with ordinary air in order to restore respiration and the circulation of the blood but, having failed, as no doubt was expected, several incisions were made in various parts of the body, and the nerves connected with the vital organs were acted on with full force by means of a rod in connection with the galvanic battery. When an incision was made on a principal nerve in the elbow, the effect of the shock was most visible. The arm was lifted up quickly and moved for some time in a tremulous manner. The chest was considerably swollen and perceptively heaved at the same time. The under jaw also occasionally moved but there was no contortion of the features. Dr Jeffray said the operations had not turned out altogether as well as could have been wished. This might be owing to a variety of causes. A good deal might depend on the way in which the rope was put around the neck. When the loop was fairly behind, it resembled a case of choking or drowning; but when it was at the one side, it might so rend and destroy the nerves as to defeat the purpose of galvanism. Having intimated that no further galvanic experiments were to be made, the audience left the hall.'

35

THE GREAT COACH ROBBERY

In 1963 the overnight mail train from Glasgow to London was stopped and robbed of £2.6 million in a daring, highly organised crime known as the Great Train Robbery. Yet more than 130 years earlier another robbery requiring ingenuity and skilled planning and in which the team of conspirators astonishingly included a dog, netted the thieves an enormous haul. It was the Great Coach Robbery. But while the crooks who stole from the train received savage prison sentences, the mastermind behind the coach robbery went to the gallows.

Until the advent of steam engines during the early 1800s and even earlier, vast amounts of money were transferred between banks and head offices on public horse-drawn coaches. In March 1831 porters from the Commercial Bank at Campbeltown in Argyll had taken a chest packed with cash on the *Duke of Lancaster* steamer to its branch in Glasgow, where it was locked overnight. Next day the money along with bags from other branches was placed in the foreboot – a locked compartment under the driver's seat – on the Prince Regent coach to Edinburgh. Security left a lot to be desired. Each week the Commercial Bank made similar transfers to its head office in the capital using the Prince Regent, a fact that did not go unnoticed by innkeeper George Gilchrist, who ran a thriving business supplying coaches – including the

Prince Regent – and horses and who knew most of the drivers on the route between Glasgow and Edinburgh.

Gilchrist had carefully watched and noted the routine; coaches set out simultaneously from the two cities, made stops to change horses and collect passengers and met at Airdrie, where the drivers changed over and took the coaches on to their destinations. He had mused over the chances of robbing one of these regular runs – there were rumours of hundreds, even thousands of pounds being carried – but had held off attempting a theft because he was well known to the drivers and realised he was bound to be recognised.

However, his opportunity came when a regular driver fell ill and an elderly replacement, a stranger, was brought in. But he needed to work fast because the robbery had to be carried out while the usual coachman was off work. Gilchrist had already mentioned his plan to his brother William, to horse dealer William Morrison, joiner Thomas Campbell from Mid-Calder where he had once lived, Falkirk cooper Robert Simpson and a friend, James Brown. It involved breaking into the foreboot, taking out the contents and getting off the coach before the theft was discovered.

Just as the Great Train Robbery depended on an accomplice at Glasgow watching and reporting to the rest of the gang that the mail train had been loaded and departed, so Gilchrist had a man stationed outside the Commercial Bank to make sure its packages, locked into a strongbox, were loaded on the Prince Regent. His task was to then gallop to the outskirts of the city to report to others waiting to board. However, the first attempt had to be aborted when other passengers were inside and on top as the coach set off from Glasgow. Gilchrist decided the answer was simply to make sure all the seats were empty. On 23 March a man went to the ticket office and paid £6 12 shillings for all six inside seats from Glasgow. Next day the Prince Regent was loaded up, temporary driver John McDowall flicked his whip and set off. There were no passengers inside but seated next to him on top was a man, Brown, with his dog, the animal held by a strong, long chain that rattled as the coach bumped along; inside the foreboot and the strongbox the bank packages contained a staggering £5,712 6 shillings – equivalent in 2017 terms to just under £600,000 in cash.

Just outside Glasgow at Shettleston a young couple signalled McDowall to stop, waving tickets entitling them to seats inside. The coachman watched as the man helped the woman to board, passing her bag to her once she was inside and soon after he had to halt again as another ticket holder, a male, climbed in. Further on he stopped again, this time to let a minister board; the man's bag was placed in the foreboot but the passenger had only been able to buy a ticket for an outside seat. It was difficult for those on top of the coach to hear one another speak over the sound of the horses and rumble of the iron-shod wheels; further the day was cold, windy and with flurries of rain while the constant and irritating rattling of the dog chain seemed to have become worse after leaving Shettleston; further the owner was frequently shouting at his animal to sit still.

The racket was deliberate; it was covering three men, the Gilchrists and Simpson, hard at work inside the coach. A few days earlier George Gilchrist had travelled to Edinburgh and in a dress shop, saying they were presents for his wife, bought a women's dress, coat, boots and straw bonnet from which hung long blue ribbons before going on to a high-class gents outfitters to buy clothing for his brother, who would pose as his companion. He was taking no chances; he did not want to risk purchasing them in Glasgow where there was always the possibility, no matter how faint, of an assistant who sold them boarding the same coach and recognising them.

While in the capital he had met up with Campbell, who handed over a number of joinery tools, including a brace, bit, hammer, chisel and screwdriver. Now he used them to bore a series of holes in the forward wall of the coach, hack out a chunk of panel with the help of the chisel, force up the lid of the strongbox and drag out most of the contents, the sound of the dog chain drowning out the noise of the drill. It had taken Gilchrist just under an hour and the three quickly replaced the wooden panel and pinned up the lining of the inside of the coach to cover the damage; now, about a mile and a half outside Airdrie, one of the men shouted for McDowall to halt and all three inside, together with the man, his dog and noisy chain, left.

The plotters hid in a plantation, where Gilchrist stripped off the woman's clothing, dressed and they then made their way to their homes. The theft was discovered when the coach, now driven by John Millan, stopped at Uphall and he saw the lining of the inside ripped and parcels addressed to the Commercial Bank strewn about.

Police made strenuous efforts to trace the robbers, trying to follow their tracks after they left the coach. The bank offered a reward of £500 (£55,000), which it quickly doubled to £1,000, for information leading to the arrest of the crooks and gradually information trickled in. Police arrested Brown and found gold sovereigns taken during the robbery hidden in a fishing basket at his home; then Morrison and Campbell were detained and, knowing they could face the death penalty, agreed to cooperate, telling all they knew about the theft and so the net gradually closed, the prize catch being Gilchrist. He was determined to save himself; following his arrest he locked a sheriff into his own office then fled, only to be caught. He was tried with his brother and Brown in the High Court at Edinburgh in July and found guilty, largely because of evidence given against him by Morrison and Campbell, although the jury decided the case against the others was not proven. The Great Coach Robber, married with a family, was executed on 3 August 1831.

In the case of the 1963 robbery the idea of stopping a train is thought to have come from an incident a year earlier at Carfin in Lanarkshire when five men successfully brought a goods train laden with cigarettes to a near halt by pouring oil on the lines, causing the wheels to lose grip. Gilchrist too may have based his remarkable plot on a robbery in March 1817, when a gang netted almost £5,000 (£395,000) through stealing a parcel being sent by coach from Edinburgh to Edie and Company at Stirling. The *Morning Post* reported, 'On arrival of the mail coach at Stirling and on examining the place where similar valuable parcels had been conveyed for a considerable time in perfect safety it was found to be missing; an alarm was spread and from circumstances the robbery was strongly suspected to be one of those called 'put up' robberies, the valuable contents of the parcel having been previously known to the thief and the part of the coach it was deposited in. The passengers had all left the coach and it was strongly suspected that some, or the whole of the inside passengers were concerned in the robbery.

'An inquiry took place respecting them and their proceedings on the road when it was ascertained that all the inside places were taken previous to the mail starting from Edinburgh. Three of the passengers of the names of McAllister, Hamilton and Carter, got into the mail coach previous to its starting and the fourth passenger was taken up on the road. As the mail was passing the top of Princes Street, Edinburgh, one of the passengers who had booked himself by the name of Hamilton suddenly stopped the mail and said he had forgotten some important papers and it would be of no use pursuing his journey without them; he was therefore obliged to return home and left the mail, taking his great coat over his arm and saying he must go on his journey the next day.' Other passengers also left the coach long before reaching their paid for destinations.

Agents acting for the bankers made extensive inquiries, but the trail went cold. Then in the late spring of the following year a man was arrested at a London opera house and accused of using a sharp knife to steal from members of the company by cutting their pockets. A search of his home uncovered items taken in the Stirling mail coach theft and he was identified as the passenger McAllister, alias Crowder. Hamilton was found in Newgate jail, awaiting transportation for theft, and all three were taken to Glasgow but then freed when the bankers suddenly announced they did not want the matter taken any further, it being rumoured most of the money had been recovered.

That episode might also have inspired another similar heist when in December 1824 packages containing notes worth around £4,200 were stolen from a mail coach on its way from Stirling to Edinburgh. By the time it stopped at Corstophine the money had vanished and it was later thought it had been taken a short time earlier while the coach horses were being changed over at Kirkliston. The hunt for the thieves took searchers south as they followed the trail of two men who had regularly changed notes in the names of the banks whose money had been in the stolen packages. At Thirsk in North Yorkshire they aroused thirty-nine-year-old Londoner Robert Murray, a former seaman, from a bed in a roadside inn and arrested him. Inquiries back in Scotland revealed that for several weeks prior to the robbery Murray had stayed at lodgings in Rose Street, Edinburgh, from where he daily went out to check on the arrival of mail coaches. He was charged with the theft but freed on a not proven verdict after a trial at Edinburgh in February 1825.

Dogs on the street barked that once again justice had been foiled because five years earlier another criminal had managed to escape his deserts. Massive rewards and extensive police investigations in Scotland and England had failed to find the killer in November 1806 of bank porter William Begbie, stabbed outside the entry leading to the British Linen Company Bank in Bank Close and robbed of a bag containing £4,392 (£347,836) he had been delivering. All that was recovered was a bag filled with large denomination notes, payment of which had been immediately stopped. Inquiries, however, did reveal that James MacCoul, an associate of notorious London villain Houghton 'Huffey' White, had been seen on a number of occasions around the spot where Begbie was murdered. However, the authorities did not have any evidence on which MacCoul could be charged.

Five years later, in July 1811, the Glasgow branch of the Paisley Union Bank was robbed of a massive £19,753, almost a million and a half pounds in present day values. Investigators discovered that a man calling himself Moffat, but who answered MacCoul's description, had lodged in the Broomielaw before the robbery along with Huffey White. Such a huge haul the investigators reasoned could only be handled by criminals with well-established contacts; MacCoul and White fitted this bill and after the latter was arrested and faced with serious charges they offered to hand over what they claimed to be the proceeds of the robbery, about £12,000, to buy him a pardon. The bank agreed even though it meant a shortfall of nearly £8,000 but then began a series of civil claims and counter claims between MacCoul and the bank, the latter claiming MacCoul was responsible for repaying the difference, he denying he was responsible.

During the middle of the legal arguments which went on for a number of years White, who had fallen out with fellow Londoner MacCoul, was hanged in 1813 for robbing a mail coach at Northampton. Finally with its patience exhausted the bank insisted MacCoul be formally accused of the robbery and in June 1820 he was convicted at the High Court in Edinburgh and sentenced to death.

MacCoul continued playing his ace card – that he knew the whereabouts of the rest of the money – and it earned him a reprieve in August. However, he was told it was replaced by a life prison sentence, news that shocked him and caused a sudden mental decline. He died in Edinburgh jail in December, aged fifty-seven, and was buried in the Calton churchyard.

London-based criminals must have looked on the banks of Scotland as easy targets, a view one more would come to regret. On Boxing Day 1830 thieves broke into the bank of Robert and James Watson in the centre of Glasgow while the porter, who lived on the premises, was at church. It was a baffling theft because there were no signs of a break-in and detectives concluded a series of false keys must have been used. The culprits made off with banknotes valued at £6,180 (£624,180) and gradually inquiries revealed that for some weeks before the theft a man calling himself Lee had taken lodgings in Warwick Street near the bank posing as the manufacturer of portable jacks. He had also arranged for a woman who gave her name as 'Mrs Allan' and who he said was his sister to lodge nearby in Blyth Court.

The pair were actually notorious London thief William Heath, an expert lock picker, and his mistress Elizabeth Crowder, who both ran brothels in London. It was established that the two of them, together with two other men had been regularly spotted hanging around the bank, causing the porter's wife to ask, after noticing Heath for the umpteenth time, 'What's he lurking about there for?' Heath had also slyly watched the movements of the porter and his family, even following them to church services.

Following the robbery the gang fled to London, but Heath's accent and constant appearances near the bank led to meetings between police in the English capital and Glasgow that resulted in the arrest of he and Crowder, who were taken north by coach. After a trial in the city Heath was found guilty but the case against the woman was adjudged to have been not proven, a verdict she did not understand, bursting into tears on hearing it until the significance was explained at which Heath took her in his arms and hugged her. Sentencing him to death the judge told Heath, 'That you have been guilty of a most extensive robbery is evident, but how it has been effected is best known to yourself.'

The following day a member of the Watson banking family applied for Crowder's arrest on grounds that she was believed to be, 'In possession of all or at least a part of the stolen property.' She was rearrested and held in prison for some time while lawyers wrangled but in the end the bank lost out. Some pointed fingers at the Watsons, questioning why it was that having been warned Heath and his associates were in Glasgow and had been seen around the premises, the bankers simply put extra bolts on their front door and had not insisted that police order the suspects out of Scotland.

Heath's execution was delayed for two weeks while attempts were made to persuade him to reveal the whereabouts of the money but when they failed he was hanged at Glasgow on 20 October 1831.

36

PASSION

'Of all base passions, fear is the most accursed,' wrote William Shakespeare in *Henry VI*. His words might have been meant for either of the wives of evil William Bennison, a cruel killer, liar and adulterer who hid behind the honest religious beliefs of others to commit two horrific murders. But then passion, for the best or the worst, was the cause of countless crimes.

On 5 November 1838 ardent churchgoer Bennison married pretty, dark-haired Mary Mullen at Tavanagh near Portadown in Ireland, swearing to love and honour her. Mary had fallen for his evident honesty; he appeared to be a man who took his religious faith very seriously but she quickly discovered he was a cruel, violent creature prone to mood swings and she shed no tears when after just a few months he left her.

Bennison headed for Scotland and once again used religious services to meet other women, among them Jean Hamilton, who quickly gave herself to him, and when the Irishman proposed marriage accepted, the couple being wed in a Wesleyan ceremony at Paisley on 5 December 1839, exactly thirteen months after he and Mary had tied the knot. They moved to Edinburgh and surprisingly Bennison took his new bride to Ireland and while there briefly introduced her to his family. Jean could never be sure, but had the impression he had been married previously;

the name 'Mary' seemed to often crop up during conversations but he told Jean that Mary was one of his sisters and had once worked in Scotland. He and Jean had not been long back in Edinburgh before she revealed she was pregnant and almost immediately he vanished, saying he needed to go back to Ireland for a short time.

Bennison's mind was made up. Ever since their trip to Ireland awkward questions had been posed about 'Mary'; it was time to get rid of her. Mary was surprised when he once more showed up but through the dual means of beatings and reminders that she had taken a marriage vow to obey him he forced her to accompany him back to Scotland. Her family never saw her again.

During the sea crossing she became unwell, her illness being blamed on seasickness. He took her to lodgings at Airdrie where, a week after they arrived, she suddenly became violently sick after eating porridge. Bennison said he could not afford to call a doctor and even when a fellow lodger offered to pay told him he had already spoken to a medical expert who advised him to simply give his wife an occasional glass of wine. Two days after taking ill Mary died. Some of the other lodgers were suspicious about the cause of her sudden sickness, her terrible pain, vomiting and craving for liquids, but her husband's apparent distress and religious fervour appeared genuine and resulted in churchgoers paying for her funeral in an unmarked grave the day after her death. The gravediggers had barely begun throwing earth on her coffin when the grieving widower was gone.

He turned up dressed in the black of a mourner on the doorstep of Jean who, not unnaturally, wanted to know what had happened. According to Bennison his family in Ireland had needed his help and so he had travelled there and resolved their problems. But he said that Mary – the woman he claimed to be his sister but who was actually his wife – announced she wanted to visit her old employer in Airdrie. However, during the sea crossing she took ill and died. In his absence Jean had given birth to his daughter but it was another girl who almost immediately attracted him. Near neighbour Margaret Robertson was a devout worshipper at the local Methodist chapel and soon Bennison was sitting with her in chapel, taking her for evening walks and joining Margaret and her mother for tea.

Jean complained he hardly spent any time with her and their daughter; her harping, continuing probing about his affairs in Ireland and questions about why he was seen so often with Margaret irritated him. Jean and her sister Margaret Ross had been with him one day at chapel when another worshipper had asked Bennison, 'I think I know your face; was it not you who buried your wife in Airdrie?' To the man's bewilderment and surprise Bennison denied that was the case and angrily stormed off. It left Jean asking even more questions. Now it was her turn to go so he could concentrate on Margaret Robertson.

In mid-April 1850, thirty-two-year-old Bennison announced Jean was desperately ill and not expected to last many more hours, news that astonished her friends and sister Margaret in particular. She rapidly deteriorated. Her husband claimed he had called a doctor who had examined her and said nothing could be done. That was yet one more in the long catalogue of lies that were the life of William Bennison. Jean died in agony and her body was still warm when he went off to sleep at the Robertson home, angrily rejecting calls for a post-mortem to find the cause of the unexplained death. 'She died happy, what more could you want?' he asked Margaret and arranged an immediate burial.

But others were wondering about the death. Just a week before Jean became sick Bennison had joined a benefit society and received £3 on her death, while the foundry where he worked had given him money and bought the dead woman's coffin. It was enough for police, tipped off by the dead woman's family, to intervene. Her body was exhumed and her final meal of porridge found to contain arsenic. Bennison was arrested and in a statement said Jean had made the porridge; that he had never been married in Ireland and never heard of Mary Mullen. Shown a copy of their marriage certificate he changed his mind, saying that after leaving her following the marriage he had been told she had died, allowing him to legitimately marry Jean, and was staggered when he discovered Mary was still alive.

His lies continued by pleading not guilty when he went on trial at the High Court in Edinburgh for bigamy and double murder, but he was convicted. Before Bennison was sentenced to death Lord Moncrieff told him, 'It has been my fortune to sit upon many trials of men tried for their lives or very serious offences and crimes; but I must say that I have seldom seen any one in which deeper criminality was involved than in this case.'

As he waited for his execution in August 1850 workmen began building the scaffold outside his cell, their efforts attracting an increasing crowd. Newspapers told how, 'A semicircle consisting of persons of all ages, thieves, prostitutes and vagabonds was formed and from their known habits and tastes it could not be expected that their conduct would be of the most orderly description. Loud laughter and discordant shouts, mingled with the noise of the preparations in anticipation of the tragic scene broke the stillness of the night and some of the female spectators relieved the tedium of the night by dancing.' Bennison's vile plot to be with another woman had ended in the ignominy of the gallows.

A year earlier another man had allowed his passions to turn him into a murderer. Crofter James Burnett's wife, Margaret, had been loyal and faithful, bearing him four sons and four daughters during their twenty-seven-year-long marriage, feeding him, warming his bed and tending him when he was sick. But when she needed his attention he instead turned his roving eye elsewhere towards the firm young body of farm servant Jane Carty, aged twenty-three. In 1843 Margaret had suffered a stroke that partially paralysed her left side; it meant she had to walk with the aid of a stick and their once vigorous sex life became dull. Her fifty-three-year-old husband was sexually active and instead of caring for his crippled wife began openly visiting Jane, gradually spending an occasional night with her until her bed became his, the pair ignoring the disgust of neighbours and distress of the abandoned Margaret.

Despite a considerable age gap Burnett from Tyrie, Aberdeenshire, had made up his mind to marry his young mistress but she was adamant that so long as his wife lived that would never happen; divorce was out of the question because Margaret would never agree to that. From Burnett's point of view there was only one thing for it. In November 1848 Margaret suddenly became ill, violent pains wracked her body causing her to scream out in agony. She died very soon after and while her friends wondered about the cause of her sickness Burnett had her buried within twenty-four hours and as if to give food to gossips had the marriage banns for he and Jane read out in church.

Rumour though had spread; local police heard whispers about the middle-aged farmer, his mistress and the wife that stood in the way. They suggested to Burnett that in order to dispel gossip he should have Margaret's body exhumed and examined, an idea he dismissed but one the authorities felt necessary and ordered the go ahead. Tests showed the presence of arsenic in Margaret's stomach and her husband was charged with her murder. He denied the offence at Aberdeen Circuit Court in April 1849 and continued maintaining his innocence even after the jury found him guilty and Lord Mackenzie sentenced him to be hanged.

However, in the condemned cell the burden of what he had done to their mother caused him much mental distress when he thought of the children particularly during, with time running out, a visit from the four youngest, three sons and a daughter. The *Aberdeen Journal* reported, 'Addressing them one by one he expressed sincere sorrow for the crime he had committed; lamented in language of the most touching character the disgrace he had brought on his family and earnestly exhorted them to pray with and for him that he might receive God. The eldest son, whose mind was evidently much impressed with a sense of the responsibility which his position involved, earnestly implored his father, as he had confessed his crime to man, to confess it with deep penitence of heart to God. The old man was deeply affected.'

At eight o'clock on the morning of 22 May Burnett was led in chains from his cell to the scaffold at Aberdeen. At ten the previous evening the town's clock had been stopped and the usual morning and evening ringing of the city bells hushed. Schools were opened earlier to stop pupils watching the grim ceremony and workers urged by employers not to take part of the day off to attend. Even so, around 10,000 people were there as the Glasgow hangman Murdoch, now in his eighties, launched him into eternity.

Inflamed desire had cost Burnett and his wife their lives; almost a century earlier another scandal had equally dire consequences for two men and another young woman. Thomas Ogilvie had lived quietly and comfortably with his mother at East Milne near Forfar, Angus, seemingly a confirmed and happy bachelor until at the age of forty he was beguiled by Catherine, daughter of Sir Thomas Nairn, third Baronet of Dunsinane in Perthshire and a rare beauty half his age. Her family encouraged Ogilvie's courtship; at twenty-one she was near to passing the age by which women were expected to have married and his proposal was accepted. The couple wed in January 1765 but it was immediately evident to Catherine that her husband lacked excitement and vigour; the marriage bed was a cold, frustrating place for a passionate young woman with hot-blooded sexual needs. Then suddenly into her life rode a knight in shining armour.

Days after the wedding the couple were visited by Thomas's brother Patrick, who had served as an army lieutenant in the East Indies. He had called to congratulate the pair but instantly Catherine fell for his good looks, stories of war and peace, and tales of adventures that were calculated to turn her head.

Her attraction for her brother-in-law was matched by his for her. The *Newgate Calendar* recorded that, 'They were seen within three weeks after the wedding by the servants walking in the fields with too great familiarity and kissing each other with all the fondness of enraptured lovers. Soon afterwards Anne Clarke, a kinswoman of Mr Ogilvie, paying a visit to the family, remarked a great intimacy between the lovers who frequently went to bed together without the precaution of shutting the chamber door. Mrs Clarke remarked on the scandalous impropriety of the lady's conduct; but so far from blushing at it, she boasted of her love for her brother-in-law with whom she said she would abscond or otherwise give a dose to her husband whom she detested.'

Blood is thicker than water. Even though he was aware of

Catherine's adultery Thomas merely told his brother he was bringing shame on the family but then gave him a generous sum of money to leave. The soldier packed his belongings and took off but the love affair continued; the couple wrote and secretly met and remarkably Thomas, realising the depth of their affection for one another, wrote to Patrick asking him to come back, saying, 'My wife cannot be happy without you.' It was an astonishing act of forgiveness, but evil had already penetrated the mind of his wife. Pregnant with his child she had asked Patrick to send her white arsenic under the guise of supplying her with medicinal salts and when her husband drank the tea she had made him one morning he instantly suffered excruciating stomach pains and died; the marriage had barely lasted four months. The lovers were arrested and in August went on trial for murder and incest – having sex with a brother or sister-in-law was then a criminal offence punishable by death – and were both found guilty and sentenced to death.

Catherine's pregnancy was confirmed by a panel of midwives and she was kept in jail until the birth, after which she would hang. Patrick meantime was executed at Edinburgh in November 1765 in terrible circumstances when the rope snapped, leaving him crashing to the ground where he was seized, tied up for a second time and sent to his death.

Catherine gave birth in January 1765 and was told she must hang the following month. But the story of the incredible beauty did not end on the scaffold, as the *Newgate Calendar* told. 'She escaped from the prison at nine at night in the uniform of an officer; and an old footman who had lived in her father's family, being waiting for her with a post-chaise, they set off together. Mrs Nairn was not missed till near noon on the following day; and persons were sent to re-apprehend her, but she had arrived in London before them. She now engaged the master of a Dutch fishing smack to convey her to Holland for 50 guineas; but the wind blew with such violence that he was obliged to land her on the Kentish coast, whence she travelled to Dover, attended by her faithful servant. They immediately got on board the packet boat bound for Calais and no authentic accounts respecting her have transpired since that period.'

The marriage had broken down in three weeks; the time it took thirty-one-year-old John Adams to get rid of his wife Jean – a time of cruelty, deceit and callous murder. When he was sentenced to death at Inverness in September 1835 Lord Moncrieff told him, 'Going on from one sin to another, from one heartless act to another, in a dark hour of your existence the Prince of Darkness took advantage of you and in a bloody action which deep as are many of the cases that come before us is almost unparalleled in enormity, has sealed your fate.'

Adams was an uncaring, selfish individual. As a young man he had been forced to leave his native Forfar by angry local people after getting a helpless deaf and dumb cousin pregnant and abandoning her. He fled to Aberdeenshire, where he made another youngster pregnant. Enlisting in the army, he deserted in Derbyshire after stealing money from comrades but met a local girl, Dorothy Elliott, and persuaded her to move to Scotland with her. They travelled to Dingwall, north of Inverness, living there together as man and wife for a year, he going under the name of Anderson.

But money was getting short and so Adams went in search of a gullible target, promising Dorothy he would soon be back. He headed east and at Montrose met shopkeeper Jean Brechin, who fell for his soft words and kisses and after a whirlwind courtship they married, Adams persuading her to move with him to Inverness, where he assured her work was plentiful. At his suggestion Jean sold her business and most of her belongings, sending what remained to Inverness where she and Adams moved into lodgings in Chapel Street, he frequently leaving her, giving the excuse he was off looking for a home for them. During the next three weeks he rarely saw his wife, spending his time with Dorothy, but then he told Jean he had found accommodation near Dingwall. To the surprise of the family who ran the lodging house he announced they were leaving late that same night. But Jean never reached her new home, ending her days in a shallow grave in a ruined hut with her head smashed in by a huge stone.

When he was arrested Adams at first denied ever having been to Montrose or knowing the dead woman. He said the furniture sent to Inverness was a gift from an aunt. But his lies were soon exposed; lots of people who knew Jean came forward, including some who had been guests at their wedding. Adams was convicted of murder, Lord Moncrieff donning the black cap to tell him he must hang, adding, 'Having deceived one young woman, bringing her away from her parents, in sad reliance on the word of man you practised on the feelings of another and brought yourself into a condition in which secrecy could no longer avail you, then you consummated all by the awful crime of murder.'

It was lust for a young woman that led to one of the most sensational murder trials to be heard in Scotland during the nineteenth century when Doctor Edward William Pritchard was accused of killing his wife and mother-in-law. Pritchard was probably fortunate not to have been convicted of being behind at least one more death. The bearded medic could not resist the other sex, particularly when they were young. He had worked as a doctor in Hunmanby near Scarborough in Yorkshire, but was forced to leave after one of his young patients fell pregnant, Pritchard denying being the father. He set up in practice not far away at Filey but there were complaints about the manner in which he examined women there and he was advised to leave, so he moved to Glasgow. There, in May 1863, he was suspected of setting fire to the bedroom of twenty-five-year-old maid Elizabeth McGrain at the family home in Berkeley Street, Glasgow, having first strangled or drugged her. The girl was dead by the time her body was recovered and although an investigation was made into the circumstances it was felt there was insufficient evidence to bring any charges against Pritchard.

Two years after arriving in Scotland the Pritchards, despite the doctor being in debt, had moved to an expensive property in Sauchiehall Street along with another young, attractive girl servant, Mary McLeod aged eighteen, who had fallen for his bedside manner. In February 1865 Mary Pritchard, aged thirty-eight, the wife who Pritchard had married fourteen years earlier, suddenly fell ill. As her condition worsened her mother Jane travelled from her Edinburgh home to help nurse her. Now she too took a sudden illness and died on 25 February. Less than a month later Mary followed her seventy-year-old mother to the grave.

A fellow doctor, James Paterson, suspicious at the way in which both women had so suddenly succumbed, had refused to put his name to death certificates necessary for a burial and so Pritchard signed them himself.

Now he was free to vent his lusts elsewhere – or so he thought because unknown to him an anonymous letter, almost certainly written by Paterson, had been sent to the authorities suggesting they looked into the circumstances of both deaths. The bodies were exhumed and discovered to contain the poison antimony. Pritchard was arrested, sparking a field day for gossips, who told stories about Mary McLeod, having boasted that her employer had promised that in the event of his wife not being around she would step into her shoes. It was enough for the girl to be taken into custody and questioned at length before being released.

Following a five-day sensational trial in Edinburgh Pritchard was convicted of double murder and, watched by a boisterous crowd estimated at up to 100,000, he was hanged at the Salt-market overlooking Glasgow Green.

37

WHISKY GALORE

Whisky Galore, the acclaimed novel by Sir Compton Mackenzie, is the story of Scottish islanders who try salvaging a cargo of whisky from a stricken ship while an officious officer tries to prevent them; it is based on the real-life grounding in 1941 of the SS *Politician* off Eriskay in the Outer Hebrides. The story, made into a successful film, might just as easily have been taken from an incident on the island of Arran in 1817, although in this case the recovery of the whisky by a team of excisemen left three islanders shot dead and the man in charge of the operation facing being hanged.

Crafty islanders all along the west coast of Scotland resented having to pay duty into the coffers to the King for spirits smuggled from illicit distilleries on the mainland or sneaked in from the continent. Equally, the Crown was determined to make them pay and a fleet of small cutters patrolled the coastline and islands looking for smugglers. The authorities had been tipped off that whisky was being regularly smuggled to Arran and on 25 March the cutter *Prince Edward*, under the command of Sir John Reid, on watch off the Ayrshire coast and with Arran three miles in the distance spotted a small boat apparently laden with casks of whisky being rowed towards the island. Warning shots were fired from the cutter's gun as a signal for the boat to stop but the rowers merely increased their efforts. Reid ordered his mate John Jeffrey to take a crew and chase the smugglers in a small boat.

Jeffrey was one of the backbones of the excise service, a man who had proved over the years that he was not one to back down in a crisis. He was just eleven when he enlisted in the Royal Navy and distinguished himself while commanding a gunboat – a responsibility normally given only to lieutenants – during the Walcheren campaign in 1809. Jeffrey was said by senior officers to have been involved in at least thirty risky operations to seize smuggled spirits and was described by superiors as, 'Not a person likely from hurry and heat of the moment to have done anything rash or violent.' It was a quality the Arran islanders would dispute.

He set off in pursuit with a crew of twelve but the locals had too great a start and Jeffrey could only watch as his quarry reached the shore, where they were met by islanders who ran off with the casks and took them into the island to hide them. The contraband was dumped in a ditch at a farm at Shannochie on the south of the island. Jeffrey's crew having beached their boat left two men to guard it while the rest, armed with muskets and cutlasses, gave chase, found four casks filled with whisky and seized them intending to take them back to the beach and then row them to the cutter. The islanders, though, were having none of it. Word spread like wildfire that excisemen had arrived and within minutes upwards of 200 angry men, women and children appeared demanding that the casks be left alone, something the mate was not prepared to allow. Some youngsters in the crowd threw stones at the seamen, but none were hurt.

At the trial at the High Court in September following the incident the prosecutor told the court, 'The crowd which was increasing and pouring down from the countryside was collected either by signals with which the people there communicate among themselves with great dexterity or by the sound of the guns fired by the cutter. It continued to increase when about a mile and a half from the shore they became violent and, attempting to carry away the smuggled goods, declared that none of the crew should return to the cutter with their lives. Jeffrey repeatedly warned the crowd, assured them he was an officer and warned them to stay clear. He tried to keep the mob away from his crew by pressing them with the flat sides of his sword. Jeffrey walked towards the shore and fired two blank shots over the heads of the mob. The mob seemed to hesitate and then with a general cheer immediately rushed forward. A few women were selected to lead the attack. Some of Jeffrey's men were knocked down. One was dragged several yards along the ground. Jeffrey was knocked down and while lying on his back gave orders to fire. Some of his men lying on the grounds and fighting with the mob fired.'

What happened when balls flew into the islanders was described by Daniel McKinnon who had watched as the excisemen came ashore then saw the stand-off turn violent as islanders demanded the return of their whisky from Jeffrey, who had a cutlass in one hand and a pistol in the other. He said his uncle William McKinnon, who had served in the excise for thirteen years before retiring to become a crofter on Arran, had told Jeffrey he would help he and his men carry the casks to the beach in exchange for a 'taste' of the whisky; the offer was refused. The situation became increasingly tense with seamen fixing bayonets to their weapons and when the order was given to 'fire' his uncle ran off but then another volley cut into him. 'Good God Donald, I am shot,' he told his nephew and fell. The ball had passed through his body but he lay bleeding heavily and as Daniel tried to comfort him a crew member fired at him, the ball going wide but hitting a boy standing nearby in the knee, crippling him.

Within an hour William was dead. Nearby lay the body of his tenant farmer son Donald, who had been shot in the chest. Daniel told the court more shots were fired at and hit islander Isabel Nicol, who had been grappling with another crewman. She was carried to a house but died that evening. Other witnesses told how angry islanders had tackled the invaders, women taking a bayonet from one of the seamen before volleys of shots sent them fleeing for their lives. Jeffrey was found not guilty, a verdict that pleased the judges but left simmering resentment on Arran over the killings.

About 200 miles to the north of Arran lies the Outer Hebridean island of Lewis; it was the starting point for a landing that led to one of the most unusual and dramatic cases to come for trial in Scotland, in this case before the High Court of Admiralty in November 1821 when Yorkshireman Peter Heaman and Frenchman Francois Gautiez were accused of a crime that might have come straight from the pages of a gruesome story of piracy and murder on the high seas. It began when customs officers on Lewis, told that the crew of a wrecked ship had managed to make their way ashore, met the survivors to make a routine inspection of their belongings in case they were trying to smuggle anything ashore to avoid paying duty. In charge of the bedraggled six-strong little party was a man who told the officers he was 'Captain George Shadwell, the merchant owner of the 100-ton *Jane of Gibraltar* that had foundered off Barra on a voyage from Liverpool to New York and they had managed to take to a small boat and row ashore on Lewis. Earlier, a schooner had been spotted at anchor in a small bay off Stornoway. Suspecting it belonged to smugglers it had been watched from Lewis but then vanished and the officials had no reason to believe this was the *Jane of Gibraltar*.

Satisfied with their examination and being told the survivors had sufficient funds to get them to the mainland, the officers allowed them to proceed. But suddenly one of the little group, a boy, ran after the officials shouting for them to stop. What he said left them astounded. Captain Shadwell, he said, was really Peter Heaman and the vessel hadn't gone down off Barra; it had been deliberately sunk not far from where they stood. The listeners were staggered, they found the boy's tale hard to believe; here was a youngster talking about murder, mutiny, piracy and even buried treasure. Theirs was a reaction that would, when he repeated his story, be echoed in the packed courtroom at Edinburgh months later. But by then the boy's version had been confirmed and while it had been checked out all six survivors from the schooner were detained.

The excise officers had climbed into a small boat, sailed out from Stornoway and almost collided with the *Jane of Gibraltar* as she lay broadside with part of her topmast carried away. During the night a storm blew up and by next morning she was in pieces. A search of Heaman's and Gautiez's bags uncovered a solitary book – *Trial of Captain Delano for Piracy.*

The full horror was again told, this time in the *Morning Post*, when it covered the trial of Heaman and Gautiez. 'The prisoners were apprehended by an officer in His Majesty's preventative service on the island of Lewis in consequence of the information of the boy whose confession was influenced by a horror at the atrocity of the crime of murder,' the newspaper said. The boy was Maltese Andrew Camelier, who said he had served on the schooner *Jane of Gibraltar* for four years when in May 1821 the crew was joined by Heaman as mate and cook Gautiez, bringing the total strength to eight. At Malta they had taken on a cargo of raisins, oils, beeswax, silk and eight barrels of dollars and on 21 May set sail for Salvador in Brazil.

After seventeen or eighteen days at sea the master of the vessel, Thomas Johnston, a kindly, well-liked and popular sailor, and crewman James Paterson were murdered. The boy said he heard a shot and ran on deck to see Heaman hitting Paterson with the butt end of a musket. The shot had also attracted skipper Johnston, who had been in bed, having stood watch but as soon as he arrived on deck he was attacked and battered unconscious with the musket first by Gautiez and then Heaman. The killers ordered other crewmen to throw the body of Paterson overboard; realising captain Johnston was still alive, weights were tied around him and he too was thrown into the waves. Two of the crew, Strachan and Smith, had angrily protested at the murders; they were threatened by Gautiez with an axe and ordered to stay below, the hatchway being nailed down by Heaman to make sure they could not get back on deck.

The evil did not end there. The boy said Heaman lit a fire in the cabin and made two holes in the wall so smoke would blow into the space in which Strachan and Smith were confined. Then Camelier was told to get flour and water and seal up seams in the hatchway to prevent smoke from escaping. The prisoners were kept below for two nights and a day and in the meantime the *Jane of Gibraltar* had altered course; instead of sailing south she turned north, with Heaman acting as captain and his accomplice, mate.

Confident that by now Strachan and Smith were dead, sure to have been overcome by smoke, the murderers opened the hatch only to find the two men still alive. Both were allowed briefly on deck to breathe in fresh air but were then forced back below desk and once more the hatchway was nailed down to stop them escaping. After a further three days both were freed but made to swear they would tell nobody what had taken place and ordered to kiss a Bible as a sign they would not go back on their word.

As the *Jane of Gibraltar* continued north she passed Ireland, Heaman and Gautiez having set a course for the west coast of Scotland. On board they opened the barrels of dollars and emptied them into sacks. Eventually they sighted the island of Barra, dropped anchor and made for shore, where they bought a small boat, telling the others it was to eventually transfer them and the money to dry land. Then they set sail for Stornoway and close to the town, off Suardail, began sinking the schooner by forcing the others to use a crowbar to open up holes in her planking. When water began pouring in the killers used the boat bought at Barra to row the money and the others ashore, on the final trip sinking the little rowing boat. On the beach Heaman and Gautiez stuffed some of the dollars – each was later found to have 6,300 of them – into their belts, buried the remainder and set off to walk into Stornoway at which point the officials met them and the horrifying story was revealed.

Strachan, aged nineteen, said he had been in the forecastle when he overheard Heaman plotting with Gautiez to murder Captain Johnston and take over the *Jane of Gibraltar*. He had been locked below when he protested at the killings but realising all hands would be needed if the schooner was to reach Scotland the plotters allowed him and Smith up on deck but they were warned by Gautiez, 'You go into the sea,' unless they joined the

311

mutiny. Heaman had promised the others a share of the money if they kept silent.

Fellow crewman Peter Smith, also nineteen, from Arbroath said he had only been on the *Jane of Gibraltar* a handful of days when Heaman told him it was planned to, 'Put away the Captain and take possession of the dollars.' He said he later heard Paterson screaming, 'Murder, murder, God save my soul for I am murdered now,' and then he was silent. As Captain Johnston was being thrown overboard Smith said he heard him groan. Following the murders and the decision by the killers to head for Scotland, Heaman called the others together and ordered them to say in the event of being boarded by any other vessel that they had been robbed by pirates and to cover their tracks even further they threw the ship's papers into the sea.

When they stood before the Admiralty Court, Heaman and Gautiez were accused of, 'The piratic seizure of the *Jane of Gibraltar* when on her voyage to the Brazils freighted with a valuable cargo including specie to the amount of 38,180 Spanish dollars; and further with the murders of Thomas Johnston and James Paterson and also with confining Peter Smith and Robert Strachan in the forecastle where, by attempting to suffocate them by smoke, they succeeded in terrifying Smith and Strachan to assist them in seizing the vessel, which they afterwards sunk off the coast of Ross-shire and landed the specie on the island of Lewis in that county.'

Although both pleaded not guilty the evidence was over-whelming and after a trial lasting through the night the jury unanimously convicted them at six o'clock in the morning.

Sentencing them to hang the judge told them, 'Providence arrested you in your bloody career. You landed on the shores of this island, a land where the innocent were always sure of asylum but the guilty of detection. If there was a punishment severer than death you deserve it. The door of mercy is always open to the penitent offender of the laws but to the pirate and murderer it must be ever shut.' He ordered a gibbet to be erected on the sands at Leith within the flood mark and the pair hanged between nine in the morning and noon. They were executed on 9 January 1822.

The sea could be a risky place and nature wasn't necessarily the cause of danger. During the Napoleonic Wars between 1803 and the final crushing of Bonaparte in 1815 thousands of French prisoners of war were shipped to Scotland. In March 1811 as 300 prisoners were on board the *Gorgon* on its way to Leith from where they would be marched to Edinburgh, a terrifying attempt was made to seize the vessel. An officer had written to friends telling them, 'The murder of all the officers was to be a part of this horrible plan. Fortunately one of the prisoners revealed the plot a few hours before it was due to be put into execution. Fifty of them, who usually had their parole on deck at one time, were to have been picked men and headed by several officers of privateers, a rush was to have been made, the officer of the watch thrown overboard and the arms seized.'

The plan was for all the prisoners below decks to be freed but the crew of the *Gorgon* foiled the scheme, clapped two ringleaders in irons and warned the rest they would be shot if there was further trouble. The quick thinking of those on the *Gorgon* meant it landed its human cargo safely. But a few months later a plot was foiled in which prisoners kept in Edinburgh Castle planned to escape, rush to Leith, seize a boat and sail to France.

38

THE LAST DROP

The spectacle of Robert Smith dangling from a gibbet was the last the public would have of a hanged convict. From 1800 to 1868 there had been 269 executions, an average of almost four a year, but parallel with the gradual reduction in the number of capital crimes had been a steady drop in hangings. Up to the turn of the century just sixteen men and one women stood on scaffolds in prisons and prison yards in Scotland – about one every two years – while from 1900 until twenty-one-year-old Henry John Burnett became the last person to be hanged in Scotland when he was put to death at Craiginches prison in Aberdeen by hangman Harry Allan in August 1963, thirty-three men and one woman, Susan Newell, were launched into hell.

The first execution to take place in what was officially termed as 'private' in Scotland was that of George Chalmers, hanged at Perth jail in October 1870 for murdering tollgate keeper John Miller near Braco, Perth and Kinross, the previous December despite a series of petitions to the government pleading for him to be reprieved on the grounds he was a lunatic. Efforts to save him failed but newspapers were no longer able to describe in detail the last moments of a condemned man or woman, his or her demise usually being limited to a single paragraph simply announcing that his execution had gone ahead.

Jessie King, aged twenty-nine, from Stockbridge, Edinburgh, became the last woman to be hanged in Scotland in the nineteenth century when she was put to death in March 1889 in the capital for the appalling crime of baby farming. Mothers paid her to adopt their children but instead of caring for the vulnerable infants Jessie killed two of them while continuing to take the money. She was accused at the High Court in Edinburgh of strangling twelve-month-old Alexander Gunn and Violet Duncan Tomlinson, just six weeks, and thanks to evidence from her older lover, Thomas Pearson, she was convicted of both charges in just four minutes by the jury and hanged at Calton jail in March. Patrick Leggett, thirty, had the dubious distinction of being the first person hanged in Scotland in the twentieth century when he was launched into eternity at Duke Street prison in Glasgow for the cowardly murder of his wife Sarah Jane. A persistent delinquent Leggett suspected Sarah Jane of having lovers and stabbed her in the back. After his execution he was buried within Duke Street prison.

The last woman to be put to death in Scotland before capital punishment ended was thirty-year-old Susan Newall, who killed newsboy John Johnston in 1923 at her Coatbridge home when he demanded money for a newspaper and she refused to pay. With the help of her daughter, Janet, the body of the thirteen-year-old was rolled inside a mat and the pair set off to Glasgow with the corpse loaded on a cart intending to dump it. Lorry driver Thomas Dickson felt sorry for them and gave them a lift to Duke Street but as he was unloading the cart the boy's head was uncovered. Dickson let them go on but police were called and first Susan then her husband John was arrested. They were tried at Glasgow but only Susan were convicted despite her defence pleading she was insane at the time of the boy's death.

Hangman John Ellis put her to death at Duke Street jail in October 1923 and in his autobiography, *Diary of a Hangman,* said she had 'behaved in an exceedingly brave manner' but did not go into detail about the execution which was not surprising because he bungled it, forgetting to strap her wrists with the result that on the trapdoor as he put the hood over her head she threw it off calling, 'Don't put that thing on me,' at which Ellis launched her into eternity bareheaded, her hands flailing and her eyes open and bulging to the horror of officials surrounding the scaffold.

Equally brave was Paul Christopher Harris, aged twenty-eight, launched into eternity at Barlinnie by Albert Pierrepoint in October 1950 for the murder in a brawl at Govan, Glasgow, of Martin Dunleavy. As the victim lay dying in hospital he refused to name his attackers, telling a policeman with his very last words, 'I will get them myself.' Paul and his older brother Claude were found guilty of killing Dunleavy and both sentenced to hang. In Barlinnie they were kept in separate condemned cells but just hours before they were due to hang Paul said he had struck the fatal blow. He knew his eleventh-hour confession meant death, but at least it won a reprieve for Claude, whose sentence was commuted to life imprisonment. He died in 1985 aged sixty-five.

Two months later history was made at Barlinnie when thirty-three-year-old police constable James Robertson became the first person to be hanged for using a car as a murder weapon. Some believed the handsome father-of-two died through being gallant, not prepared to save himself but as a consequence distress his family by pleading guilty to manslaughter, a charge likely to have been accepted by the prosecution and leading to lengthy imprisonment. Such a plea would have meant sordid details of his affair with the victim coming out.

One night while a colleague covered for him, Robertson sloped off from his beat in the centre of Glasgow. When he turned up two hours later other officers were already dealing with the death of single mother Catherine McCluskey, whose body was found lying in a road. It was thought she had been the victim of a hit-and-run driver until a post-mortem examination revealed she had been battered senseless before a car ran backwards and forwards over her as she lay unconscious. Investigations revealed she had a policeman lover named Robertson and when he was arrested detectives discovered he used a stolen car that still bore traces of the dead woman's body. Robertson said he had run over her but it was an accident. He was advised that confessing to having an affair with Catherine and saying she pestered him to set up home with her could get the murder charge reduced to manslaughter but he refused saying that admitting he had been cheating on his wife would unfairly embarrass her, a decision that cost him his life.

Throughout the history of crime and punishment in Scotland, one name stands out above all others as the worst that evil can devise. Officially Peter Thomas Anthony Manuel murdered seven people between January 1956 and January 1958 but it is beyond doubt that he killed two others and very probably even more. He had a string of convictions and served a long stretch in Peterhead prison in Aberdeenshire for rape but after his release he turned to murder. He was arrested when he used new bank-notes stolen from the home of his last victims to buy drinks and he was held in Barlinnie jail from where each day he was taken to Glasgow High Court for his trial starting in late May 1958. On the ninth day he fired his lawyers and conducted his own defence, but he was convicted and told he would hang.

On the day he was sentenced Barlinnie officials moved him to the condemned cell on the third floor of 'D' hall, where he was joined by specially selected prison officers who would stay with him round the clock until his death. His behaviour became increasingly erratic as he began feigning insanity in the hope of saving himself, refusing to speak to the officers with him and spending twenty-four hours a day listening to a radio. At one stage he slyly put soap in his mouth and started foaming through his lips; at other times he would only utter the word 'chips'. His family were constant and loyal visitors but as the end neared his antics irritated his mother Bridget so much that she slapped his face and told her son, 'You can't fool me.'

As is so often the case where men and women commit acts of terrible evil, Manuel attracted a considerable fan base. Letters addressed to him regularly arrived at Barlinnie from strangers begging him to send them souvenirs, including personal items, postcards or one of his handkerchiefs. Some of the requests were said to be ghoulish and one of these was suspected by prison staff who examined the writing on it and its contents to have been sent by two schoolboys living in the south of England.

On the night before the execution an official from the visiting committee, who had kept a regular watch on Manuel and his treatment, recorded details of his meeting with the murderer in the condemned cell describing him as being in 'good spirits'. Early next morning, Friday 11 July, executioner Harry Allan and his assistant Harold Smith were admitted to the condemned cell to pinion Manuel's arms. 'Turn up the radio and I'll go quietly,' Manuel told Allan. At eight o'clock when the cell door was opened Allan led the way a few paces across the landing to the execution suite opposite where the noose dangled from a beam placed in the cell above, the floor of which had been removed. Manuel stood on the trapdoor cut in the floor of the suite and eight seconds later dropped into the cell below. He was pronounced dead by the prison medical officer and the body taken into the jail's mortuary, which was below the cell into which Manuel had dropped. His corpse was carried outside to a waiting grave and still lies within the Barlinnie walls.

Like other executions, the cost of that of Manuel had to be borne by the Lord Provost of Glasgow whose responsibility it was to organise and pay for hangings. The rope used by Allan and Smith, and the straps with which they pinioned the mass killer's arms and, as he stood on the trapdoor, his legs, were officially rented from the Home Office in London. Two sets of equipment – one a reserve in case the other was faulty – were crated and sent by train to Glasgow Central station in the days before the execution where they were collected and taken to Barlinnie in readiness for the hangmen, who worked out the length of drop from a government chart based on the height and weight of a victim.

Manuel was the second last convict to hang at Barlinnie, the last being nineteen-year-old Anthony Miller just under two and a half years later for murder.

During the 1970s, while carrying out the realignment of pipework at Barlinnie, workmen discovered the remains of a number of executed convicts. These were carefully exhumed, with some being offered to known relatives for them to rebury elsewhere while those whose families could not be found or did not claim them were reinterred within the prison grounds.

Following the ending of transportation to Australia in 1886 the government of the day needed another dumping ground for the scum and riff-raff that it wanted to be kept well away from decent, respectable society. It chose two sites, Dartmoor on the wild moors of Devon and Peterhead on Aberdeenshire's north-east coast. Convicts were sent to Peterhead to build not only their own prison, but to help construct a nearby harbour.

In October 1881 a horrendous storm had lashed Berwickshire and south-east Scotland, swamping at least fifty fishing boats and leaving about 200 men drowned. The freak weather devastated communities and the authorities decided to create a harbour at Peterhead that could act as a haven for fishermen in the event of any repetition. Work on building Peterhead jail started around 1888 and granite for the jail and the immense walls of the harbour was quarried at nearby Stirling. A railway line was constructed, allowing prisoners to be taken directly each day out of the jail to the quarry and trucks then carried the stone both to the prison and harbour. One of the carriages remained at the prison until the site was redeveloped in 2013 and when it was examined, to the astonishment of historians and prison staff, hidden within one of its walls was a long blade, clearly intended as a weapon to be used in an escape attempt.

Peterhead would become the most dreaded prison in Scotland, not only because of the fact that being so remote meant difficulties for the families of inmates to visit. It was a grim, damp place, forever cold. The original convicts had slept in hammocks slung from hooks in the ceilings of narrow cells, two of which had to be later knocked into one to accommodate single beds. Until shortly before the outbreak of the Second World War staff at Peterhead carried cutlasses instead of batons and inmates were warned never to approach to closer than 'two cutlass lengths' from any officer. It was the last jail in Britain where staff carried guns, the officer in charge of the quarry being issued with a rifle, a practice which it was decided to discontinue when the officer on guard dropped the weapon one day and it went off by accident.

In addition to Manuel, Peterhead housed many of Scotland's

most notorious criminals, including Oscar Slater, whose wrongful conviction for the murder of an elderly Glasgow spinster in 1908 resulted in him spending nineteen years incarcerated there. Campaigners who included *Sherlock Holmes* author Sir Arthur Conan Doyle persisted in claims he was innocent but it was July 1928 before the conviction was quashed.

Safecracker Johnny Ramensky was one of the few men to escape from Peterhead, while revolutionary socialist John Maclean served part of a five-year sentence for sedition in Peterhead, during which he was force-fed. Prison conditions were blamed for a severe deterioration in his health and he died in 1923 of pneumonia aged forty-four.

Peterhead was also the only jail to which the SAS were called in to put down a riot after inmates took an officer hostage in October 1987. Then Prime Minister Margaret Thatcher authorised the controversial operation in which special forces armed with stun grenades, gas canisters, batons and pistols stormed 'D' Wing, rescued the hostage and handcuffed the rioters.

Workmen carrying out renovations at Saughton prison in Edinburgh discovered a discarded handwritten document showing the calculations scribbled down by the hangman for an execution there. Bodies found during the work were moved to another site within the jail, their resting place marked by a memorial stone.

Perth jail was originally a prisoner of war camp for up to 7,000 French prisoners captured during the Napoleonic Wars and who built the prison between 1810 and 1812. While renovations were being carried out at Perth twenty graves were discovered and investigations revealed them to be those of French prisoners who had died of sickness or disease during their incarceration. The remains were reinterred.

The nooses were finally curled away for the last time with Scotland's final execution, that of twenty-one-year-old Henry John Burnett on 15 August 1963, who became the only person to die in the then newly opened execution block at Craiginches jail, Aberdeen. Burnett was convicted of murdering Thomas Guyan, the seaman husband of his married mistress Margaret, at the Guyans' Aberdeen home. He was executed by Harry Allan, his body buried within the jail. Craiginches closed in 2013 and the following year his remains were handed over to relatives who arranged for them to be cremated at a private ceremony. It was yet one more tragically premature ending to a young life, a young man with everything to live for but whom love launched into eternity.